1-67

Helen Ball
II C - June 22, 1945
Mills College
Oakland, Cal.

RACE DIFFERENCES

A GROUP OF BOOKS IN PSYCHOLOGY
UNDER THE GENERAL EDITORSHIP OF
GARDNER MURPHY
COLUMBIA UNIVERSITY

○

GENERAL PSYCHOLOGY
by Gardner Murphy

A BRIEFER GENERAL PSYCHOLOGY
by Gardner Murphy

EXPERIMENTAL SOCIAL PSYCHOLOGY
by Gardner and Lois Murphy

PSYCHOLOGICAL TESTS, METHODS, AND RESULTS
by H. E. Garrett and M. R. Schneck

PSYCHOLOGY AND THE NEW EDUCATION
by S. L. Pressey

APPLIED PSYCHOLOGY
by Richard W. Husband

A STUDENT'S DICTIONARY OF PSYCHOLOGICAL TERMS
by Horace B. English

THE PSYCHOLOGY OF LEARNING
by E. R. Guthrie

RACE DIFFERENCES
by Otto Klineberg

○

Harper & Brothers
Publishers

RACE DIFFERENCES

BY

OTTO KLINEBERG

Columbia University

HARPER & BROTHERS PUBLISHERS

NEW YORK AND LONDON

RACE DIFFERENCES

This book is complete and unabridged
in contents, and is manufactured in strict
conformity with Government regulations
for saving paper.

To Franz Boas

PREFACE

THERE is undoubtedly a great deal of curiosity concerning race. Students are always asking questions which touch upon a wide variety of scattered problems. One wishes to know whether the Negro brain differs from the White; another has heard that the glands of internal secretion explain racial psychology; another is interested in differences in the crime rate; still another asks whether it is true that race mixture results in degeneration and loss of vigor. There is a great deal of material bearing on these and many other questions, and it has seemed worth while to collect the most important parts of it and make them more readily accessible.

The book is written primarily for students. The subject matter is in part technical, although the attempt has been made to present it as clearly and as simply as possible, so that no special background or training is needed in order to follow the argument. The interest and emphasis are primarily psychological, but the relevant material has been gathered from a number of the natural and the social sciences. The last part of the book makes use of ethnological data which seem to have a special pertinence for psychological problems. It is hoped that the rather extensive documentation throughout the book will be of some help to advanced students who wish to continue their work in this field.

The problem of race is, however, more than an academic problem. In most parts of the world it has a practical significance which cannot be ignored. The conclusions to which this book lead, namely, that there is no adequate proof of fundamental race differences in mentality, and that those differences which are found are in all probability due to culture and the social environment, have as a consequence a definite significance outside the confines of the university. The book is therefore addressed also to the "intelligent layman," in the hope that he will overlook its more academic aspects and will be interested in examining the evidence that the world has been taking "race" much too seriously.

There are many people who in one way or another have made a contribution to this book. My graduate students at Columbia University have helped by their discussions and criticism to clarify the problems, and several of them have assisted much more concretely by their research, experimental as well as bibliographic. It is a pleasure to record my thanks to Dr. A. Franzblau for his many important suggestions; to my mother for her great help in connection with the index; to my sister, Miss Nettye V. Klineberg, for her valuable assistance with the bibliography; and to Professor Ruth F. Benedict, of the Department of Anthropology at Columbia University, for her helpful criticism of the material dealing with Culture. My special thanks go to Professor Gardner Murphy, the editor of this series, who has helped with his encouragement and advice at all times, and to Professor Franz Boas whose teaching made this book possible.

I would express my thanks to my wife, if this book were not hers as well as mine.

Otto Klineberg

New York
June 15, 1935.

Table of Contents

RACE DIFFERENCES

Chapter I

INTRODUCTION: AN OUTLINE OF RACIAL THEORIES

EARLY HISTORY

"OF ALL the vulgar modes of escaping from the consideration of the effect of social and moral influences upon the human mind, the most vulgar is that of attributing the diversities of conduct and character to inherent natural differences." Buckle (7, p. 37) quotes with complete approval this opinion of John Stuart Mill (23); but the vulgar mode of which he spoke has apparently always been popular, and has expressed itself in a literature of ever-increasing proportions. Naturally enough, the argument and the conclusions vary with each writer, and are usually directed toward the glorification of his particular people. This fact alone will probably convince the serious student that in the field of racial theories he cannot hope for objectivity. The greater frequency with which one race or one people is praised may depend upon an accidental majority among those who write the books, and truth is not necessarily on the side of the most articulate. It may still be instructive, however, to look at racial theories in their historical setting.

The earliest theories that have come down to us found in the physical environment the explanation of the group differences that were observed. (See Thomas, 30.) Aristotle in the fifth century B.C. said that whereas the peoples living in the cold climate of northern Europe were conspicuous for their spirit and bravery, their lack of intelligence unfitted them for political organization and dominion. Asiatics were intelligent and inventive, but they lacked spirit. The Greeks were geographically intermediate, and therefore by nature fitted to rule the earth (2). About three hundred years later, Vitruvius (31), a writer on Roman architecture, described the southern peoples as having a keen intelligence, due to the rarity of the atmosphere and the heat, whereas the "northern nations, being enveloped in a dense atmosphere, and chilled by moisture from the obstructing air, have but a sluggish intelligence." (Book VI, Chap. 1, Sec. 9.) Between the two extremes was situated the best people, in this case, the Romans. A later writer, Ibn Khaldun (20), changed the argument slightly to fit his own requirements; Arabia was in the warm zone, but the water around the Arabian peninsula had a cooling effect that made the climate really temperate. The Arabians were therefore superior.

In more modern times these racial theories become complicated by the "science" of the period. In the case of Jean Bodin (6) in the sixteenth century, it is astrology that furnishes the needed support. In France the planets exert their benign influence in the most favorable combination, and so France is designed by nature to be mistress of the world.

At about the same time the problem of race became the very practical concern of the early conquerors of the New World. Simar (28) points out that the Spanish *conquistadores* felt the need of justifying their enslavement of the Indians; their apologists, Sepulveda, Quevedo, and others, did so on the ground that the Indians were an absolutely different race, not human in the same sense as were the Spaniards, and therefore not requiring to be treated in the same way. These writers, says Simar, were the first "polygenists"; the first who believed in the multiple origin of the human races.

The opposite view was most clearly expressed by Buffon (8), who has sometimes been called the "first anthropologist." He was a monogenist, believing that man was originally one type, and that all observed differences are due to the effect of the environment. If the Negroes return to a temperate climate, he maintained, they will be white in a few generations. Herder (17) a little later adopted much the same point of view, although he was less ready to make extreme generalizations like the last. During the early years of the following century a number of English writers began to glorify the Anglo-Saxon "race," and to speak of the English as destined to inhabit and civilize the whole world. This was the beginning of the "White man's burden." Then came Gobineau.

GOBINEAU AND HIS FOLLOWERS

Count Arthur Joseph de Gobineau (1816-82) is usually regarded as the father of modern racial theories. He wrote his four-volume *Essai sur l'Inégalité des Races Humaines* (12) in consequence of researches begun on his family tree, and by his own admission it was written in part to prove the superiority of his own race. He preached the superiority of the White race over the other races, and of the Aryans over all other Whites. The Black race, in Gobineau's theory, represents passion and is the source of lyricism and the artistic temperament; the Yellow man represents utility, order, mediocrity; the White is the expression of reason and honor.

The supreme race is the Aryan, and the Teutons are its purest modern representative. Civilization sprang from the Aryans, declining when the Aryan blood became diluted. The Indian civilization was Aryan; the Egyptian was created by an Aryan colony from India; the Greek was due to Aryans with some Semitic intermixture. Civilization without an Aryan creator is unthinkable.

Gobineau never defined the Aryans very clearly from the

physical point of view. The term was used later by Max
Müller (24) in a purely linguistic sense, and in his opinion
it was devoid of any racial or anatomical implications. (See
Chapter II.) Gobineau adopted and popularized it and began
the Aryan movement, which has reached its climax in our
own day. His theory achieved immediate recognition in
Germany, and Gobineau societies sprang up all over the
country. Among others, Richard Wagner was an enthusias-
tic supporter. The fact that nothing was known of an Aryan
"race" did not detract from the popularity of the theory.

Gobineau's most important follower was Houston Stewart
Chamberlain (9), who published his *Grundlagen des 19ten
Jahrhunderts* in 1899. He was a member of the Gobineau
Society, and his writings were so popular with the ruling
class in Germany that he was known as the Kaiser's anthropologist. Though born in England, he found Germany
much more congenial, and lived and wrote in that country.

Chamberlain, too, is not quite certain what the Aryans
are; but he speaks of their most important representatives, the
Teutons, as being for the most part tall, fair and dolichocephalic (long-headed). The Aryans were first characterized
in this way by Pösche (25), and Chamberlain follows him,
though not too strictly. He admits that in many cases a
Teuton or Aryan cannot easily be recognized, and it is
sometimes necessary to use intuition or a "spiritual divina-
tion," which Chamberlain speaks of as rational anthropology. For example, Dante's noble countenance shows that he
must have been a Teuton.

According to Chamberlain, the Teuton is everywhere
triumphant. The Renaissance was due to the Teutons of
Italy. All the great creative minds of western Europe were
Teutons. Paul and Jesus were Aryans, not Jews.

Chamberlain is sometimes at a loss to find an adequate

physical characterization of the "races" he is attempting to describe. The Jews, for example, are discussed at great length, and are regarded as an alien people, but it is not always easy to define the nature of their difference from the Germans. Chamberlain confesses that there are many Jews who are not recognizable as such, and who would usually be mistaken for Germans; but even in their case it often happens that when one of them enters a room, a German child, usually a girl, will unaccountably begin to cry. This is the "rational" anthropology on which Chamberlain's theory is based.

In the ascription of all of civilization to the Teutons, Ludwig Woltmann (32) went even further than Chamberlain. In his *Politische Anthropologie*, Woltmann "proved" that all the great Italians were really Germans, and that even their names had originally been German. Giordano Bruno was Braun, Leonardo da Vinci was Wincke, Giotto was Jothe. The same was true of the great Frenchmen—Diderot was Tietroh, Gounod was Gundiwald, and so with many others.

The more purely physical aspects of race, and especially the cult of dolichocephaly, were developed by Otto Ammon in Germany (1) and G. Vacher de Lapouge in France (21). Ammon made a large number of anthropometric measurements on army recruits in Baden, and found that the urban population had longer and narrower heads than the rural. He formulated what is known as "Ammon's Law," to the effect that dolichocephals have a greater inclination for city life and a greater aptitude for success than brachycephals (round-heads). The dolichocephal has a taste for novelty and adventure; the brachycephal is pacific, thrifty, reflective, conservative and attached to the soil.

This was perhaps the first important formulation of a law of selective migration, some of the more recent implications of which we shall discuss in a later chapter. Unfortunately for the law, it does not hold everywhere. Livi (22), for example, found exactly the opposite result in southern Italy; the population of Naples was more brachycephalic than that of the surrounding country. His explanation was that Naples attracted to itself a number of migrants from the northern and central portions of Italy, which are much more brachycephalic (Alpine) than the south, which is predominantly Mediterranean. Naples was less dolichocephalic than the surrounding country because it was less purely Mediterranean. Ammon's results may be similarly explained. In the cities of Baden there are a number of migrants from more dolichocephalic portions of Germany; the cities are less purely Alpine than the surrounding rural districts, and therefore less brachycephalic. Livi argues that the less homogeneous population of the cities will necessarily vary in the opposite direction from that of the surrounding country. It may be added that Beddoe (5) in England also failed to verify Ammon's theory. It follows that the inferences which Ammon drew with reference to the relation between psychological characteristics and shape of the head have no foundation.

De Lapouge gave as one of the arguments for the superiority of the dolichocephals the fact that in a cemetery of the superior social and economic classes in Paris there were more dolichocephalic skulls than in the cemetery of the lower classes. Largely on the basis of head form, he attempted a psychological characterization of the *Homo Europæus* (the Nordic, or northern European) and the *Homo Alpinus*. The former was domineering, self-reliant, courageous, adventurous, had great foresight, loved liberty and independence, and tended to be a Protestant. The Alpine was industrious, frugal, conservative, the perfect serf, produced few geniuses and was usually a Catholic. De Lapouge wrote: "I am convinced that in the next century millions will cut each others' throats because of one or two degrees more or less of cephalic index." (See Hankins, 16, p. 128.)

In the United States Gobineau's mantle seems to have fallen mainly on the shoulders of Madison Grant, who in his early book, *The Passing of the Great Race,* (13) and his more recent *The Conquest of a Continent* (14) has taken up arms in favor of the Nordics. In the first book he described the Nordics as a race of soldiers, sailors, adventurers, explorers and, above all, rulers, organizers and aristocrats. The Alpines are a race of peasants. The Mediterraneans are superior to the Alpines in intellect, and superior even to the Nordics in the field of art. In Europe today, "the amount of Nordic blood in each nation is a very fair measure of its strength in war and standing in civilization" (13, p. 175). The decline of Spain was due to the dilution of Gothic blood when the scepter fell into the hands of the Iberians. In France, the vigor of the nation declined when the Alpines and Mediterraneans replaced the Nordics. Germany has suffered obvious ruin; its people are now descendants of Alpine peasants, among whom chivalry and generosity are rare. In America, the greatest danger lies in the "gradual dying out among our people of those hereditary traits through which the principles of our religious, political or social foundations were laid down, and their insidious replacement by traits of less noble character" (13, p. ix). This is what is meant by the "passing of the great race."

This point is developed in the second book, which is a history of the United States from the racial point of view. It is again argued that the original as well as the best stock in America is Nordic, and that care must be taken not to allow it to be smothered by the more recent arrivals from

southern and central Europe. In this connection it is important to note that Hrdlička (18) in his study of "Old Americans" found the oldest American stock not to be predominantly blond or dolichocephalic. Among the males, there
were 16.6 per cent dolichocephalic, and 21.7 per cent brachycephalic; of the females, only 8.1 per cent were dolichocephalic and 41.9 per cent were brachycephalic, the remainder
in both cases being intermediate. In hair color also, most of
the "Old Americans" were neither very blond nor very dark,
but somewhere between the two. We may conclude, therefore, that the Nordic character of the first settlers has been
considerably exaggerated.

Grant's was not the only attempt to write American history in terms of race. Eckenrode (11) wrote a book on Jefferson Davis in which he characterized the Civil War as a
struggle between Nordic and non-Nordic elements. This
was (see Hankins, p. 223) "the last great effort of the Nordic
race to save itself; having lost, it has moved steadily toward
nothingness." "The victory of the North meant the predominance of the non-Nordic elements in American life.
. . . The chief result of the Civil War was the ruin it brought
to the Nordic race in America" (11, p. 361).

In modern Germany, before the recent flood of pro-Nor-
dic or pro-Aryan propaganda, the most important expressions of this point of view were to be found in Baur, Fischer
and Lenz (4), and in the writings of Günther (15). In the
former, the attempt is made by men of standing in the
exact sciences to give a characterization of the various human races, in which, however, objectivity is unfortunately
subordinate to personal impression. Negroes are described as
lacking in foresight, not inclined to work hard in the present
to provide for the future, influenced by the immediate impressions of the senses, vacillating between cheerful indif-

ference and hopeless depression, poor in imagination and devoid of the power of mental creation. Their childish traits are conspicuous, especially their cruelty and lack of sympathy; their notorious lack of sexual control is due not so much to the exceptional strength of the sexual impulse as to a general childish lack of the power of restraint. They have great oratorical ability, and their musical gifts are remarkable. Their organizational and political faculties are poorly developed, and they have never produced any kind of social structure worthy of comparison with those of Europe and Asia.

The Mongols are treated rather more kindly. They are described as having quick apprehension and an excellent memory, but they do not excel in imagination, critical faculty or abstraction; they have little interest in any of the pure sciences. Brilliant thinkers, investigators, inventors, or men of genius can hardly be said to have existed among the Mongols. It is doubtful whether Chinese civilization and the Chinese state were mainly originated by true Mongols. "In northern China there are millions of persons having a slender build, a narrow head, a narrow face and a narrow, prominent nose, whose general type, therefore, suggests a European origin" (p. 636). Yet their powers of resistance, their frugality and their determination lead the authors to conclude that "there is much to indicate that the future of the earth belongs to the Mongols" (p. 637).

The European races are likewise characterized according to the usual stereotypes. The Alpines are persistent and energetic workers, lacking in imagination, but with marked tenacity and considerable intelligence. The Mediterraneans are restless, lively, frivolous, with a taste for gesture and oratory; they have less sense of truth and honor than the Nordics, and a low general intelligence. The Nordic race marches in the van of mankind. It owes its leading position not only to its high intellectual endowments, but also to its character traits—individualism, self-control, courage, imagination, foresight, constancy of will.

Günther is even more extreme in his striking contrast between the Nordics and all others. The Alpines, who constitute such a large part of the German people, receive special marks of his disfavor. They are described as petty, narrow-minded, spiteful, envious, crafty, furtive, sullen, dirty, devoid of any creative energy, persistent in uninspired activities. The Nordics, on the other hand, are the bearers of all conceivable virtues, and the leaders in civilization everywhere. It may be added that Günther's books have obtained in Germany an almost unlimited popularity; one of them (15a) has gone into a great many editions.

These characterizations are subjective and therefore not susceptible of proof; they are as a result almost as difficult to disprove. Some of the statements by Baur, Fischer and Lenz even have a certain plausibility, although the best indication of their wholly arbitrary nature, especially as far as value-judgments are concerned, is to be found in the fact that other writers have glorified different races with similar enthusiasm.

In Favor of Other Races

One of the most illuminating examples of a different point of view is to be found in a letter from the Chinese Emperor Ch'ien Lung to George III of England in 1793. The English king had written requesting the establishment of a British representative and a trading center at Peking, and the Emperor declined in the following words: "If you assert that your reverence for Our Celestial dynasty fills you with a desire to acquire our civilization, our ceremonies and code of laws differ so completely from your own that, even if your Envoy were able to acquire the rudiments of our civilization, you could not possibly transplant our manners and customs to your alien soil. . . . Swaying the wide world, I have but one aim in view, namely to maintain a perfect governance and to fulfil the duties of the State; strange and costly objects do not interest me. If I have commanded that the tribute offerings sent by you, O King, are to be accepted, this was solely in consideration for the spirit which prompted you to dispatch them from afar. . . . We possess all things. I set no value on objects strange or ingenious, and have no use for your country's manufactures. Therefore, . . . it behoves you, O King, to respect my sentiments and to display even greater devotion and loyalty in future, so that, by perpetual submission to our Throne, you may secure peace and prosperity for your country hereafter." (See Backhouse and Bland, 3, p. 332.)

The Harvard anthropologist Dixon believes that the Nordics have played an important rôle in the world's history, but that they are now gradually passing from the stage. In the future, it is the Alpine type which "seems destined to play perhaps the leading part" (10, p. 521). There is no special virtue in race purity; it is only where the three European races have met and blended that the highest achievements have been obtained, nor does the Nordic component appear to be the most important. From the fusion of Alpine and Mediterranean types, whose brains in size surpass all the rest, have come the greatest achievements (p. 518).

Sergi (26) regards the Mediterraneans as the true bearers of civilization; the Asiatics and the Germans only destroyed what they had created. The true Aryans were not blond, but dark, and of short stature. In a special study with Frassetto (27) of the bones of Dante, Sergi writes: "These

characteristics correspond perfectly to those of the Mediterranean race, that is to say, that great race which has a glorious history of about five thousand years, and which created
all the various phases of Mediterranean civilization from the
pre-Hellenic to the Latin, and later the Italian Renaissance.
Dante, therefore, represents the most authentic and most
glorious type of the Mediterranean stock." Dante was not a
Teuton; he was "Italian in blood and in heredity" (Author's translation).

Huntington (19) is best known for his advocacy of the
view that geographical environment, rather than race, determines the characteristics of human groups. The ability of
the Germans is due not to inherent biological factors, but to
the stimulating climate. Civilization flourishes where there
is the greatest climatic energy. When Huntington does
commit himself, however, as to racial differences, it is the
brachycephalic Alpines rather than the dolichocephalic
Nordics whom he regards as superior, largely on the basis
of the greater average size of their brains. He writes: "There
has been a series of steps toward a round head. Such a head
is biologically the highest and most specialized, because it
can hold the largest brain in proportion to its surface and
weight" (p. 75). In central Europe and America, the round
heads are replacing the long heads gradually but unmis-
takably.

THE PROBLEM

If there is ever to be any agreement among scientists concerning the problem of racial differences, it will not emerge
from the type of subjective theorizing which has been reviewed in this chapter. The serious student demands objectivity, and will not content himself with value-judgments
that cannot be verified. In the field of race there is, however,
available at the present time a large mass of material, repre-

senting a wide variety of objective approaches in several different though not unrelated disciplines. Anthropologists, anatomists, physiologists, clinicians, psychologists, sociologists, and others—all have made their contribution, and the results of their studies have at various times been interpreted as proving beyond any doubt that races differ in their psychological endowment. The scattered nature of the evidence, and the complexity of the methodological problems involved, have suggested the need of a careful analysis of all the relevant material, so that each study and each conclusion may be seen in proper perspective.

Such an analysis is attempted in the following chapters. The writer has sought to present and evaluate the available objective data, and to approach the problem of race from as many different viewpoints as possible.

Bibliography

1. Ammon, Otto. *Zur Anthropologie der Badener*. Jena, 1899.
2. Aristotle. *The Politics of Aristotle*. Oxford, 1885. (Trans.)
3. Backhouse, E., and Bland, J. O. P. *Annals and Memoirs of the Court of Peking*. New York, 1914.
4. Baur, E., Fischer, E., and Lenz, F. *Human Heredity*. New York, 1931. (Trans.)
5. Beddoe, J. *The Races of Britain; a Contribution to the Anthropology of Western Europe*. Bristol, 1885.
6. Bodin, J. *The Six Books of a Commonweale*. London, 1606. (Trans.)
7. Buckle, H. T. *The History of Civilization in England*. London, 1864. 4th ed. (2 vols.)
8. Buffon, G. L. *Histoire Naturelle*. Paris, 1749-88. (Complete Ed., 36 vols.)
9. Chamberlain, H. S. *Grundlagen des 19ten Jahrhunderts*. Berlin, 1899.
10. Dixon, R. B. *The Racial History of Man*. New York, 1923.
11. Eckenrode, H. J. *Jefferson Davis, President of the South*. New York, 1923.

12. de Gobineau, Count A. J. *Essai sur l'Inégalité des Races Humaines.* Paris, 1853-55. (2 vols.)

13. Grant, M. *The Passing of the Great Race, or The Racial Basis of European History.* New York, 1916.

14. Grant, M. *The Conquest of a Continent; or, The Expansion of Races in America.* New York, 1933.

15a. Günther, H. F. K. *Rassenkunde des Deutschen Volkes.* Munich, 1924. (5th Ed.)

15b. Günther, H. F. K. *The Racial Elements of European History.* London, 1927. (Trans.)

15c. Günther, H. F. K. *Adel und Rasse.* Munich, 1927. (2nd Ed.)

15d. Günther, H. F. K. *Rasse und Stil.* Munich, 1927. (2nd Ed.)

16. Hankins, F. H. *The Racial Basis of Civilization: A Critique of the Nordic Doctrine.* New York, 1926.

17. Herder, J. G. *Ideen zur Philosophie der Geschichte der Menschheit.* Berlin, 1784-91.

18. Hrdlička, A. *The Old Americans.* Baltimore, 1925.

19. Huntington, E. *The Character of Races.* New York, 1924.

20. Ibn Khaldun. *Prolégomènes Historiques.* Paris, 1862. (Trans.)

21. de Lapouge, G. V. *Les Sélections Sociales.* Paris, 1896.

22. Livi, R. *Anthropometria Militare.* Rome, 1896.

23. Mill, J. S. *Principles of Political Economy.* Boston, 1848.

24. Müller, M. *Lectures on the Science of Language.* London, 1864.

25. Poesche, T. *Die Arier.* Jena, 1878.

26. Sergi, G. *The Mediterranean Race.* Rome, 1895.

27. Sergi, G., and Frassetto, F. "Esame antropologico delle ossa di Dante." *Riv. Antrop.,* 26:1925.

28. Simar, T. *Étude Critique sur la Formation de la Doctrine des Races, au 18ième siècle, et son expansion au 19ième siècle.* Brussels, 1922.

29. Stoddard, T. L. *The Rising Tide of Color Against White World Supremacy,* New York, 1920.

30. Thomas, F. *The Environmental Basis of Society.* New York, 1925.

31. Vitruvius, P. *The Ten Books on Architecture.* Cambridge, 1914. (Trans.)

32. Woltmann, L. *Politische Anthropologie.* Eisenach, 1903.

33. Woltmann, L. *Die Germanen und die Renaissance in Italien.* Leipzig, 1905.

PART I

THE BIOLOGICAL APPROACH

Chapter II

RACE

Definition

THE universal interest in racial problems has so far not been accompanied by anything like universal agreement as to the meaning of race. There is certainly no field of study in which terms have been used more loosely or more ambiguously, or in which social and political preoccupations have played more havoc with scientific method. Even among academic anthropologists there is no approach to unanimity, and the task of formulating the problems of this book in terms acceptable to all is by no means an easy one.

There is, however, one point on which it is safe to assume substantial agreement. Whatever else the term "race" may be found to include, it must at least refer to the presence in a population of certain *physical* characteristics. One writer (Hankins, 14) defines a race as "a group of human beings set apart from others by one or more marks of physical difference" (p. 262). To this simple definition one further qualification should be added, namely, that if this group is to be regarded as a race, the physical traits distinguishing it must be determined by heredity. Obviously, a group of men who have lost their legs in a war, or whose growth has been stunted by defective nourishment, will not constitute a race. The physical traits used as a criterion of race must be at least relatively (though not absolutely, as will be seen later) independent of the more obvious environmental influences; they must "breed true," they must be handed on from generation to generation.

A race, then, may be defined as a large group of men possessing in common certain physical characteristics which are determined by heredity. The other, non-physical, qualities which have been ascribed to races are in this sense secondary, in that they do not belong to the concept or definition of race; they are not used, for example, in race classification. When a psychologist (Moss, 30) writes that "a distinct race is a group of people having the same remote ancestry, and consequently having certain physical *and mental* [italics ours] traits different from those of other races with a totally different ancestry" (p. 93), he incorporates into his definition a judgment for which proof is required, and upon which there is in the meantime no agreement. Similarly, when an anthropologist (Hrdlička, 19) states that "the characters that distinguish human races are morphological, physiological, chemical, psychological, and even pathological" (p. 159), he is definitely outside the limits of accepted anthropological doctrine. By definition, the characters that distinguish human races are morphological; the rest remain to be proved.

Even in connection with physical or morphological characters, it is important to bear in mind certain qualifications to which the concept of race is subject. When two races are described as differing in any particular physical feature— for example, in stature—strictly speaking, this ought to mean that every member of the one race differs in that respect from every member of the other. (Boas, 3c.) Actually, when Mongoloids (for example, Japanese) are described as short, and North Europeans (for example, Swedes) as tall, this does not mean that all Japanese have the same (short) stature, nor that every Japanese is shorter than every Swede. Japanese vary greatly, and so do Swedes, and there is a great deal of overlapping—that is to say, there are many Japanese who are taller than many Swedes. This variability within any one racial group is recognized in the definition of a race (Hooton, 17) as "a great division of mankind, the members of which, though *individually varying*, are characterized *as a group* [all italics ours] by a certain combination of morphological and metrical features, principally non-adaptive, which have been derived from their common descent" (p. 397). There is no homogeneity within each race, and no sharp line between one race and another. "All the diversities which exist are variable, and pass into each other by insensible gradations." (Pritchard, 34, p. 644.)

It follows that when two races are being compared, it usually means little to say that one race is characterized by the possession of one trait, and the other race by the possession of another. There is too much variability within each race to permit of such a comparison. Evidently the so-called racial traits are not inherited equally in the case of every individual or every family belonging to that particular race. Inheritance takes place in family lines; and among both Japanese and Swedes, to revert to the example cited, there are both tall and short families, and therefore tall and short individuals. The two groups do differ, however, in the measure of central tendency (the average or median stature), and in the distribution of statures in the total population; they may still be compared from this point of view, and the amount of difference noted, as well as the amount of overlapping in the two distributions.

This has an important practical consequence which is, however, seldom fully recognized. If there is always overlapping, general statements made about a race will not necessarily apply to any particular member of that race. North Europeans are, as a group, tall, but many of them are short. If a certain individual is known to be a North European, it cannot be assumed that he will be tall. Any extension of group descriptions to the individual will always be open to question. This point has especial significance in connection with psychological comparisons; even if we believe, let us say, that Negroes as a group differ from Whites as a group in any of the aspects of intelligence or personality, we have no right to regard every Negro as differing from every White, or to expect that all Negroes will behave similarly in similar situations. This may seem too obvious to require emphasis; yet there is probably no error in the study of race into which it is easier to fall. It is permissible to speak of group differences only when care is taken not to apply the results of group comparisons to individuals. (Boas, 3c.)

CLASSIFICATION

A race, then, is characterized by the possession of certain inherited physical traits, and racial classification is based upon the distribution of physical traits in different populations. So far there may be said to be substantial agreement among physical anthropologists, but with this the agreement ceases. Granting that physical traits are important, it remains to be decided which trait is most important for purposes of classification; it is clear that the classifications will not be the same if, let us say, skin color is selected by one anthropologist and the shape of the head by another. Since there appears to be no objective way of deciding which trait is to be preferred, there are a great many different racial classifications, all of them equally subjective and equally arbitrary. A few illustrations will make this point clearer.

The earliest classifications were based almost exclusively on skin color, the most obvious of physical characteristics. Linnæus (26) had four races—*Europæus albus, Asiaticus luridus, Americanus rufus, Afer niger*. Blumenbach's (2) widely used classification changed the terminology slightly and added one race; his groups were the Caucasian, Mongolian, Ethiopian, American, Malayan. Nott and Gliddon (32) kept these five under the names of European, Asiatic, Negro, American and Malay, and added to them the Australian and the Arctic.

On the other hand, F. Müller (see 23), using hair texture as a criterion, reached a classification which naturally gave results entirely different from those of his predecessors. His scheme is as follows:

A. Ulotrichi, or Wooly-haired
    1. Lopochomi, or Tuft-haired; Papuans, Hottentot-Bushmen
    2. Eriocomi, or Fleecy-haired; African Negroes
B. Lissotrichi, or Straight-haired
    1. Euthycomi, or Stiff-haired; Australian, Malay, Mongolian, Arctic, American
    2. Euplocomi, or Wavy-haired; Dravidian (Southern India), Nubian (Sudan), Mediterranean (Europe, North Africa, etc.)

The arbitrariness of racial divisions, and the impossibility of determining whether there ought to be three races or three hundred, is perhaps nowhere better exemplified than in the classification by Deniker (6), who used a combination of hair texture, skin color, eye color and shape of nose, to arrive at no less than seventeen main races and twenty-nine sub-races. At the other extreme, Sergi (37), interested mainly in the skeletal characters of the face and head, divided mankind into two species, the dolichocephalic (long-headed) Eurafricans, and the brachycephalic (round-headed) Eurasiatics. (Note: The *cephalic index* is calculated from the formula $\dfrac{\text{width of head} \times 100}{\text{length of head}}$. If the resulting figure is seventy-five or less, the head is usually regarded as dolichocephalic; if eighty or more, as brachycephalic; between seventy-five and eighty, as mesocephalic. Kroeber [23] suggests seventy-seven and eighty-one as more appropriate limits for dolicho- and brachycephaly, respectively.)

The Eurafrican species, in Sergi's view, arose in Africa and spread in prehistoric times into Europe; it is represented by the African, Mediterranean and Nordic "races"; and since differences in skin color are explained by Sergi as the effect of temperature, climate, food and manner of life, these three groups are regarded as very closely related. The Eurasiatic species presumably arose in Asia, and also invaded Europe very early; it formed the brachycephalic wedge now found in central Europe, and includes Celts, Germans and Slavs, as well as Asiatics.

Head shape is here made to unite the African and the North European, differing as to skin color, hair texture, nasal index and a host of other characters. On the other hand, if skin color is used as a criterion of race, there is very little difference between the North and the Central European, who differ markedly in cephalic index; the skin color of the Negro and the Australian is almost the same, but their hair texture is altogether different. If hair texture is used, the Australian and Mongolian belong together; but they differ in skin color, in the hairiness of the body, and in a great many other morphological features. It is hardly necessary to multiply instances of the discrepancies in the field of race classification.

The classification which is in fairly general use, and which, with one modification or another, has the sanction of a great many anthropologists (see Kroeber, 23; Hrdlička, 19; Ripley, 36), is by no means free from this inevitable arbitrariness, but is presented here as a convenient starting point for further discussion. It describes three main races: the Negroid or "black," the Mongoloid or "yellow-brown," and the Caucasian or "white." The Australian, dark-skinned like the Negro, but with straight hair and great hairiness of the body, is sometimes regarded as an independent race (Elliott-Smith, 8), sometimes set to one side as of doubtful classification (Kroeber, 23).

The Negroid race, dark brown or black in color, is characterized by frizzly hair, relatively little hair on the face or body, full lips, a flat nose and rather long arms and legs, and is found in Africa and Melanesia; the Dwarf Black (Bushman and Hottentot) is a specialized variety. The Mongoloid race, "yellow" or brown, has straight hair, very little hair on the face or body, thin lips, usually short arms and legs, and frequently the epicanthic fold which gives the impression of slanting eyes. It includes not only the Mongolian proper, but also the Malay and the American Indian, the latter having migrated from Asia to North America via the neck of land now covered by Bering Straits.

The "white" race has, of course, been studied with much the greatest care, and several subvarieties have been described, of which the best known are the Nordic, the Alpine and the Mediterranean. The Nordic, or North European type, is characterized by tall stature, blond hair, blue eyes, a fair skin and dolichocephaly, and is found in greatest frequency in the Scandinavian countries, England, Scotland, northern Germany, northern France, Holland, the Flemish portion of Belgium, and in some of the Baltic countries. The Alpine or Central European is a little shorter and a little darker than the North European, and is brachycephalic; this type is found in Switzerland, Austria, southern Germany, central France, the Walloon portion of Belgium, northern Italy, Russia, Poland, the Balkans, and parts of western and central Asia. (Fischer, 9, and Deniker, 6, speak of a Dinaric race, tall, dark and brachycephalic, as inhabiting the Balkans, but other anthropologists see in the Dinaric race only a subvariety of the Alpine.) The Mediterranean or South European type is still darker, still shorter, and dolichocephalic, and is most frequently met with in Spain and Portugal, southern France, southern Italy, Greece, northern Africa, parts of East Africa, Arabia, Persia and India. (Kroeber, 23, however, prefers to regard the Hindu as an independent physical type.) Other types have been described, but these are perhaps the most widely known and the most frequently recognized.

A word of caution is necessary at this point. When it is said that the Scandinavian countries, for example, are Nordic, it is usually implied that almost all, if not all, Scandinavians are tall, blond and dolichocephalic. This is far from being the case. The Swedish anthropologist Retzius (35) found among recruits in the Swedish army only 11 per cent pure or "typical" Nordics. In another study using a somewhat less rigorous criterion, the figure was raised to 30 per cent. Even in a country like Sweden, which has frequently been described as 100 per cent Nordic, the typical Nordics still appear to be very much in the minority. The present writer had occasion in connection with a psychological investigation conducted in Europe some years ago (22) to visit certain regions which have been regarded as "purely" Nordic, Alpine and Mediterranean, respectively; he found only 20 to 25 per cent of boys between the ages of ten and twelve who conformed to the physical type supposedly predominating in their particular community. "Pure races," that is to say, populations all the members of which are of the same physical type, are occasionally found in small inbred communities (Boas, 3c), but not as constituting any of the existing European nations. To preach in favor of race purity, as has been done so often in recent times, is therefore just anthropological nonsense. It is many thousands of years too late, not only for Europe and Europeans, but for other parts of the world as well; there are no longer any pure races to be kept pure.

It may be, however, that this whole manner of stating the problem is a misleading one. The relative rarity of pure racial types may be due to countless generations of race mixture; it may also be due to the fact that the pure race never existed in the form in which it has been described by the anthropologist. The type may be an entirely artificial creation, introduced for purposes of classification, but with little or no basis in reality. If we compare Swedes and Bavarians, we find the former to be on the average taller, fairer and more long-headed; if now we combine these three characteristics of tallness, blondness and dolichocephaly into a "type" or "race" and assume that originally it was a pure race, every member of which showed this same combination of characteristics, we are definitely going beyond the evidence. We have no way of knowing whether such a homogeneous group ever existed.

RACE AND NATION

It follows from the above that to assume any sort of identity between race and nation is clearly unjustified. Race is a zoological concept; it refers to physical type; nation is a political concept implying boundaries and an independent government. The absurdity of identifying the two is clearest in the case of the American "melting pot" nations, each with an almost boundless heterogeneity of physical characteristics. Similarly among the European nations, it is at once clear that the political boundaries have nothing to do with physical type. References to a French or German or Italian race are meaningless. In France, the Nordic type is found in the extreme north (Flanders, Normandy), the Alpine type in the large central area (Auvergne and Velay, for example), and the Mediterranean type in the south (the Pyrenees, Provence, the Riviera). In Germany the northern portions (Schleswig-Holstein, Hanover) contain many "Nordics," but the whole south (Baden, Bavaria, Wurtemberg) is predominantly Alpine; it is said that at one time anthropometric work in Germany was halted because it yielded too many non-Nordic components. (Dixon, 7.) In Italy the Alpine type occurs most frequently in the north (Lombardy, Piedmont), while the south, including Sicily and Sardinia, is predominantly Mediterranean or South European. In all three countries the "unclassifiable" or "mixed" types are definitely in the majority, and there are large regions in which "pure" racial types are very rare exceptions. The same situation prevails in most European nations, and it is therefore important to bear in mind that the terms *race* and *nation* belong in entirely different categories.

It is only fair to point out, however, that one anthropologist (Keith, 20a) views the relation between race and nation quite differently. "If evolution is true, we ought to find human races in every stage of differentiation. This is what anthropological investigation is now revealing. There are not only . . . completely differentiated racial types, but there are nationalities and peoples which represent every stage in the process of differentiation from a zero-point upwards." There are different kinds of races:

Pandiacritic races........every individual recognizable
Macrodiacritic races...80 per cent or more recognizable
Mesodiacritic races........30-80 per cent recognizable
Microdiacritic races...less than 30 per cent recognizable

British nationalities are regarded as being only at the microdiacritic stage of racial differentiation. "The politician's conception of race is thus justified and should be regarded as having a true biological significance." Keith's view, however, can hardly be said to be identical with that of the "racial" politician, to whom race is something fixed and immutable, not something which can be created out of the accident that a large number of people now live near one another and intermarry. To the racially minded politician it is not enough that his nation is becoming a race; he regards his nation as a complete race now, and is therefore resentful of all intermixture. In that sense, existing nations are clearly not races. In any case, Keith's racial criterion of recognizability may reside in a host of secondary factors— clothes, gait, posture, facial expression—and may have no biological or genetic significance whatsoever.

RACE AND LANGUAGE

There is even more confusion between race and language, and many terms which properly apply only to language have been used as if they had also a racial connotation. It is wrong, for example, to speak of a "Latin" race, in spite of the frequency with which that phrase appears in popular literature. Latin is of course a language, and "Latins" can mean only those groups whose languages are of Latin origin —among others, the French, Italians, Spaniards, Portuguese and Roumanians. Of these, the Spaniards and Portuguese are mostly Mediterranean in type, Roumanians are largely Alpine, Italians are partly Alpine and partly Mediterranean, and the French are a mixture of all three European types, with the Alpine predominating. Clearly, there is no race or physical type to which all Latins may be said to belong.

The term "Aryan" as applied to race is also meaningless.

Students of linguistic science have given the name Aryan to
the parent language from which most European languages
presumably developed. Aryans, then, would be the people
who speak a language derived from the original Aryan or
Indo-European; if such a language is spoken by Negroes or
Polynesians, they too may legitimately be called by that
name. If it is preferred to restrict the term to those who
were the first to use an Aryan language, it is still impossible
to give it a precise racial significance, for no one knows to
what physical type these original Aryans belonged. Max
Müller (31), who at one time believed that one could speak
of the Aryans as a race, later realized his error, and gave it
as his opinion that an ethnologist who speaks of Aryan
race, Aryan blood, Aryan eyes and hair, is as great a sinner
as a linguist who speaks of a dolichocephalic dictionary or
a brachycephalic grammar. Dolichocephaly refers to physical type, and Aryan to language; the two categories require
to be kept separate. It need hardly be added that the recent
agitation in favor of preserving the purity of the Aryan race
and rigidly excluding all non-Aryans has no foundation in
anthropology.

There is no "Semitic" race; when Arabs and Jews are
described as Semites, all that can legitimately be meant is
that Arabic and Hebrew both belong to a group of languages known as Semitic. As to physical type, Arabs are
predominantly Mediterranean. Many Jews belong to the
same general type, but these are definitely in the minority;
if there is any one type which occurs more frequently than
another, it is the Alpine. There is clearly no one physical
type which can be described as Semitic. As far as the Jews
are concerned, a very large number of investigations have revealed so much variability in physical type, with skin color
ranging from very blond to very dark, and cephalic index

from extreme dolichocephaly to extreme brachycephaly, that almost all anthropologists (with the exception of those whose views are influenced by purely political considerations) agree that a distinctively "Jewish race" does not exist. In every country there seems to be a clearly marked tendency for Jews to approximate the physical type of the people among whom they live. Presumably distinctive Jewish characteristics, like the "Jewish" nose, are relatively rare, and, in any case, are probably due to intermixture with groups which were originally not Jewish. (See Ripley, 36; Dixon, 7; Fishberg, 10.)

Needless confusion in the whole field of race is caused by this loose use of terms, and by the failure to keep constantly in mind the kind of group to which the word "race" may legitimately be applied. When problems of race are involved, it is important to leave political and linguistic categories in the background. If it were not for established usage, it would certainly be wiser to discard the term altogether, and start with another which would be free from all these entangling connotations. As it is, the word will have to be used, but always with the understanding that it refers to physical type, and that all the other implications with which it has been popularly and historically associated require to be examined very carefully before they can be accepted.

INSTABILITY OF PHYSICAL TYPE

The concept of race or physical type, usually regarded as referring to fixed group characteristics, has undergone a very serious limitation as the result of the important studies conducted by Franz Boas (3a) on the changes in bodily form of descendants of immigrants. Boas was interested in discovering whether the change from the European to the American (particularly New York City) environment would be accompanied by any change in the bodily form of the immigrant and his descendants.

The results as they affect cephalic index are of special interest in this connection. Sicilians (males) born in Sicily were found to have an average index of 77.7; those born in America, 81.5; Hebrews (males) born in central Europe, 83.0; in America, 81.4. For the female subjects, the results are similar, though not quite so striking. The changes are statistically significant and point clearly to a definite influence of the American environment; the head of the American-born Sicilian becomes rounder, that of the American-born central European Jew becomes longer. The northwest European (Scotch) subjects show no change in head form, but a definite increase in weight and stature. Boas concludes that "all the evidence is now in favor of a great plasticity of human types" (p. 3). This does not necessarily mean that there is in America a definite approach to a general uniform American type; "we do not yet know how long the changes continue, and whether they would all lead to the same result; the proof of the plasticity of types does not imply that the plasticity is unlimited" (p. 13). In view of the frequency with which Boas has been misquoted to the effect that race is entirely a function of environment, and that the American environment is gradually producing a distinctively American race, his own much more conservative appraisal of his results should be borne in mind.

A number of explanations of the change in head form have been advanced, but no one of them appears to be entirely satisfactory. Fischer (9), for example, points out that the form of the head may be markedly influenced by external conditions in childhood, particularly by habits of cradling and bedding. If the infant lies on its back, its head will become broad with a flat occiput; if on its side, it will be long and narrow. A pair of identical twins were so treated by Walcher (39), and at the age of two and a half years there was a cephalic index of 78.8 in one case, and of 86.2 in the other. (Similarly, the type of cushion will also have an effect, though a rather curious one; a hard cushion will cause dolichocephaly because the head will sink to one side; a soft cushion will cause brachycephaly because the infant will remain on its back.) As Boas points out, however, it is difficult to see why a change in the form of cradling should affect one group one way, and another group quite differently.

Martin (29) indicates that in animal experimentation there are many parallels to the findings of Boas. A lack of certain vitamins in the diet of rats, for example, results in a more dolichocephalic form of skull. The effect of domestication is marked; in the wild form, wolves have a long, narrow, low head; in captivity, the head is short, wide and high, with an increase in cranial capacity. Similar changes have been reported in the case of other domesticated animals. (Kruse, 24.)

It has also been suggested that the movement from country to city may be responsible. Ammon, as we have seen in the preceding chapter (see page 5), evolved the so-called Ammon's Law to explain why the inhabitants of the city of Karlsruhe in Baden were found to be more dolichocephalic than the surrounding rural population. His theory, however, offers no possible explanation for the very different results in the case of the Sicilian and of the central European Hebrew immigrants, respectively.

In any case, whatever the explanation, there seems to be no doubt as to the partial instability of the physical traits used in racial classification. Boas' results have been confirmed for head index by Guthe (13), Hirsch (16), and others; and Spier (38) has shown that Japanese born in America are taller than those who are born in Japan. Racial distinctions, even on the physical side, are by no means so hard and fixed as many of the racial classifications would suggest. (Note: The variations in the physical type of the Jew the world over may also be explained, at least in part, by this same plasticity under varying conditions. Fishberg [10] and others are inclined to account for it entirely as the result of intermarriage; it is probable that both factors have contributed.)

Primitive and Advanced Races

The question of the origin or origins of the human race, as well as of its subdivisions, has important practical as well as theoretical implications. If various human groups differ in their origin, there is a greater presumption in favor of a fundamental difference in their stage of biological development, and therefore also of their mental level. The history of colonization illustrates the manner in which the theory of polygenesis was used to justify the exploitation of dark-skinned natives by the conquering Whites. Negro slavery in the United States was frequently justified on similar grounds; the Negro was regarded as an inferior and totally different species of man, and ordinary human or humane treatment was more or less unnecessary in his case.

At present there is almost no scientific opinion in favor of the polygenic theory; with the one important exception of Sergi (37), who regards the Eurafrican and Eurasiatic types as two distinct species, most anthropologists and prehistorians have been content to seek but one cradle of humanity. (See MacCurdy, 27.) Klaatsch's (21) polygenic theory is little more than a scientific curiosity; his notion was that the Negro and the gorilla are closely related and descended from one ancestral stock of ape-men, and that the orang is similarly related to the races of Europe, Asia and Australia. The theory was later modified or misinterpreted by Klaatsch's followers to mean that the Negro descended from the gorilla, the Mongolian from the orang, and the Caucasian from the chimpanzee. The evidence for both the original and the later theory was equally trivial, and it hardly needs to be taken very seriously.

Even in terms of a single origin of the human race, it is still possible to ask whether in the evolutionary scheme certain human varieties represent earlier, more primitive types, a little more closely related than others to the pre-human ancestor. Attempts have been made to construct a human family tree, showing which races separated from the human stem earlier, and which represent later, more advanced varieties. Of the three important races, it is customary to place the Negro a little below the others in the scale of development, with the Mongolian somewhat higher, and the Caucasian flowering at the top of the tree. (See Osborn, 33; Warden, 40; Elliott-Smith, 8.) The evidence usually cited in support of this scheme is that the Negro shows a number of primitive traits—dark pigmentation, prognathism, receding forehead, and low, broad nose—which presumably indicate his closer relationship to the ape-like ancestor from whom we are all descended. (See Warden, 40.)

Unfortunately there is at present no means of reconstructing in detail all the morphological features of the immediate percursor of man, although some information can be obtained from prehistoric human material. It seems quite certain that man did not descend from any of the existing anthropoids, but that the anthropoids and man had a common ancestor. It is mainly by a study of the anthropoid, however, that some idea of this common ancestor may be obtained; and it is relatively safe to assume that the features now shown by the three great primates—the gorilla, the chimpanzee and the orang—may be regarded as biologically earlier or more primitive than those which occur only among human beings.

From this point of view, some of the traits of the Negro referred to above do lend support to the notion of his greater primitiveness; in others, however, the Negro is by no means the most ape-like of the three races. The ape, for example, has practically no lips, and the thick everted lips of the Negro may therefore be regarded as the most human and the most advanced; in this respect the Mongolian is closest to the anthropoid, and the Caucasian intermediate. In the hairiness of the face and the body, the Caucasian, and particularly the North European, resembles the ape most closely (the Australian is not included in these comparisons); the Negro is next, and the Mongolian furthest removed. In hair texture the Caucasian is again closest; the Mongolian is intermediate, while the frizzly hair of the Negro is the least ape-like of the three. The hierarchy will evidently depend entirely on the features which are singled out for observation. (Boas, 3c; Kroeber, 23.) In the length of his arms the Negro may seem to be the most closely related to the gorilla and the other great apes, but it is only fair to note also that in the length of his legs he is the furthest removed.

Pigmentation offers a special problem. It is usually assumed that the dark pigmentation of the Negro is an indication of greater primitiveness. The gorilla is of course black, and the skin of the chimpanzee and of the orang frequently contains some black pigment, though the prevailing color is brown rather than black. Keith (20b) is of the opinion that the stock from which the human races have arisen had brown pigmented skin, and that the very black African and very fair European may represent comparatively recent products in the evolution of modern races. In that case, the dark pigmentation of the Negro could hardly be regarded as an especially primitive character.

Marked supra-orbital ridges—rounded bony prominences just above and in extreme cases overhanging the eyes—are present in the gorilla and the chimpanzee (though not in the orang) and in many of the early human finds like Pithecanthropus, Neanderthal man, Rhodesian man, and others. Keith (20b) writes: "There is not a shadow of doubt that the stock from which modern man is descended had great supra-orbital ridges" (p. 177). Supra-orbital ridges are much more pronounced in Whites than in Negroes.

The dolichocephaly of the Negro has also been referred to as a primitive trait (Warden, 40), but here again the matter is far too complicated to be disposed of so simply. It is true that early man appears to have been long-headed; the cephalic indices which have been calculated for the paleolithic specimens range from 70.0 to about 75. (La Chapelle, 75.0; Neanderthal, 73.9; Spy I, 70.0; Spy II, 75.7; Gibraltar, 74.0. See Osborn, 33; Martin, 29; Hooton, 17; MacCurdy, 27.) The fact, however, that all the great apes are brachycephalic makes it very difficult to regard dolichocephaly as necessarily more primitive. The male orang has an average cephalic index of 88.0; the male gorilla, 82.4; and the male chimpanzee, 83.5. (Martin, 29.)

In this connection it is maintained by Martin, Dixon (7), and others, that brachycephaly is dominant over dolicho- and mesocephaly, and that it seems also to be more persistent. They see dolichocephaly slowly giving way to brachycephaly in many countries of Europe; this would suggest that brachycephaly is the later and more advanced form. Recent very careful statistical analyses by Boas (3b) of Dutch material collected by Frets (12) have failed, however, to show any brachycephalic dominance; inheritance of head form does not follow any simple Mendelian rule, and it is impossible to regard any one variety as dominant over any other. (See also Bryn, 5; Hilden, 15.)

In any case, since many of the so-called advanced groups, like the Nordic and the Mediterranean among the Whites, also show dolichocephaly and would therefore have to be regarded as more primitive than the round-headed Mongoloid Eskimo or Malays, the racial hierarchy referred to above would receive no support from the use of head form as a criterion of development.

Finally it may be noted that a number of attempts have been made to discover whether there is any difference in the degree of relationship between the blood of various races and that of the anthropoid apes. Various techniques have been used, but they have all failed to demonstrate such a difference. Landsteiner and Miller (25) found the differences between White and American Negro bloods to be imperceptible by the techniques which they used. Bruck (4) reports that the differences between the various human races (White, Mongolian, Malay) cannot be demonstrated by the use of serum which has been immunized against apes. Similar results are reported also by Marshall and Teague (28) and Fitzgerald (11), although the agreement is not complete.

It seems fair to conclude that there is no racial hierarchy which is consistently supported by all the available evidence, and that the notion that one race is more primitive than another has no acceptable scientific foundation.

BIBLIOGRAPHY

1. Blumenbach, J. F. *Anthropological Treatises*. London, 1865. (Trans.)
2. Boas, F. *The Mind of Primitive Man*. New York, 1911.

3a. Boas, F. *Abstract of the Report on Changes in Bodily Form of Descendants of Immigrants.* Washington, 1911.

3b. Boas, F. "The Cephalic Index in Holland and Its Heredity." *Human Biol.,* 5:1933, pp. 587-599.

3c. Boas, F. *Anthropology and Modern Life.* New York, 1928.

4. Bruck, C. "Die biologische Differenzierung von Affenarten und menschlichen Rassen durch spezifische Blutreaktion." *Berliner Klin. Woch.,* 44:1907, p. 793.

5. Bryn, R. "Researches into Anthropological Heredity." *Hereditas,* 1:1920, p. 186.

6. Deniker, J. *The Races of Man.* New York, 1900. (Trans.)

7. Dixon, R. B. *The Racial History of Man.* New York, 1923.

8. Elliot-Smith, G. *Human History.* London, 1929.

9. Fischer, E. *Anthropologie.* Leipzig, 1923. (In *Kultur der Gegenwart,* Schwalbe, Ed.)

10. Fishberg, M. *The Jews: A Study of Race and Environment.* New York, 1911.

11. Fitzgerald, G. G. "An Attempt to Show Specific Racial Differences in Human Blood by Means of the Reaction of Fixation." *J. Med. Res.,* 21:1909, p. 41.

12. Frets, G. P. *Heredity of Headform in Man.* The Hague, 1921.

13. Guthe, C. E. "Notes on the Cephalic Index of Russian Jews in Boston." *Amer. J. Phys. Anthrop.,* 1:1918, pp. 213-223.

14. Hankins, F. H. *The Racial Basis of Civilization: A Critique of the Nordic Doctrine.* New York, 1926.

15. Hildén, K. "Zur Kenntnis der menschlichen Kopfform in genetischer Beziehung." *Hereditas,* 6: 1925, pp. 127-146.

16. Hirsch, N. D. M. "Cephalic Index of American-born Children of Three Foreign Groups." *Amer. J. Phys. Anthrop.,* 10: 1927, p. 79.

17. Hooton, E. A. *Up from the Ape.* New York, 1931.

18. Hrdlička, A. *The Old Americans.* Baltimore, 1925.

19. Hrdlička, A. "Human Races" in *Human Biology and Racial Welfare.* (E. V. Cowdry, Ed.) New York, 1930.

20a. Keith, Sir A. "The Evolution of the Human Races." *J. Royal Anthrop. Inst.,* 58:1928, pp. 305-321.

20b. Keith, Sir A. *Man, a History of the Human Body.* New York, 1912.

21. Klaatsch, H. *The Evolution and Progress of Mankind.* London, 1923. (Trans.)

22. Klineberg, O. "A Study of Psychological Differences between Racial and National Groups in Europe." *Arch. Psych.,* No. 132:1931.

23. Kroeber, A. L. *Anthropology.* New York, 1923.

24. Kruse, W. *Die Deutschen und Ihre Nachbarvölker.* Leipzig, 1929.

25. Landsteiner, K., and Miller, C. P. "Serological Studies on the Blood of the Primates." *J. Exp. Medicine,* 42:1925, pp. 841-872.

26. Linnaeus C. v. *Systema Naturæ.* London, 1747. (5th Ed.)

27. MacCurdy, G. G. *Human Origins.* New York, 1924.

28. Marshall, H. T., and Teague, O. "A Study of the Precipitin and Complement Fixation Reactions." *Philippine J. Sci.,* 3:1908, pp. 357-377.

29. Martin, R. *Lehrbuch der Anthropologie.* Jena, 1928. (3 vols.)

30. Moss, F. *Your Mind in Action.* Cambridge, Mass., 1929.

31a. Müller, M. *Lectures on the Science of Language.* London, 1864.

31b. Müller, M. *Biographies of Words and the Home of the Aryas.* London, 1888.

32. Nott, J. C., and Gliddon, G. R. *Types of Mankind.* Philadelphia, 1854.

33. Osborn, H. F. *Men of the Old Stone Age.* New York, 1918.

34. Pritchard, A. *The Natural History of Man.* London, 1885.

35. Retzius, G., and Fürst, C. M. *Anthropologia suecica.* Stockholm, 1902.

36. Ripley, W. Z. *The Races of Europe.* New York, 1899.

37. Sergi, G. *L'Uomo, secondo le origini, l'antichità, le variazioni e la distribuzione geografica.* Milan, 1911.

38. Spier, L. "Growth of Japanese Children Born in America and in Japan." *Univ. Wash. Publ. in Anthrop.,* 3:No. 1, 1929, pp. 1-30.

39. Walcher, G. "Entstehung von Brachy- und Dolichozephalie." *Zentrlbl. f. Gynäk.,* 29:1905, pp. 193-196; *Münch. Med. Woch.,* 1911, p. 134.

40. Warden, C. J. *The Evolution of Human Behavior.* New York, 1932.

Chapter III

BIOCHEMICAL AND CONSTITUTIONAL
DIFFERENCES

THE BLOOD GROUPS

THE arbitrary nature of racial classifications based upon physical characteristics, and the consequent difference of opinion as to how races are really divided, has led anthropologists to look for a criterion of race in a totally different field. It seemed for a time as if certain properties of the blood, more particularly the agglutinative reactions of the red blood corpuscles (that is to say, the tendency of the corpuscles to clump together under certain conditions), might offer a satisfactory basis for distinguishing race, and might introduce at least some degree of order into the chaotic field of physical anthropology.

Landsteiner (32) pointed out in 1900 that bloods might be classified into various groups according to these agglutinative reactions. Every blood contains, of course, red blood cells or corpuscles which float freely in the clear, straw-colored fluid, the serum. It frequently happens that when serum from one blood is added to the red blood cells of another, agglutination or clumping occurs. The substances in the serum which cause the clumping are known as *agglutinins*, and the materials in the red blood cells which make them susceptible to agglutination are the *agglutinogens*. There are two different agglutinogens, A and B, which may be found in the red blood cells; any particular blood may contain either A or B, or both, or neither. There are also two different agglutinins, anti-A and anti-B, which may bc found in serum; any particular serum may contain either anti-A or anti-B, or both, or neither. If an individual has in his corpuscles only the A property, he must have in his serum, anti-B; the serum always contains the agglutinins which react against the qualities lacking in the corpuscles. It is clear that A and anti-A cannot co-exist in the same blood, for in that case the serum would cause the agglutination of its own red blood cells.

There are four possible combinations of these characteristics, and they constitute the four blood groups.

I. Group O   The red blood cells contain neither A nor B, and are therefore not agglutinable by any serum. The serum contains both anti-A and anti-B, and agglutinates the red blood cells of all the other groups.

II. Group A   The red blood cells contain A, and are agglutinable by the serum of I and III. The serum contains agglutinin anti-B, and agglutinates the red blood cells of III and IV.

III. Group B   The red blood cells contain B, and are agglutinable by the serum of I and II. The serum contains agglutinin anti-A, and agglutinates the red blood cells of II and IV.

IV. Group AB   The red blood cells contain both A and B, and are agglutinable by the serum of I, II and III. The serum contains no agglutinins.

(Note: The above classification is the one suggested by Jansky [24]. Moss [39] changes groups I and IV around. In order to avoid ambiguity it is much better, as Verzar [65] suggests, to use the letters rather than the numerals. In this country the Moss classification is in general clinical use. It should be added that still other sub-groups have since been discovered. See 32c.)

In determining the group to which an unknown blood belongs, it is necessary to start with test sera known to belong to Groups A and B. A drop of each test serum is placed upon a slide, and a drop of an emulsion of the red cells of the unknown blood is added to it. If the cells are not agglutinated by either serum, the blood belongs to Group O; if they are agglutinated by both sera, the blood belongs to Group AB; if agglutinated by the B serum alone, the blood is A; if by the A serum alone, the blood is B.

In transfusion fatal effects may result when the red blood corpuscles of the donor are agglutinated by the serum of the recipient; it is clearly of the greatest importance, therefore, to make certain that the A and B groups be kept separate. Since it usually does very little harm if some of the red blood cells of the recipient are agglutinated by the serum of the donor, Group O is the universal donor, and Group AB the universal recipient. (See Gates, 17.)

The blood groups have attracted considerable popular notice because of their use in medico-legal cases, particularly in those concerned with disputed parentage. Whatever agglutinogens are found in the red blood cells of the child must be present in the cells of one or the other parent. For example, if both parents belong to Group O, the child's blood can contain neither A nor B and he must therefore also belong to Group O. In such a case, if the child's blood should turn out to contain either A or B or AB, it may be concluded that the child is illegitimate. Similarly, if both parents belong to Group A, the child may belong to Groups A or O, but not to either B or AB; if one parent is A and the other B, the child may belong to any one of the four groups. Other possibilities can easily be worked out along these general lines. It is important to note that an examination of the blood in medico-legal cases can yield only negative evidence, that is to say, it can in certain cases determine that a given individual cannot be the father of a particular child. It is obvious that blood examination can never show who the father really is. (For discussion of heredity of blood groups, see Ottenberg, 42; Snyder, 59; Bernstein, 7.)

BIOCHEMICAL "RACES"

The application of blood groupings to the question of racial classifications is originally the work of Hirszfeld and Hirszfeld (21), who examined the blood of a large number of soldiers of different nationalities interned in a camp in Salonika during the latter part of the World War. They found such marked differences in the frequency of the various blood pictures that they reached the conclusion that the blood groupings were fundamental to race differences. The tables which they present make a very good case in favor of their theory of two distinct serological races, A and B, one originating in Europe, the other in Asia, and mixing so as to produce the races and the nationalities which we now know. A portion of their results is presented in Table 1.

TABLE 1: DISTRIBUTION OF BLOOD GROUPS (HIRSZFELD)

Nationality	Per Cent A	Per Cent B	Per Cent O
German	48.0	17.0	40.0
English	46.4	10.2	46.4
Serbian	46.4	20.2	38.0
Greek	45.6	20.2	38.2
French	45.6	14.2	43.2
Turk	44.6	25.2	36.8
Italian	41.8	14.8	47.2
Russian	37.5	28.1	40.7
Arab	37.4	24.0	43.6
Malagasy	30.7	28.2	45.5
Annamite	29.6	35.6	42.0
Negro (Senegal)	27.6	34.2	43.2
Hindu	27.5	49.7	31.3

(Note: These percentages in each case add up to more than 100. This is due to the fact that the table is so arranged that the cases of AB are listed with both A and B, because they indicate the presence of both A and B.)

As the Hirszfelds point out, Group A is more plentiful in central and northern Europe (over 40 per cent); as we go east and south, the amount of A decreases (between 30 and 40 per cent around the Mediterranean, less than 30 per cent among the groups from Asia and Africa). The percentage of B shows a corresponding, though not quite so regular, increase, as may be seen from the table.

Unfortunately for this theory and classification, the results obtained by later investigators complicated the picture tremendously. (See table in Snyder, 59.) The figure for the Japanese, for example, is 54.8 per cent A, 32.3 per cent B, 26.8 per cent O; this is almost the same blood picture as is shown by the Germans, who are certainly far removed from them, not only on the basis of this theory, but also in all the physical characteristics used in the more conventional racial classifications. The figure for the Poles is 46.6 per cent A, 29.9 per cent B, and 32.5 per cent O; almost exactly the same proportions are found for the northern Chinese—44.4 per cent, 31.0 per cent, and 31.1 per cent. Kruse (31) points out that a similar blood picture is found in other groups as far apart as these—for example, the English and the Sardinians, the Tyrolese and the Berbers. Various groups of Chinese differ as much from one another as they do from a number of European groups. Evidently the classification into serological races is not nearly so simple or so certain as the original investigations would suggest.

In order to allow for this greater complexity, Ottenberg (44) introduced a classification into six biochemical races, which was later slightly modified by Snyder (59), who described seven races altogether. These more elaborate classifications, however, simply illustrate again exactly the same difficulty encountered by the orthodox physical anthropologists; here also racial divisions depend upon arbitrary limits set by the special interests of the investigator. Snyder himself makes this clear in his statement that until more extensive work has been done on the peoples of Africa and the Orient no very definite conclusions can be drawn from the blood group data. Even then we cannot be too cautious in our applications (p. 257).

Perhaps the most striking result in this whole field is that found in the case of the American Indians, who show an exceedingly high percentage of Group O. For pure-blood Indians, Coca and Deibert (10) obtained a figure of 77.7 per cent, and Nigg (41), of 72.7 per cent. In a later study Snyder (59), after a very careful separation of pure from mixed-blood American Indians, reported that 91.3 per cent of the former and 64.8 per cent of the latter belonged to Group O; he believes that really pure-blood Indians would belong entirely to this group. (Somewhat similar results have also been reported for the Filipinos by Cabrera and Wade [8]; 64.7 per cent O.) It has been suggested that the American Indians branched off from the human stem before the mutation to either A or B occurred in the blood; this would mean that the original blood formula was O, and that A, B and AB are relatively late developments.

The most important objection to this otherwise plausible theory is that the blood groups occur among the anthropoids also, which makes it a little less likely that A and B represent late mutations. Landsteiner and Miller (33) found among 55 chimpanzees, 50 in Group A and 5 in O; of 6 orangs, 2 were A, 3 were B and 1 AB; the one gibbon tested was in Group A. The presence of A and B in the apes does not necessarily mean that man derived his agglutinogens from the anthropoids. As Gates points out (17), it is possible also that they represent independent parallel mutations in the anthropoid and the human lines of descent. Gates' further point, that otherwise "it is difficult to see how blood groupings of different human races can be significant as showing racial relationships" (p. 202), can hardly be taken very seriously. It still remains to be proved just how significant the blood groupings really are. A recent survey by Wyman and Boyd (69) concludes that "the blood groups are probably older than the present races."

In any case there seems to be very little relationship between the usual types of anthropological classification and the division of races according to the blood groupings. For example, the so-called Hunan type (Snyder's classification) includes Poles, Ukrainians and Roumanian Jews, as well as a number of definitely Mongoloid types; the Africo-Malaysian type combines groups as different as the Senegalese and the American Negroes on the one hand, and the people of Annam, Java and part of China on the other. In Europe the Nordic, Alpine and Mediterranean "races" show no clearcut differentiation in the frequencies of their blood groups. This may of course mean that there has been so much intermingling in Europe for thousands of years as to result in a general uniformity of type, in which the original elements have been obscured. In that event blood groupings are now just as valueless as skin color or stature in revealing fundamental race differences. It has also been suggested that geographic and other environmental factors may have a definite effect upon racial blood pictures; Kruse (31) explains in this way the great variability among the Jews.

On the psychological side, there has so far been little attempt to discover whether differences in blood grouping correspond to differences in mentality. If it should develop, after a great deal more work has been done, that blood is a better criterion of race than is physical type, the study of racial psychology will necessarily change from a comparison of Nordics and Mediterraneans to that of Groups A and B and O. One such investigation was made by Furukawa (15), but the results are difficult to interpret. With this exception, all that has been done in the meantime is to look for some biochemical basis in the blood for the psychological differences found among various members of the same general racial group. The components of human blood—hæmoglobin, creatinin, phosphate, sugar, calcium, and many others—have been quantitatively studied in the attempt to throw some light on the biochemical basis of personality. (See, for example, Starr [61], and Rich [48].) A very recent study in this field has, however, shown so much variability in the day-to-day determinations of the biochemical components of the blood of the same individual as to make it doubtful whether these can be used with any accuracy in the study of psychological characteristics. (Goldstein, 18.) It is clear that this whole field has at present little to offer to the student of psychological race differences.

The Endocrine Glands

The approach to the problem of race differences from the standpoint of the endocrines, or internal secretions, has attracted special attention, because it offers a basis for some degree of correspondence between physical and mental characteristics. Recent work, mostly of a clinical nature, has suggested that personality may be at least partially under the control of endocrine factors; if it can be shown that the physical characteristics used in race classification are also due to excess or deficiency in the internal secretions, it may be possible in this way to lay a foundation for a scientific race psychology.

Baur, Fischer and Lenz (3) are of this opinion. "Racial differences mainly depend upon differences in the internal secretions. Inasmuch as the effects of the internal secretions are of great importance in determining the outward bodily configuration, and inasmuch as their effects are also closely connected with the mental life, it should be possible on this ground to trace connections between mental aptitudes and bodily racial characters, and to do this scientifically" (p. 688). Berman (6a) writes: "It seems to him [the writer] manifest that in the explanation of similarities and dissimilarities in racial and geographical groups, their investigation [of the endocrine glands] opens the road to a series of researches the value of which cannot be overestimated" (p. 165).

The most important work in this field has been done by Sir Arthur Keith (25a; 25b; 25c), who has considered in detail the functioning of the various endocrine glands in connection with physical racial characteristics. It will be convenient in this discussion to take up one by one the principal endocrines, and to discuss critically the psychological and racial significance of each. (For a convenient summary of the material on the endocrines, see Hoskins, 23.)

1. *The Thyroid.* This gland, consisting of two lobes and a connecting isthmus, and situated at the base of the neck, controls metabolic activity, or the rate of physical and chemical change in the body. Its normal activity is necessary for the regulation of energy transformations in the organism. When it is overactive, there results a condition known as hyperthyroidism, the most important symptoms of which are exhaustion, increased excitability and a rapid heart rate. Diminished activity, or hypothyroidism, is psychologically

more significant. When it occurs early in life, it may in extreme cases result in cretinism, characterized by dwarfism and general physical underdevelopment, as well as by mental sluggishness and subnormality. When this same condition develops after puberty, it is known as myxedema. Both myxedema and cretinism can be counteracted and in many cases entirely cured by the administration of thyroid.

In cretinism the character of the face, the hair and the skin may be markedly altered, and Keith believes that some of these alterations tend to bring about a resemblance to the Mongoloid facies. For example, there is a flattening of the face and, in particular, a reduction in the bony scaffolding of the nose, which in many cases gives a definitely Mongoloid appearance. The Mongolian, then, would be relatively hypothyroid as compared with the European. Keith is also of the opinion that the condition known as *Mongolian idiocy*, so-called because of a somewhat superficial resemblance to the Mongoloid type, and regarded by Crookshank (11) as a reversion to a Mongolian component in the ancestry of Europeans, is also due to a thyroid deficiency. It is important to note, however, that Mongolian idiocy is not improved by the administration of thyroid, and that it is therefore probably not due entirely, if at all, to a thyroid condition.

Stockard (63) attempts to explain the characteristics of African pygmies on the basis of thyroid deficiency. He points out that the human cretin will not develop into an adult unless thyroid is administered. The individual with a subnormal amount of thyroid may be expected to be more childlike than the normal, and also much shorter in stature because of the metabolic disturbance. The African pygmy he regards as a childish African of low intelligence as well as of small size—a not fully metamorphosed large Negro, suffering from a mild and slow-going cretinism. He suggests the experiment of administering thyroid to the young pygmy to see whether he would develop into a normal, full-grown Negro. It should be pointed out, however, that the analogy between the pygmy and the cretin is a very doubtful one, and depends almost entirely upon the similarity in size; the "low intelligence" of the pygmy is an unproved assumption for which no objective evidence is at present available. Hooton (22) writes: "The pygmies are the most skillful huntsmen and woodsmen of the African forests . . . the pygmies present no features of morphological inferiority which justify the assumption that they belong to a lower evolutionary grade than other men" (p. 468).

A very interesting attempt was made by Muller (40) to obtain some quantitative evidence in this field by actual measurement of the size of the thyroid gland in a Mongoloid group. He noted that the Malay population of Java had on the average a much smaller thyroid than the European Whites. His conclusion was that although the activity of a gland is not proportional to its volume, yet the facts are of importance for the acceptableness of a relation between race and the endocrine system. Recently a much more important body of material has been accumulated on racial differences in basal metabolic rate, which is a better index of thyroid activity. The metabolic data will be discussed in a later chapter. (See Chapter VI.)

2. *The Pituitary.* The pituitary is situated at the base of the brain in a bony depression known as the *sella turcica.* Its most important function is to regulate the growth of bone; an overactive anterior pituitary may cause giantism, and an underactive one, dwarfism. If the overactivity comes relatively late in life when the long bones have stopped growing, the increase in size affects mainly the extremities (hands and feet) and the bones of the face, and the condition

is then known as acromegaly. There may occur a combination of giantism and acromegaly, or either may be present by itself. On the psychological side it has been suggested that the pituitary controls the rhythmic functions (see Langdon Brown, 34) and also that acromegaly is accompanied by apathy, lack of initiative and slow speech, while giantism tends to be associated with an even temperament, laziness and self-satisfaction. These characterizations should, however, not be taken too seriously.

One of the characteristics used in race classification is of course stature, and the degree of functioning of the anterior pituitary may therefore be regarded as an important factor in race differences. Keith points out further that the European shows a pituitary predominance in the marked development of his bony structure; the sharp nasalization, the tendency to strong eyebrow ridges, the prominent chin, the bulk of body and the high average stature may all be accounted for in this way. Neanderthal man was even more markedly acromegalic, and the belief of one British craniologist that Neanderthal characters still occasionally appear among modern Europeans is, according to Keith, undoubtedly due to the occurrence of acromegalic disturbances. (Keith, 25e.)

There is a clinical condition known as *dystrophia adiposogenitalis*, or Fröhlich's syndrome, which is due to an enlargement of the pituitary and is accompanied by atrophy of the sexual system. One of the signs is the deposition of a large amount of fat on the buttocks. It is well known that Hottentot women as a rule also show a marked deposition of fat in that region (steatopygia); Darwin (12) suggested that its presence could be accounted for by sexual selection. Keith believes that there must be some relation between these two conditions, even though the occurrence of steatopygia among the Hottentots is not accompanied by any disturbance in sexual function. Miller (38) describes the case of a Spanish woman suffering from acromegaly and steatopygia, and shows in a photograph the close resemblance to the normal Hottentot contours. The Spanish woman responded very well to treatment, and it is interesting to speculate what might happen to young Hottentot women if they could be treated in the same manner.

Royster and Moriarty (54) measured the size of the *sella turcica* in White and Colored boys and girls by means of X-ray pictures. They found the largest in the case of the Negro boys, followed by the White boys, the White girls and the Negro girls, in that order. Here again it is impossible to assume a direct relationship between the size of the pituitary and its function; but as far as these results go, they offer no indication of a greater pituitary predominance in the Whites.

3. *The Adrenals*. These glands are situated just above the kidneys, one on either side. They appear to control the distribution of hair on the body, and also play an important part in the pigmentation of the skin. Each one consists of two portions, the cortex and the medulla; an overactive adrenal cortex is influential in precocity of physiological development. Addison's disease, which is usually due to a tubercular condition of the medulla, is accompanied by a marked production of brown pigmentation over the whole body. These two characteristics, hairiness and pigmentation, are among those used in racial classifications. Keith believes that originally man's skin was of a dark color, and that the function of healthy adrenals is to clear away the pigment. This would mean that the Negro is relatively deficient in adrenal functioning. It may be added that on the psychological side the adrenals have been shown by Cannon (9) and

others to play a very important rôle in emotional behavior; Berman (6a) believes that the person with an active adrenal will be particularly masculine and aggressive.

4. *The Thymus.* The thymus is situated a little above and to the right of the heart region; it is large during childhood, but undergoes a process of involution at about the time of adolescence. Its function appears to be the regulation of the pubertal changes. In cases of precocious involution of the thymus, the individual may differentiate too rapidly and become old long before his time, whereas in thymic sub-involution the infantile characteristics may last far beyond the age at which a normal person becomes adult. Keith's view is that the more childlike appearance of the Mongolian is probably due to a greater persistence of the thymus. Shellshear (57) investigated the size of the thymus among the Chinese in one hundred post-mortems and found it to be definitely larger than in Whites of the corresponding ages. He also believes that this is associated with the childish appearance of the Chinese and suggests that a form of sexual selection—a preference for placid, childlike characters—may have played a part.

5. *The Gonads.* The gonads, or sex glands, have both an external and an internal secretion, the former concerned with procreation, and the latter with the development of the so-called secondary sex characters. It has been noted that eunuchs are taller and longer-limbed than normal men of the same place and race; what is known as the eunuchoid constitution is marked by these characteristics. There are certain tribes of Negroes along the Nile who are particularly tall and slender (the Nilotic Negroes), and Keith suggests that this may be due to a lesser activity of the interstitial cells of the gonads. Usually at puberty the body begins

to broaden, but in the eunuch and in the Nilotic Negro slenderness appears to persist much longer.

CRITICISM OF THE ENDOCRINE THEORY

There are a number of points in which this interesting theory of Keith's is of doubtful validity. It rests in general upon an inference from pathological to normal conditions, and such an inference is always dangerous. The fact that among Whites a disease of the adrenals is accompanied by brown pigmentation is no proof that among normal Negroes pigmentation must have the same cause. If it did, it would be reasonable to expect that Negroes should show also the functional disturbances which go with adrenal deficiency, for example, the lack of bodily strength; this is characteristic of Addison's disease, but certainly not of the Negro. The Nilotic Negro and the female Hottentot show none of the loss in sexual function that accompanies the endocrine conditions which their physical type is said to resemble. The similarity between the pygmy and the cretin is hardly a close one, and the "childlike" Chinese shows no real arrest in his physiological and mental development. On the functional side, there is no evidence that the endocrines are of importance in the differences among races. At this point it should be mentioned that environmental factors may contribute markedly to endocrine activity; for example, the presence or absence of iodine in the water supply may so affect the thyroid as to transform the whole bodily constitution. (Stockard, 63, 64.)

As far as psychological differences are concerned, too little is known at the present time, in spite of the confident assertions of certain endocrinologists, to warrant the attitude that racial psychology has now been given a scientific basis. It is only in extreme clinical cases that any relationship between the endocrines and personality is at all clear; the explanation of personality differences among normal individuals has not yet been clarified by the study of the endocrines. This whole field is, however, a suggestive one; and further objective and quantitative studies of endocrine functioning in the various races, as well as of its relation to personality, may yield material of great value. In the meantime, Keith's theory remains only an interesting speculation.

It is clearly a distortion of the problem to study the influence of each endocrine gland in isolation. The endocrines together form a system, affecting and influencing one another in various ways, and by their balanced action determining their total contribution to the whole make-up of the individual. Shellshear (57) writes: "It would be more correct to say that the general appearance of any individual has been brought about by the combined influence of a great number of different factors, and that his growth is capable of being influenced in particular by any or all of the ductless glands" (p. 647). In certain recent studies the emphasis has been placed not on a single gland, but on the total constitution, and it is to the problem of the relation between constitution and race that we turn in the next section.

Constitutional Types

Constitution may be defined as the totality of individual characteristics as determined by heredity. No two persons (with the exception of identical twins) have exactly the same constitution, but it has frequently been suggested that there is enough similarity between individuals to permit of a classification into types. In that case, both "race" and "constitutional type" would refer to groups of individuals who have certain physical (and possibly also mental) characteristics in common. The question arises as to how these two kinds of classification are related, and more particularly as to whether a study of constitutional types throws any light on the subject of race differences.

The interest in the problem of constitution has arisen mainly out of clinical considerations. Since the days of Hippocrates medical men have been concerned with the possibility that a certain constitution may predispose to a particular form of disease, and have suggested that a knowledge of constitution may aid in the understanding of fundamental physiological reactions. Hippocrates is probably responsible for the original description of the "habitus phthisicus" and the "habitus apoplecticus," constitutional types susceptible to respiratory and circulatory disturbances, respectively. Beneke (5) went somewhat further with his division into (a) scrofulous-phthisical, (b) carcinomatous, (c) rachitic. Bauer (2) has developed the study of constitutional factors in disease; and recently Draper (13) has given to this whole approach a more objective and statistical basis, and has carefully measured the physical traits of a number of patients suffering from pulmonary tuberculosis, gastric and duodenal ulcer, pernicious anemia and other diseases in an attempt to trace their relation to the whole constitution.

Divisions into types, like divisions into races, are necessarily arbitrary. What has usually happened in the history of this subject is that certain extreme cases have been singled out as typical, and that all others have been interpreted in the light of their approximation or resemblance to these. As Saller (55) points out, the types do not represent the most frequent, but rather the most "beautiful" cases, that is to say, the cases conforming most perfectly to the ideal set up by the investigator. The classical types are based not directly upon objective measures but upon an abstraction which, although it is suggested by the observation of a great many cases, does not by any means represent the characteristics of the majority of them. On the statistical side, therefore, the division into constitutional types is almost always open to question.

It may very well be, however, that it is unfair to apply to this approach the usual criteria of statistical method. The types may be extremes, or they may be ideals; but if in either case they show a relationship to certain definite forms of activity or behavior they may contribute to an understanding of the functional significance of constitution. The recent emphasis, particularly by Kretschmer (29), on the relation between constitution and mentality makes it all the more important to see whether this approach is able to furnish any foundation for a racial psychology.

In the actual classifications there is naturally a marked degree of variation, depending upon the special interest and emphasis of the investigator. There is also considerable overlapping, and it is especially interesting to note the common tendency to recognize the division into the long-narrow and the short-thick types, though the names for them differ widely, and though other types may occasionally be added. Table 2 which follows presents some of the better-known classifications, and indicates the points at which they are in substantial agreement. (See Wertheimer and Hesketh, 68; Saller, 55; Weidenreich, 67.)

Of these various classifications, the one by Kretschmer has had the most important psychological implications, and will be discussed in the greatest detail.

KRETSCHMER'S TYPES

Kretschmer takes issue with the classification of Sigaud (58) and his collaborators on the ground that it lays too ex-

TABLE 2: CLASSIFICATIONS OF CONSTITUTIONAL TYPES

Investigator	Long-narrow	Short-thick	Other Types
Hippocrates	habitus phthisicus	habitus apoplecticus	
Beneke	scrofulous-phthisical	carcinomatous	rachitic
Stiller	atonic or asthenic	hypertonic, apoplectic	
De Giovanni	phthisic	plethoric	athletic
Manouvrier	makroskele	brachyskele	
MacAuliffe	type plat	type rond	
Sigaud	respiratory	digestive	muscular, cerebral
Viola	microsplanchnic	macrosplanchnic	
Pende	katabolic (longitype)	anabolic (brevitype)	
Kretschmer	leptosome (asthenic)	pyknic	athletic, dysplastic
Bean	hypermorph	mesomorph	hypomorph
Weidenreich	leptosome	eurysome	
Stockard	linear	lateral	

clusive emphasis upon the characteristics of the face, leaving out of account the rest of the body. The "type cérébral," for example, shows a marked development of the region of the forehead; the "type respiratoire," of the middle part of the face; the "type digestif," of the chin and mouth; and the "type musculaire," of all these parts equally. Kretschmer also regards the face as having special importance; it is a sort of mirror of the constitution, or it may be regarded as its "visiting card." He insists, however, that it must be studied in relation to the whole constitution, and that no physical characteristic should be ignored in the diagnosis. "Not a hair of his head, and not a peculiarity of his nose is indifferent to us" (p. 38).

Kretschmer has described four main types. The *leptosome* is characterized as tall, slender, with a relatively narrow chest, long legs, an elongated face, long and narrow hands and feet—in general, with small body volume relative to stature. The *pyknic* is short, thick-set, with a heavy trunk and short legs, a round chest and rounded shoulders, short hands and feet—a large body volume relative to stature. The *athletic*, as the name suggests, is strong and muscular, with a well-developed bony structure, wide shoulders, a heavy torso and large hands and feet. The *dysplastic* may be regarded as an abnormal type, showing deficiencies or distortions in structure, asymmetrical development, or glandular imbalance.

The psychological significance of these types arises primarily from Kretschmer's report that they differ in the frequency with which they are found among patients suffering from two main types of mental disease, namely, schizophrenia or dementia precox, and manic-depressive or circular insanity. In the original material, Kretschmer presented the results which appear in Table 3.

TABLE 3: CONSTITUTION AND PSYCHOSIS (KRETSCHMER)

Constitutional Type	Circular Insanity	Schizophrenia
Leptosome	4	81
Athletic	3	31
Leptosome and athletic mixed	2	11
Pyknic	58	2
Pyknic, mixed forms	14	3
Dysplastic	0	34
Unclear	4	13
	85	175

Kretschmer concluded that there is an intimate relationship between manic-depressive insanity and the pyknic constitution, whereas schizophrenia is much more likely to occur among individuals of the leptosome, athletic or dysplastic type. This finding attracted a great deal of attention in psychiatric circles, and a large number of investigations were undertaken, particularly in Germany, in the attempt to test the validity of Kretschmer's theory. In 1926 Kretschmer (29a) summarized the results obtained by twenty-three different investigators on a body of psychiatric material consisting of over four thousand cases, and found in general a substantial agreement with his original study. See Table 4.

TABLE 4: CONSTITUTION AND PYSCHOSIS (COMBINED STUDIES)

Constitutional Type	Circular Insanity (Per Cent Cases)	Schizophrenia (Per Cent Cases)
Pyknic and pyknoid....................	66.7	12.8
Leptosome and athletic................	23.6	66.0
Dysplastic...........................	0.4	11.3
Atypical.............................	9.3	9.9

In the subsequent development of this theory Kretschmer pointed out that even in those cases in which there is no clearly marked psychotic condition, there is still a relationship between physique and personality. Schizophrenia, for example, is a disease marked by a very high degree of introversion, a withdrawal from reality and a development of autistic thinking; these same characteristics may, however, be found to a lesser degree in individuals who are not psychotic, but who will nevertheless tend to belong to the same constitutional categories as do the true schizophrenics. Kretschmer describes two temperaments which fluctuate between the normal and the psychotic and can be studied in the case histories of patients who later develop mental disease. These are the cycloid and the schizoid, resembling manic-depressive insanity and schizophrenia, respectively. The cycloid tends to be social, good-hearted, friendly, or gay, humorous, lively; he is usually practical and realistic. The schizoid, on the other hand, is unsocial, quiet, reserved, a little odd, or he may be timid, sensitive, a lover of books and of nature; he is very difficult to know because of his hidden, deeper side, his autism, his "in-sich-hineinleben"; there is always a glass cage between him and the world. The cycloid is usually pyknic; the schizoid, leptosome or athletic, and more rarely dysplastic. When the characteristics of the cycloid and the schizoid are reduced still further, Kretschmer speaks of the normal cyclothyme and schizothyme biotypes, also related to the various constitutional types in the same fashion.

The normal biotypes have also been studied by the techniques of experimental psychology. The Rorschach test, for example, showed more "extroverts" among the pyknics, and more "introverts" among the leptosomes. A self-diagnosis by means of a questionnaire indicated that most pyknics described themselves as cyclothyme, and most leptosomes as schizothyme. Pyknics are said to be more directly influenced by the external environment; they are more distractible, they show a better "incidental memory" (i.e., for things to which they were not explicitly directed to attend), and a greater perception span. Leptosomes, on the other hand, show a superior power of abstraction, and can much more successfully carry on two different mental operations at the same time. These and other findings are regarded by Kretschmer as corroborative of his theory.

Results of this type, as well as those obtained by Kretschmer's clinical approach, have been severely criticized on methodological grounds. It has been pointed out, for example, that the two groups, pyknics and leptosomes, have not always been carefully equated for various factors which may have real importance. It has been shown (Kolle, 27; 28; Garvey, 16; Farber[1]) that differences in age between the two groups may play a part. There is a tendency for leptosomes to become more pyknic as they grow older; and as manic-depressive insanity usually occurs later in life than does schizophrenia, it may be that the age factor is responsible for the coincidence of manic-depressive insanity and the pyknic constitution. Kretschmer does not believe that age affects the results to any considerable extent, but the most recent studies in this field have shown that it is by no means negligible.

[1] Unpublished Master's Essay, Columbia University Library.

It may be added that an experimental study by Klineberg, Asch and Block (26) of pyknics and leptosomes among
college students carefully equated for factors of age, social
and economic status and intelligence, failed to verify any
of the results obtained in the German experimental studies.

CONSTITUTION AND RACE

There have been a number of suggestions of an intimate
relation between Kretschmer's constitutional types and the
various European sub-races. Sofer (60), even before the development of Kretschmer's theory, suggested that the "habitus phthisicus" was simply a somewhat pathological Nordic
type, and that the "habitus apoplecticus" was similarly connected with the Alpine. Stern-Piper (62) regards the leptosome as a pure Nordic, the pyknic as Alpine, and the athletic
as a stronger Nordic, as well as a Dinaric type, and suggests
that the apparent psychiatric and psychological differences
between pyknics and leptosomes are racially determined.
Lenz (35) also believes that every race has its specific constitutional type, and Pfuhl (47) regards the Mediterraneans
and Dinarics as schizothyme and leptosome. (The constitutional types of Sigaud have also been associated with races;
Mayerhofer [37] identifies the "type cérébral" with the Nordic, the "type digestif" with the Alpine, the "type musculaire" with the Mediterranean, and the "type respiratoire"
with the Dinaric.)

Weidenreich (67), after a very careful survey of the literature in this field, concludes that any such identification of
constitution with race is entirely unjustified. He shows that
his two main types, leptosome and eurysome (pyknic), can
be found in all racial populations, throughout Asia and
Africa as well as in Germany and other European countries. His conclusion is strengthened by the quantitative

findings of a number of investigators. If the pyknic is identical with the Alpine, and the leptosome with the Nordic, the two constitutional types should differ in the characteristics which differentiate the two races. It has been shown, however, by Rösler (53), Henckel (20) and Von Rohden (51) that there is about the same distribution in the color of the eyes and of the hair in the two types, and also by Von Rohden and Gründler (52) that they do not differ appreciably in cephalic index or in stature. Evidently constitutional type differences do not coincide with differences in race.

It may still be, however, that even though race and constitution are not completely identical, the relative frequency of constitutional types in the various races will differ greatly. This is Kretschmer's belief; he notes a tendency for the leptosome type to predominate in the Nordic parts of Germany, and the pyknic type in the Alpine regions. Guber-Gritz (19) comes to the same conclusion. Scaglia (56) reports that in Sardinia there is a much larger proportion of longitypes (that is, individuals with long legs and relatively small trunks, as among leptosomes) than in the northern parts of Italy. Von Verschuer (66) found among German students in south Germany 24 per cent leptosomes, 38 per cent athletics, and 38 per cent pyknics, whereas in central and north Germany the proportions were 43 per cent leptosomes, 29 per cent athletics, and 28 per cent pyknics.

It is interesting to compare with these figures the relative frequency of the psychoses in the various parts of Europe. Henckel (20), for example, has shown that in Sweden there are 49 cases of circular insanity to 350 of schizophrenia (15:100); in Bavaria, which is mainly Alpine, the proportion is 73 to 100, and in Wurtemberg, 85 to 175 (50 : 100); Rittershaus (50) has also insisted that there is more schizophrenia among pure Nordics than among Alpines. On the other hand, a questionnaire sent by Von Rohden (51) to a large number of psychiatric institutions in Germany, Austria and Switzerland showed German Switzerland (predominantly Alpine) to have about the smallest proportion of manic-depressive insanity, whereas the Nordic provinces of Hanover and Oldenburg were among those with, relatively, the smallest proportion of dementia precox. In the German regions regarded as most purely Nordic, there were 76 cases of schizophrenia to 24 of manic-depressive insanity; in the most purely Alpine regions, the proportion was almost exactly the same—74 to 26. In Switzerland the proportion in 1923 was 86 to 14. In any case, it must not be overlooked that apparent racial differences in the incidence of various forms of insanity may have a cultural as well as a biological or constitutional basis, and also that statistical comparisons of this kind are always doubtful. This problem will be discussed in a later chapter (Chapter XIII).

Kretschmer believes that although race and constitution are by no means identical, there are races which are relatively more pyknic or leptosome, and therefore relatively more cyclothyme or schizothyme, respectively. He is of the opinion that this may account for the differing psychological characteristics of northern and southern Germans, as well as for those of other European groups. The Swiss, for example, are pyknic and cyclothyme—realistic, capable, fond of festivity, home-loving, industrious. The Bavarians and Austrians, like the Swiss in constitution and race, are relatively hypomanic, cheerful in thought, sensual, gay, lively and talkative. In the areas of purest Nordic (and therefore largely leptosome) settlement, the people are serious, sadly earnest in their attitude toward life, and in their old epic lays consistently gloomy (30). The Alpine race in France and Italy is also pyknic-cyclothyme (the so-called Gallic temperament). The Mediterraneans, especially in Spain and Corsica, are strongly schizothyme. In Spain, for example, Kretschmer finds a tendency to serious earnestness, to grandiloquence of style, and to a solemn and ceremonious aristocracy.

CRITICISM OF KRETSCHMER'S RACIAL THEORY

This characterization might be more plausible if there were not so many important exceptions. Kretschmer finds very little of the schizothyme temperament in southern France and Italy, although these are definitely Mediterranean and predominantly leptosome in type; the assumption is made that they have been so mixed with Alpines that the true Mediterranean character has been lost. Kretschmer suggests also that the schizothyme genius of north Germany tends to philosophy and science, and the southern temperament to music and art; here again there are a great many exceptions requiring to be explained. Wurtemberg in south Germany has had many philosophers and little music, but "Wurtemberg," says Kretschmer, "has a strong Nordic ingredient." The Netherlands and Flanders are eminent in painting rather than in philosophy, but that is explained by Kretschmer as due to the fact that the Netherlands have a number of Alpine racial islands. These exceptions necessitate so many modifications in the theory as to make it of little use for scientific purposes. There is no indication that Wurtemberg is more Nordic than Baden, or that there are more Alpine islands in the Netherlands than in north Germany. In any case the difference in the proportion of constitutional types in north and south Germany is hardly great enough, even on the basis of Kretschmer's theory, to affect culture or psychology very considerably. Von Verschuer's results referred to above show that leptosomes and athletics combined constitute 62 per cent of the student group in south Germany and 72 per cent in central and north Germany.

This whole question is complicated by the relation between constitutional type and a large number of factors which have no racial significance. The effect of age has already been mentioned. It has also been shown (see Stockard, 64) that social and economic status may play a part, and that in general the upper social class is more leptosome than the lower. Even in Japan Baelz (1) has shown that the Choshiu or upper class is distinctly leptosome in type, and the Satsuma, or lower class, is predominantly pyknic. Pfaundler (46) believes that these differences may be due to earlier maturation in the upper classes, resulting from differences in food and manner of living. It is interesting to speculate as to how much of the observed relationship between constitution and psychosis may be due to the fact that both are determined by the social environment. If high social status develops a certain amount of introversion and withdrawal from life, as well as a leptosome physique, a possible relation between this physique and schizophrenia may more easily be understood. Much more work is needed before this hypothesis can be verified.

There has been considerable discussion as to whether type and occupation are related. Sigaud (58) suggested, for example, that there are more cerebral and respiratory types among brainworkers than among handworkers. Lubinski (36) believes that hard work on a farm, with muscular exercise and fresh air during the early years, tends to broaden the skeleton and result in pyknoid types. Kretschmer's own view is that constitution is the cause, rather than the effect of this relationship. Pyknic types tend to engage in certain occupations because they find them psychologically more congenial. It is no accident, he says (see von Rohden, 51), that pyknics, who are fond of material things, should constitute the majority of butchers and bakers and innkeepers, and that leptosomes should find their way to the secluded regions of the university or the laboratory. (It is interesting to note that in a recent study at Barnard College in New York [26] there was a very marked preponderance of the leptosome type.) It has been urged against Kretschmer, however (by Kolle, 27; 28), that he has never proved the priority of constitutional types, and that all of these environmental factors, including occupation as one of the most important, require to be considered. Until this has been done adequately, the relation between constitution and race will remain obscure, and will be of very little assistance in the study of racial psychology.

OTHER THEORIES

Stockard (63), whose distinction between the linear and lateral types has been included in the table (see page 57), has also attempted an application to problems of race. The linear type is active, energetic and nervous, with a great deal of emotional control; it is a rapidly growing type, with early puberty; it is dolichocephalic. The lateral type shows late puberty and slow differentiation, and is brachycephalic. These types are mainly dependent upon the activity of the thyroid. Where there is much iodine, as in maritime climates and along the coastal plains, the thyroid tends to be overactive, and a linear type develops. The lateral type occurs rather in a continental, inland environment, where iodine is rare. The English, says Stockard, are a linear type race; the Germans, a lateral type. This theory has, however, little foundation. There is no proof that the linear type has a more active thyroid or an earlier puberty than the lateral.

No differences in this respect have been reported between the Germans and the English, nor is it possible to describe in the same psychological terms a linear group like the south Italians and one like the Scotch or the Scandinavians.

Bean (4) also believes that his constitutional types have a racial significance, even though they may cut across racial classifications. The tall hypermorph is usually found near the sea, in Britain and Japan and in the Mediterranean and Baltic regions. The mesomorph of medium stature and a bulky body is found in the interior of continental areas; and the short hypomorph, in tropical and arctic regions. The conquering race is the hypermorph—long-limbed, long-headed, and usually, though not necessarily, blond. This appears to be a variation on the old theme of the superiority of the northwest European, which was discussed in the first chapter.

Pende attempts to understand the psychology of the Italians on the basis of his two constitutional types. The longitype, governed by sentiment and intuition, and the brevitype, dominated by logic and thought, are found in all races, though their proportions may differ. In Italy both are present in a proper harmony; and as a result of this biological and psychological polyvalence, the Italians possess muscles and hearts and brains capable of securing for Italy "a new and glorious future, and the leadership in the most varied fields of activity and of human progress" (45).

BIBLIOGRAPHY

1. Baelz, E. "Die körperlichen Eigenschaften der Japaner." *Mitteilungen der deutschen gesellschaft für Natur und Völkerkunde Ostasiens,* 3:1883; 4:1885.
2. Bauer, J. *Die Konstitutionelle Disposition zu inneren Krankheiten.* Berlin, 1924 (3rd Ed.)

3. Baur, E., Fischer, E., and Lenz, F. *Human Heredity.* New York, 1931. (Trans.)

4. Bean, R. B. "Human Types." *Quart. Rev. Biol.,* 1:1926, pp. 360-392.

5a. Beneke, F. W. *Die anatomischen Grundlagen der Konstitutions-anormalien.* 1878.

5b. Beneke, F. W. *Konstitution u. konstitutionelles Kranksein des Menschen.* 1881.

6a. Berman, L. "Anthropology and the Endocrine Glands." *Sci. Mo.,* 21:1925, pp. 157-165.

6b. Berman, L. *The Glands Regulating Personality.* New York, 1921.

7. Bernstein, F. "Zusammenfassende Betrachtungen über die erb-lichen Blutstrukturen des Menschen." *Ztschr. für Induk-tive Abstammung- und Vererbungslehre,* 37:1925, 237-270.

8. Cabrera, C., and Wade, H. W. "Iso-agglutination. Group Per-centages of Filipino Bloods." *J. Philipp. Is. Med. Ass.,* 1: 1921, pp. 100-103.

9. Cannon, W. B. *Bodily Changes in Pain, Hunger, Fear and Rage.* New York, 1915.

10. Coca, A., and Deibert, O. "A Study of the Occurrence of the Blood Groups Among the American Indians." *J. Immunol-ogy,* 8:1923, 487-491.

11. Crookshank, F. G. *The Mongol in Our Midst: A Study of Man and His Three Faces.* New York, 1924.

12. Darwin, C. *The Descent of Man.* New York, 1871.

13. Draper, G. *The Human Constitution.* Philadelphia, 1924.

14. Draper, G. *Disease and the Man.* London, 1930.

15. Furukawa, T. "A Study of Temperament and Blood-groups." *J. Soc. Psychol.,* 1:1930, pp. 494-508.

16. Garvey, C. R. "Comparative Body Build of Manic-Depressives and Schizophrenic Patients." *Psych. Bull.,* 30:1933, pp. 567-568.

17. Gates, R. R. *Heredity in Man.* New York, 1923.

18. Goldstein, H. "A Biochemical Study of the Metabolism of Men-tal Work." *Arch. Psych.,* No. 164:1934.

19. Guber-Gritz, D. S. "Somatische Konstitution der Schizo-phreniker." *Arch. f. Psychiatrie u. Nervenkrankh.* 77:1926, pp. 789-814.

20. Henckel, K. O. "Konstitutionstypen und europäische Rassen." *Klin.-Wochenschrift,* 4:1925, pp. 2145-2148.

21. Hirszfeld, L., and Hirszfeld, H. "Serologic Differences Between the Blood of Different Races." *Lancet,* 2, No. 5016:1919, pp. 675-678.

22. Hooton, E. A. *Up from the Ape.* New York, 1931.

23. Hoskins, R. G. *The Tides of Life: The Endocrine Glands in Bodily Adjustment.* New York, 1933.

24. Jansky, J. "Haematologicke Studie u Psychotiku." *Sborne Klinicky,* 8:1907, pp. 85-139.

25a. Keith, Sir A. "On the Differentiation of Mankind into Racial Types." *Lancet,* No. 5013:1911, April 15th.

25b. Keith, Sir A. "Differentiation of Man into Racial Types." *J. Roy. Soc. of Arts,* 1919, October 17th.

25c. Keith, Sir A. "The Evolution of Human Races in the Light of the Hormone Theory." *Bull. Johns Hopk. Hosp.,* Baltimore, 33:1922, pp. 155-159.

25d. Keith, Sir A. "The Evolution of the Human Races." *J. Roy. Anthrop. Inst.,* 58:1928, pp. 305-332.

25e. Keith, Sir A. *The Antiquity of Man.* London, 1915.

26. Klineberg, O., Asch, S. E., and Block, H. "An Experimental Study of Constitutional Types." *Gen. Psych. Mono.,* No. 3, 16:1934.

27. Kolle, K. "Körperbau der Schizophrenen." *Arch. f. Psych. u. Nervenkrh.,* 72:1924, pp. 40-88; 75:1925, pp. 21-61.

28. Kolle, K. "Klinische Beiträge zum Konstitutionsproblem." *Arch. f. Psychiat. u. Nervenkrh.,* 77:1926, pp. 183-238.

29a. Kretschmer, E. *Körperbau und Charakter.* Berlin, 1931. (10th Ed.)

29b. Kretschmer, E. *Physique and Character.* New York, 1925. (Trans.)

30. Kretschmer, E. *The Psychology of Men of Genius.* New York, 1931. (Trans.)

31. Kruse, W. *Die Deutschen u. ihre Nachbarvölker.* Leipzig, 1929.

32a. Landsteiner, K. "Zur Kenntnis der antifermentativen lytischen und agglutinierenden Wirkungen des Blutserums." *Zentlbl. f. Bakt., Parasit. u. Infekt.,* 27:1900, pp. 357-362.

32b. Landsteiner, K. "Über Agglutinationserscheinungen Normales

Menschlichen Blutes." *Wiener Klinische Wochenschrift,* 14:1901, p. 1132.

32c. Landsteiner, K. "The Human Blood Groups." *The Newer Knowledge of Bacteriology and Immunology,* 68:1928, pp. 892-908.

33a. Landsteiner, K., and Miller, C. P. "Serological Studies on the Blood of the Primates." *J. Exp. Med.,* 42:1925, pp. 841-872.

33b. Landsteiner, K., and Miller, C. P. "Serological Observations on the Relationship of the Bloods of Man and the Anthropoid Apes." *Science,* 61:1925, pp. 492-493.

34. Langdon-Brown, W. *The Endocrines in General Medicine.* London, 1927.

35. Lenz, F. "Psychological Differences Between the Leading Races of Mankind." Chapter 15 in Baur, Fischer and Lenz, *Human Heredity,* New York, 1931.

36. Lubinski, H. "Körperbau u. Wachstum von Stadt- und Landkindern." *Monatschrift für Kinderheilkunde,* 15:1919, p. 264.

37. Mayerhofer, E. "Die Menschenrassen (Günther) verglichen mit den Menschentypen (Sigaud)." *Ztschr. f. d. ges. Anat.* (Abt. 2) 13:1927, pp. 252-259.

38. Miller, G. S., Jr. "Steatopygy and Acromegaly." *Amer. J. Phys. Anthrop.,* 14:1930, pp. 79-82.

39. Moss, W. L. "Studies on Isoagglutinins and Isohemolysins." *Johns Hopk. Hosp. Bull.,* 21:1910, pp. 63-70.

40. Müller, H. "Über das Gefässsystems und die Thyroidea der malaiischen Rasse." *Janus,* 1922, 334-350.

41. Nigg, C. "A Study of the Blood Groups Among American Indians." *J. Immunol.,* 11:1926, p. 319.

42. Ottenberg, R. "Medico-legal Application of Human Blood Grouping." *J. Am. Med. Asso.,* 77:1921, pp. 682-683; 78:1922, pp. 873-877.

43. Ottenberg, R. "Hereditary Blood Qualities." *J. Immunol.,* 6:1921, pp. 363-386; 8:1923, pp. 11-19.

44. Ottenberg, R. "A Classification of Human Races, Based on Geographical Distribution of the Blood Groups." *J. Am. Med. Asso.,* 84:1925, pp. 1393-1395.

45. Pende, N. "Psicologia individuale e psicologia di razza." *Riv. di Psicol.,* 26:1930, p. 22.

46. Pfaundler, M. "Körpermass-Studien an Kindern." *Ztschr. f. Kinderheilk,* 14:1916, p. 1.

47. Pfuhl, W. "Die Beziehungen zw. Rassen u. Konstitutionsforschungen." *Ztsch. f. die. ges. Anat. Pt. 2. Ztsch. f. Konstitutionslehre,* 9:1923, p. 172.

48. Rich, G. J. "A Biochemical Approach to the Study of Personality." *J. Abn. & Soc. Psych.,* 23:1928, pp. 158-175.

49. Rich, G. J. "Body Acidity as Related to Emotional Excitability." *Arch. Neur. & Psychiatry,* 20:1928, pp. 589-594.

50. Rittershaus, E. "Körperbau, Rasse u. Psychose." *Zentralbl. f. d. ges. Neurol. u. Psychiat.,* 42:1926, p. 334.

51. v. Rohden, F. "Über Beziehungen zw. Konstitution u. Rasse." *Ztschr. f. die ges. Neurol. u. Psychiatrie,* 98:1925, pp. 255-278.

52. v. Rohden, F., and Gründler, W. "Über Körperbau und Psyche." *Ztsch. f. d. ges. Neurol. u. Psychiatrie,* 95:1925, p. 37.

53. Rösler, C. "Ein Beitrag zu der Frage: Zusammenhänge zwischen Rasse und Konstitutionstypen." *Ztschr. f. d. ges. Neurol. u. Psychiatrie,* 95:1925, p. 108.

54. Royster, L. R., and Moriarty, M. E. "A Study of the Size of the Sella Turcica in White and Colored Males and Females between the 8th and 9th Years, as Measured on Flat X-ray Films." *Amer. J. Phys. Anthrop.,* 14:1930, p. 451.

55. Saller, K. "Konstitution u. Rasse beim Menschen." *Ztschr. f. d. ges. Anat.,* Pt. 3, 28:1929, pp. 250-422.

56. Scaglia, G., "Sardi." *Scritti biol. di Castaldi,* 1928.

57. Shellshear, J. L. "Thymus Gland in the Chinese." *China Med. J.,* 38:1924, pp. 646-657.

58. Sigaud, C. *La Forme Humaine.* Paris, 1914.

59. Snyder, L. H. "Human Blood Groups: Their Inheritance and Racial Significance." *Amer. J. Phys. Anthrop.,* 9:1926, pp. 233-263.

60. Sofer, L. "Beiträge zur Rassenphysiologie und Rassenpathologie." *Polit. Anthrop. Rev.,* 8:1909, pp. 337-344.

61. Starr, H. E. *Psychobiochemistry in Clinical Psychology: Studies in Honour of Lightner Witmer to Commemorate the 35th Anniversary of the Founding of the First Psychological Clinic.* Philadelphia, 1931, pp. 155-166.

62. Stern-Piper, L. "Konstitution und Rasse." *Ztschr. f. d. ges. Neurol. u. Psychiatrie,* 86:1923, p. 265.

63. Stockard, C. R. "Human Types and Growth Reactions." *Amer. J. Anatomy,* 31:1923 (No. 3), pp. 261-288.

64. Stockard, C. R. *The Physical Basis of Personality.* New York, 1931.

65. Verzár, F. "Die Unsicherheiten in der Nomenklatur der Blutgruppen und ihre praktischen Folgen." *Klinische Wochenschrift,* 6:1927, pp. 347-348.

66. v. Verschuer, O. "Zur Frage Körperbau u. Rasse." *Ztschr. f. d. ges. Anat. Pt. 2; Ztschr. f. Konstitutionslehre,* 2:1925, p. 754.

67. Weidenreich, F. *Rasse u. Körperbau.* Springer, Berlin, 1927.

68. Wertheimer, F. I., and Hesketh, F. E. "The Significance of the Physical Constitution in Mental Disease." *Med. Mono.,* No. 10:1926. Baltimore.

69. Wyman, L. C., and Boyd, W. C. "Human Blood Groups and Anthropology." *Amer. Anthrop.,* New Ser., 37:1935, pp. 181-200.

Chapter IV

PHYSIQUE AND MENTALITY

INTRODUCTION

BY DEFINITION, races differ in physical characteristics. It has often been suggested that if groups differ physically, the presumption is that they also differ mentally. Kroeber (26) writes: "There is . . . no sound reason to expect anything else but that races which differ anatomically also differ in some degree physiologically and psychologically" (p. 352). Such an inference is possible only on the assumption that physical characteristics which are used in race classification have also a psychological significance. There is a substantial body of material pertinent to the problem of this relationship.

PHYSIOGNOMY

The attempt to judge personality from facial characteristics has been traced back to the earliest days of Greek speculation. Aristotle was somewhat sceptical of current beliefs, but even he was willing to concede an association between broad, flat noses and frivolity, staring eyes and stupidity, and short stub-noses and love of pleasure. In fairly recent times Lavater's (27) four volumes with One Hundred Physiognomical Rules have had a considerable vogue, and even at the present time followers are by no means lacking.

Blackford and Newcomb (6), for example, insist upon a psychological difference between individuals with "convex" and with "concave" profiles. The convex type is said to be keen, alert, quick, eager, aggressive, impatient, positive and

73

penetrating. The concave type is mild, slow of thought, slow of action, patient and plodding. The theory was tested by Hull and Evans (23), who measured the facial angle of 25 women students and correlated it with ratings by their sorority sisters on the character traits listed by Blackford and Newcomb. The correlations varied from − .27 to + .39, with an average of + .01—which means of course that the study failed to show the alleged psychological difference between convex and concave profiles. The number of cases studied is so small, however, that these correlations should not be taken too literally.

In an early study it was suggested by MacDonald (28) that there was a positive relation between dolichocephaly and intelligence, a conclusion in line with some of the popular racial theories. Röse (42) was of the same opinion, but his results showed only trifling differences between the brightest and dullest Dresden schoolboys whom he studied. Matiegka (31), in fact, found among Czech scholars that the best ones were neither very long- nor very round-headed, but rather moderately brachycephalic. More recently Baldwin (1), who made the physical measurements in connection with the genetic studies of genius by Terman and his collaborators, found that the gifted children tended to be meso- and brachy- rather than dolichocephalic. Sommerville (45) obtained a correlation of + .01 between the cephalic index of 105 students and their standing in the Thorndike intelligence test. On the basis of this and similar material, Paterson (33) concludes that "the trend of available evidence is definitely against the dolichocephalic hypothesis" (p. 121).

The same may be said for other physiognomical features which have popularly been regarded as significant. Cleeton and Knight (10) correlated various facial measures with psychological traits and found that the correlations averaged exactly zero. Viteles (51) in a recent review of the quantitative studies of physiognomy concludes that no relation to psychological traits has as yet been demonstrated.

PIGMENTATION

Havelock Ellis (13) believed that skin color is to a marked degree an index to mentality. He counted the number of blonds and brunettes in the National Portrait Gallery in London, and thought he found a definite difference, blondness being characteristic of men of restless and ambitious temperament; men of action tend to be fair, men of thought tend to be dark. He devised an index of blondness by dividing the number of blonds by the number of brunettes in each class and multiplying by one hundred. His results are presented in Table 5.

TABLE 5: THE INDEX OF BLONDNESS (HAVELOCK ELLIS)

Class	Number	Index of Blondness
Political reformers and agitators..............	20	233
Sailors.....................................	45	150
Men of science.............................	53	121
Soldiers....................................	42	113
Artists.....................................	74	111
Poets.......................................	56	107
Royal family...............................	66	107
Lawyers....................................	56	107
Created peers and their sons..................	53	89
Men and women of letters...................	87	85
Hereditary aristocracy.......................	149	82
Divines.....................................	57	58
Men of low birth...........................	12	50
Explorers...................................	8	33
Actors and actresses.........................	16	33

This table has been presented in full as a curiosity rather than as science, and even a casual glance at it will show glaring discrepancies. For example, men of science, who ought certainly to be regarded as men of thought rather than as men of action, are in this group predominantly fair;

artists and poets, too, fall into the wrong category. At the other extreme, explorers, who are surely men of action, have the lowest index of blondness.

There has been a recent revival of this notion of the psychological significance of skin color in the writings of Katherine Blackford (6), who has applied her theory to the problems of vocational guidance. She describes the blond as positive, dynamic, aggressive, quick, hopeful, variety-loving; the brunette is negative, static, conservative, cautious, patient, slow, thoughtful, specializing. The blonds are the best salesmen, and are much more successful in their dealings with other people. Paterson and Ludgate (34) attempted a quantitative check of this theory by having 187 blonds and the same number of brunettes rated for a large number of personality traits listed by Blackford. They found just as large a proportion of "blond" traits in both groups, and rejected the whole theory as of no value.

Estabrooks (14a) gave the Dearborn C group test of intelligence to 444 children in the sixth, seventh and eighth grades of the public schools of New Rochelle, New York, and found an apparent superiority of the blond over the brunette children. Those with blue eyes had an average I.Q. of 108.9; those with brown eyes, 105.0; light hair, 109.1; dark hair, 106.3. This superiority turned out, however, to be a spurious one. It is a well-known fact that children tend to become somewhat darker as they grow older; it is also true that the I.Q. is usually higher at the earlier ages. The slight superiority of the fairer children might therefore be due to the accident that they were a little younger. Estabrooks tested another sample of 139 children from Medford and Revere, Massachusetts, with the Dearborn A group test, but in this study he was careful to take only children of the same age (eight years). The results were: brown eyes, 112.6;

blue eyes, 104.9; light hair, 104.7; dark hair, 104.8. There is evidently no demonstrable relationship between pigmentation and intelligence.

CRANIAL CAPACITY

It is popularly believed that the size of the head, and therefore presumably the size of the brain, is closely related to intelligence. If there should also be a definite and consistent difference in the size of the brain in the various races, this would lend some support to the notion that there are inherent, biologically determined racial differences in intelligence.

There is ample evidence that in the process of evolution the brain has come to occupy an increasingly greater space in relation to the rest of the body. The brain of man is both absolutely and relatively heavier than that of almost all other mammals; only the elephant and allied species have an absolutely greater brain weight. The relation of brain weight to body weight is in the case of the elephant, 1:560; lion, 1:546; dog, 1:350; gorilla, 1:220; chimpanzee, 1:75; and man, 1:35 to 1:40. There are certain South American apes (Midas, Atelles) which have indices of 1:26 to 1:15, so that the superiority of man in this respect is not entirely unchallenged. (See Fischer, 15.)

Paterson (33) suggests a correspondence between head volume and cultural evolution, as indicated in the cranial capacities reported in Table 6.

This table is, however, misleading, because it does not take sufficient account of variability within the different groups, and the great amount of overlapping which results. The relation to cultural evolution is also very doubtful. As it happens, the Eskimo have on the average larger heads than the Parisians (see below). Martin (30) points out further that

TABLE 6: CULTURAL EVOLUTION AND CRANIAL CAPACITY (PATERSON)

Group	Cranial Capacity in c.c.
Anthropoid apes	621
Pithecanthropus erectus	855
Veddas	1277
Andamanese	1300
Australians	1340
Negroes	1350
Ainus	1462
Europeans	1490
Parisians	1555

there has been no essential increase in cranial capacity since the days of Neanderthal man and other fossil men of the Quaternary Period; in fact, the average of Neanderthal and, more particularly, of Cromagnon man probably exceeded the average of the present-day European. (Hooton, 22.)

Other investigators have also sought a relationship between cranial capacity and cultural development. Broca (8) thought that cranial capacity was increasing in France, but his comparison of skulls from the twelfth, eighteenth and nineteenth centuries showed no substantial difference. On the other hand, Retzius (41) found medieval skulls in Sweden to be smaller than the Neolithic, and it has also been shown that early Italian groups had larger heads than modern Italians. (See Martin, 30.) It seems to be clear that there is no obvious relationship between culture and head size.

There are undoubtedly some cases in which the relation between intelligence and cranial capacity seems very close. There is, for instance, a form of idiocy which is accompanied by microcephaly, a condition in which the head may be extraordinarily small, with a brain weight of less than 950 grams. These cases are, however, definitely abnormal, and no inference can be drawn as to the usual relationship. The fact that idiocy also frequently accompanies macrocephaly, or an abnormally large head, shows how dangerous such an inference would be.

Within the normal population there have been a large number of studies dealing directly with this problem, and the suggestion of the phrenologist Fowler (16), that the brain increases and decreases in size as mental capacities increase and decrease, has been subjected as far as possible to quantitative investigation. Francis Galton (17), for example, showed that honor men at Cambridge had slightly larger heads than ordinary pass students; and a number of succeeding studies, especially those by Porter (38), Gladstone (19) and Peterson (37), tended to confirm this finding. On the other hand, Binet (4; 5) and Simon (44) found cephalometry to be of secondary value in the diagnosis of intelligence and regarded it as having the function of confirming rather than indicating such a diagnosis. (See Paterson [33] for a review of this material.)

These studies were made before the days of modern statistical technique, and it was felt by subsequent investigators that a more careful quantitative analysis of this material was needed. Karl Pearson (36) correlated the length and breadth of the head with the scholastic records of 4500 twelve-year-old boys and girls and 1010 Cambridge students, and obtained results so close to zero that he concluded that "head measurements are not of real service as intelligence tests" (p. 122). Reed and Mulligan (40) correlated cranial capacity with examination marks of 449 male Scotch students at the University of Aberdeen, and obtained the insignificant figure of $+.07$. Sommerville (45) obtained a similar result with Columbia University students, his correlations between head measurements and intelligence ranging from $+.03$ to $+.11$. One study, that by Murdock and Sullivan (32), obtained a correlation of $+.22$ between head diameter and

I.Q. in the case of 600 school children, but this correlation is unusually high. In general there appears to be an exceedingly small, though positive, correlation between head size and intelligence.

In the interpretation of these results it is important to bear in mind the relationship between cranial capacity and social and economic status. A study made in Portugal (Da Costa Ferreira; see Martin, 30; II, p. 752) yielded the results presented in Table 7.

TABLE 7: CRANIAL CAPACITY AND ECONOMIC STATUS (DA COSTA FERREIRA)

Group	Number	Average c.c.
Upper class	23	1629
Merchant	49	1598
Higher employees	11	1590
Petty employees	52	1584
Skilled workers	150	1573
Day laborers	164	1570

A study by Matiegka (see Martin, 30; II, p. 754) in Prague gave a similar result. See Table 8.

TABLE 8: BRAIN WEIGHT AND OCCUPATION (MATIEGKA)

Occupation	Number	Average Brain Weight in Grams
Physicians and teachers	22	1500
Business men, employees and musicians	28	1469
Skilled workers	123	1450
Door-keepers and servants	14	1436
Laborers	34	1433
Day laborers	14	1410

Martin (30), in discussing these results, points out that brain weight and cranial capacity depend on a whole group of factors—age, body size, muscular mass, nourishment, pathological state—all of which must be taken into account before any conclusion may be reached as to the relation with intelligence. He does, however, conclude that to a certain extent position and achievement are dependent upon the size of the brain. It must not be overlooked that the relationship may be just the opposite, the favorable living conditions of the higher social and economic classes resulting in a larger and better-nourished brain. This is the opinion of Raymond Pearl (35), who finds a slight tendency for high intelligence to be associated with a larger head circumference, but who explains it as due merely to vigor in the growth process and to the action of good conditions of nurture, reflected also in greater stature and body weight. He reports approximately the same degree of relation between stature and brain weight as between intelligence and brain weight, and believes that the whole relationship may be explained as a case of "mens sana in corpore sano." Boas (7) is of the same opinion, suggesting that the somewhat larger brains of eminent men may be due to the fact that they belong to the better-nourished classes.

This general position has received experimental corroboration in a recent study by Estabrooks (14b), who found a positive correlation between *gross* cranial capacity and intelligence, but no relation whatsoever with *relative* cranial capacity. This suggests that great care must be taken in the interpretation of previous results. Porteus and Berry (39), for instance, found that feeble-minded children have somewhat smaller heads than the normal; but they failed to take into account the fact that the norms were obtained from children of superior economic status, and that the lower economic level of the feeble-minded may have been entirely responsible for the difference.

The question of sex differences deserves a word of comment in this connection. It has been shown that the brain of woman is both absolutely and relatively smaller than that of man. Pearl (35) found that the brains of Swedish women were 130 to 150 grams lighter than in the case of males of the same size and weight. Since no sex differences have been observed in intelligence quotient or school grades or any other criteria of ability, this may perhaps be regarded as one further argument against the notion that head size and intelligence are closely related.

QUALITATIVE DIFFERENCES IN BRAIN STRUCTURE

The attempt has also been made to discover whether special regions of the brain, rather than its total size, may be related to intelligence. The widespread belief that a high forehead, probably representing a marked development of the frontal lobes, is a sign of superior intelligence, has been subjected to quantitative study. The English criminologist Goring (20) asked a warden and a prison physician to rate 300 convicts for intelligence and height of the forehead. The results showed that those who were judged to have the highest grade of intellect were judged also to have the highest foreheads. Goring then actually measured the height of the forehead in each case and obtained the averages presented in Table 9.

TABLE 9: INTELLIGENCE AND HEIGHT OF FOREHEAD (GORING)

Group	Average Height in Mm.
Intelligent	50
Unintelligent	52
Weak-minded	54
Imbeciles	52

It is clear that there had been a pronounced error in the estimation of the height of the forehead, due to the belief of the judges in the intellectual significance of a high or low brow. A recent study by Sherman (43) showed a correlation of —.15 between the height of the forehead and scholastic achievement. Clark Hull (23) comments: "If the results of these studies should be confirmed by further investigation, it will be an interesting case of the overturning of a popular belief which is to the effect that a high forehead indicates excellent academic aptitude. In short, it would necessitate a reversal of the current use of the expressions 'highbrow' and 'low-brow' " (p. 136). Martin's (30) view that the capacity of the frontal portion of the skull is of special importance is not corroborated by this material.

The depth and complexity of the cerebral convolutions have often been considered particularly significant. The careful comparison by Donaldson (12), however, of the brains of three scholars with those of three men of ordinary intelligence yielded results so inconclusive as to rule out the use of variations in the convolutions to explain mental traits and abilities. The scholars did have somewhat better-grown and better-nourished brains, and there was a slightly greater extent of cortex in the frontal area. Donaldson suggests that favorable nutritional adjustment constitutes a fundamental condition favoring superior performance.

RACIAL DIFFERENCES IN BRAIN SIZE AND STRUCTURE

In the light of the above findings any possible racial differences in brain size or structure may not have so much significance as is popularly supposed. It is, however, important to look a little more carefully into the nature of these differences.

Racial and national differences in average cranial capacity are reported by Martin (30), although the results have been obtained by a larger number of different investigators. The figures are interesting enough for part of his material to be reproduced in some detail. Table 10 gives the average cranial capacity as determined by the seed or water method. (Note: The cranium is filled with seeds or water after the foramina have been plugged, and the contents are then poured into a

TABLE 10: GROUP DIFFERENCES IN CRANIAL CAPACITY (MARTIN; SEED OR WATER METHOD)

Group	Average Cranial Capacity in Cc.	Range	Investigator
Europe			
Tyrolese (Laas).............	1359	1080–2020	Frizzi
Dutch......................	1382	1025–1796	Bolk
Czechs.....................	1415	1230–1800	Schiff
Swiss (Disentis)............	1429	1170–1760	Wettstein
Tyrolese (Walser)...........	1436	1160–1700	Wacker
Poles......................	1440	1220–1650	Loth
Saxons.....................	1460	1290–1720	Welcker
Bavarians (Alpine foothills).	1464	1170–1750	Ried
Swiss (Danis)..............	1467	1200–1660	Reicher
Alemanni...................	1474	....	Schwerz
Alsatians..................	1484	....	Rebentisch
Wurtembergers.............	1494	....	Häcker
Bavarians (Altbayern).......	1503	1260–1780	Ranke
Africa			
Bushmen...................	1324	....	Sarasin
Negroes....................	1330	....	Welcker
Ancient Egyptians..........	1336	1060–1610	Oetteking
Cameroons.................	1422	1195–1680	Drontschilow
Kaffirs....................	1460	....	Shrubsall
Asia			
Veddas....................	1250	1012–1408	Sarasin
Hindus....................	1275	1171–1408	Welcker
Andamanese................	1281	....	Flower
Tamilis....................	1336	1236–1498	Sarasin
Chinese....................	1456	....	Haberer
Kalmucks..................	1466	....	Reicher
Buriats....................	1496	1280–1620	Reicher
America			
Indians....................	1440	1232–1660	Welcker
Greenland Eskimo..........	1452	1276–1572	Welcker
Arkansas Indians...........	1455	1310–1670	Hrdlička
Eskimo....................	1563	1410–1775	Hrdlička
Oceania			
Papuans...................	1236	....	Sergi and Moschen
Australians................	1310	....	Sarasin
Papuans...................	1398	1312–1448	Meyer
New Caledonians...........	1420	1125–1630	Sarasin
Marquesans................	1427	1230–1685	v. Luschan
Loyalty Islanders...........	1463	1245–1755	Sarasin
Maori.....................	1479	1270–1795	v. Luschan
Tahitians..................	1487	1380–1720	v. Luschan

capacity measure.) These figures are for males only; unfortunately the number of cases is not reported.

The racial differences are by no means clear or consistent. The average cranial capacity for European males by this method is 1450 cc., and for females 1300 cc. Since the above figures are for males only, we find that among the peoples listed the European average is exceeded by a Negro group like the Kaffirs, as well as by the Chinese, Kalmucks, Buriats, Eskimo, American Indians, Maori, Tahitians and others. There is also such wide variation within any one race, and consequently so much overlapping, that any direct relation between brain size and race cannot be postulated. It is interesting in this connection to note that the largest brains, on the average, were found among the Eskimo, whose culture is comparatively simple.

Table 11 similarly presents average cranial capacity as determined by the shot method. (Note: The cranium is filled with small shot, which are then emptied into a capacity measure.)

In this table the Europeans show up somewhat better. Their average is 1550 for males and 1380 for females; this male average is exceeded only by the African Amaxosa and the Javanese, although the Kaffirs, the Chukchee and the Eskimo approach it very closely. It must be borne in mind, however, that the stature of most of these groups is inferior to that of the Europeans, and that the relative cranial capacity would therefore in many cases be greater. It should also be noted that between these various groups there is a great deal of overlapping; though the Hottentot average is low, individual Hottentots may, and often do, have a cranial capacity exceeding that of the average European. This racial overlapping is also illustrated by the fact that the average for the Scotch is exceeded by the Kaffirs, Amaxosa, Chukchee,

TABLE 11: GROUP DIFFERENCES IN CRANIAL CAPACITY (MARTIN; SHOT METHOD)

Group	Average Cranial Capacity in Cc.	Range	Investigator
Europe			
Scotch..............................	1478	1230–1855	Turner
Alsatians...........................	1501	1130–1635	Adachi
Tyrolese...........................	1508	900–1990	Tappeiner
Ancient Gauls......................	1529	1364–1775	Broca
Dutch.............................	1530	1292–1680	"
Savoyards.........................	1538	1327–1712	"
French Basques....................	1544	1395–1932	"
Swiss (Wallis)....................	1546	1250–1930	Pittard
Parisians..........................	1559	1308–1900	Broca
Bretons...........................	1564	1362–1887	"
Spanish Basques...................	1584	1395–1932	"
Auvergnats........................	1609	1310–1894	"
Africa			
Hottentots and Bushmen............	1317	1183–1620	Broca
Nubians...........................	1329	1244–1429	"
Egyptians (X Dynasty).............	1443	1213–1700	"
Negroes...........................	1462	1227–1627	"
Arabs.............................	1474	1314–1628	"
Egyptians (IV Dynasty)............	1532	1213–1700	"
Kaffirs...........................	1540	.....	Shrubsall
Amaxosa...........................	1570	.....	"
Asia			
Burmese...........................	1389	.....	Turner
Ainu..............................	1462	1140–1705	Koganei
Japanese..........................	1485	1110–1630	Adachi
Chinese...........................	1518	1355–1674	Broca
Chukchee..........................	1530	.....	Montandon
Javanese..........................	1590	1321–1799	Broca
America			
Caribs............................	1410	.....	Quatrefages
Eskimo............................	1535	1418–1624	Broca
Oceania			
Australians.......................	1347	1222–1507	Broca
Tasmanians........................	1406	1220–1518	"
New Caledonians...................	1460	1287–1632	"
Maori.............................	1476	1183–1725	Scott
Polynesians.......................	1500	1338–1742	Broca

Eskimo, Polynesians, Javanese, as well as by the Chinese and Japanese.

In connection with the importance of social and economic status (see above), it is interesting to note that a recent study by Todd and Lindala (49), in which the crania of Negroes and Whites of approximately the same social status were compared, concluded that the cranial dimensions—length, breadth and vertical height above the ear—showed no significant stock differences.

The obvious impossibility of associating brain capacity with culture is recognized by Bushmakin (9), who notes that the Buriats who "have entered the zone of cultural development only with the new state organization" (p. 226), have an average brain weight greatly surpassing that of Europeans, and greater than that of Russians with a stature higher than theirs. This and similar material removes the force from the argument that a smaller cranial capacity necessarily points to inferior intelligence.

In the comparison of racial averages, one further fact must be noted. As Virchow (50) long ago pointed out, and as has recently been stressed by Huntington (24) and Dixon (11), there is a definite tendency for brachycephalic heads to have a slightly greater cranial capacity than dolichocephalic. As most Negro heads fall into the latter category, it may very well be that at least part of the deficiency in size is due to differences in head shape. In the above tables, for example, the Scotch, Dutch and other north European groups tend on the average to have a smaller cranial capacity than brachycephalic samples from Auvergne, Bavaria and Wurtemberg. Here, too, there are many exceptions— for example, the round-headed Tyrolese have smaller skulls than the long-headed Dutch—but the general trend is suggestive. The smaller size of Negro heads may therefore be even less important than it seems.

Attempts have also been made to find qualitative differences in the brain structure of various races. Bean (2), for instance, reported that Negro brains show a depression of the anterior association center (the frontal area) and a relative bulging of the posterior association center. He writes that "from the deduced difference between the functions of the anterior and the posterior association centers and from the known characteristics of the two races, the conclusion is that the Negro is more objective and the Caucasian more subjective. The Negro has the lower mental faculties (smell, sight, handicraftsmanship, body-sense, melody) well-developed, the Caucasian the higher (self-control, will power, ethical and æsthetic senses and reason)" (p. 412). This finding was based on a study of 152 brains, mostly from the anatomical collection in the Johns Hopkins Hospital. Hankins (21), commenting on these results, says that in them "one can perceive a neurological basis for racial differences in behavior and in characteristic rôles in cultural history" (p. 318). Todd (47) also suggests that the Negro skulls may have contours very different from those of the Whites, but he draws from his data no special implications with regard to behavior or mentality.

A later study by Mall (29) failed to confirm Bean's suggestion of a qualitative difference between the brains of the two races. He divided about 100 Negro and White brains into three separate divisions according to the richness of the convolutions and found almost exactly the same results for both racial groups; there was no indication that the White brains were more complex. He also weighed the frontal lobes in the case of both groups, being careful not to know in advance which were Negro and which were White, and found that although the Negro brains were somewhat lighter as a whole, the frontal lobes were relatively just as heavy. He failed also to confirm Bean's suggestion that the shape of the *corpus callosum* differed in the two groups. His general conclusion was that there are no observable qualitative race differences in brain structure.

Benington (3) collected 250 cases of Congo and Gaboon crania, and found them also to be somewhat smaller than those of modern European races. He reported, however, that the greatest deficiency lay in the occipital rather than in the frontal region. Another study of Negro brains was made by Genna (18) working with Sergi in Rome, and a careful investigation of eleven Cameroon brains yielded the result that it is not possible to arrive at any definite conclusion with respect to racial differences. A similar conclusion was reached by Keegan (25), who studied three American Indian brains, and found no constant racial differences. Fischer's (15) general conclusion is that "the convolutions and the furrows or sulci between them vary so much from individual to individual that no racial distinctions can be ascertained."

BIBLIOGRAPHY

1. Baldwin, B. T. (in L. M. Terman, *et al.*). "Mental and Physical Traits of 1000 Gifted Children." *Genetic Studies of Genius,* Vol. I. Stanford University, 1925.
2. Bean, R. B. "Some Racial Peculiarities of the Negro Brain." *Amer. J. Anat.,* 5:1906, pp. 353-432.
3. Benington, R. C. "A Study of the Negro Skull with Special Reference to the Congo and Gaboon Crania." *Biometrika,* 8:1912, pp. 292-337.
4. Binet, A. "Recherches sur la Technique de la Mensuration de la tête vivante." *L'Année Psych.,* 7:1900, pp. 314-368.
5. Binet, A. "Les Signes Physiques de l'Intelligence chez les Enfants." *L'Année Psych.,* 16:1910, pp. 1-30.

6. Blackford, K. M. H., and Newcomb, A. *The Job, the Man, the Boss*. Garden City, N. Y., 1914.

7. Boas, F. *Anthropology and Modern Life*. New York, 1928.

8. Broca, P. "Sur la capacité des crânes parisiens des diverses époques." *Bull. Soc. Anthrop.*, Ser. I, 3:1862, p. 102.

9. Bushmakin, N. "Characteristics of the Brain of the Mongol Race." *Amer. J. Phys. Anthrop.*, 12:1928, pp. 221-243.

10. Cleeton, G. U., and Knight, F. B. "Validity of Character Judgments Based on External Criteria." *J. App. Psych.*, 8:1924, pp. 215-231.

11. Dixon, R. B. *The Racial History of Man*. New York, 1923.

12. Donaldson, H. H., and Canavan, M. M., "A Study of the Brains of Three Scholars." *J. Comp. Neurol.*, 46:1928, pp. 1-95.

13. Ellis, H. *A Study of British Genius*. London, 1904. (Revised Ed., London, 1927.)

14a. Estabrooks, G. H. "Intelligence and Pigmentation of Hair and Eyes in Elementary School Children." *Amer. J. Psych.*, 41: 1929, pp. 106-108.

14b. Estabrooks, G. H. "Relation between Cranial Capacity and Intelligence in School Children." *J. App. Psych.*, 12:1928, pp. 524-529.

15. Fischer, E. "Variable Characters in Human Beings." Chapter 5 in Baur, Fischer and Lenz, *Human Heredity*, pp. 114-166. New York, 1931. (Trans.)

16. Fowler, O. S., *Human Science or Phrenology*. Philadelphia, 1873.

17. Galton, F. "Headgrowth in Students at the University of Cambridge." *Nature*, 38:1888, pp. 14-15.

18. Genna, G. E. "Sulla morfologia dei solchi cerebrali dell'uomo, con osservazioni su cervelli di indagini del Camerun." *Riv. di Antropologia*, 26:1924-1925, pp. 19-173.

19. Gladstone, R. J. "A Preliminary Communication on Some Cephalometric Data Bearing upon the Relation of the Size and the Shape of the Head to Mental Ability." *J. Anat. and Physiol.*, 37:1902-1903, pp. 333-346.

20. Goring, Sir C. *The English Convict*. London, 1913.

21. Hankins, F. H. *The Racial Basis of Civilization: A Critique of the Nordic Doctrine*. New York, 1926.

22. Hooton, E. A. *Up from the Ape*. New York, 1931.

23. Hull, C. L. *Aptitude Testing*. New York, 1928.

24. Huntington, E. *The Character of Races*. New York, 1924.

25. Keegan, J. J. "The Indian Brain." *Amer. J. Phys. Anthrop.*, 3: 1920, pp. 25-62.

26. Kroeber, A. L. "Cultural Anthropology," in *The Problem of Mental Disorder*. New York, 1934, pp. 346-353.

27. Lavater, J. C. *Physiognomik*. Vienna, 1829.

28. MacDonald, A. "An Experimental Study of Children," in *Report of the U. S. Commission of Education, 1897-98*. Washington, 1899. Vol. I, pp. 985-1204.

29. Mall, F. P. "On Several Anatomical Characters of the Human Brain," *Amer. J. Anat.*, 9:1909, pp. 1-32.

30. Martin, R. *Lehrbuch der Anthropologie*. Jena, 1928. (3 vols.)

31a. Matiegka, H. "Über die Beziehungen des Hirngewicht zum Berufe." *Politisch-Anthropologische Revue*, 3:1904, pp. 7-22.

31b. Matiegka, H. "Körperbeschaffenheit und geistige Tätigkeit bei Schulkindern." *Mitt. Anthrop. Gesellsch. Wien.*, 28:1898, p. 122.

32. Murdock, K., and Sullivan, L. R. "A Contribution to the Study of Mental and Physical Measurements in Normal Children." *Amer. Phys. Educ. Rev.*, 28:1923, pp. 209-215, 276-280, 328-330.

33. Paterson, D. G. *Physique and Intellect*. New York, 1930.

34. Paterson, D. G., and Ludgate, K. E. "Blond and Brunette Traits: A Quantitative Study." *J. Personnel Research*, 1: 1922, pp. 122-127.

35. Pearl, R. *Studies in Human Biology*. Baltimore, 1924.

36. Pearson, K. "Relationship of Intelligence to Size and Shape of the Head and Other Mental and Physical Characters." *Biometrika*, 5:1906, pp. 105-146.

37. Peterson, F. "Craniometry and Cephalometry in Relation to Idiocy and Imbecility." *Amer. J. Insanity*, 52:1895, pp. 72-89.

38. Porter, W. T. "The Physical Basis of Precocity and Dullness." *Transactions of the Acad. of Sci. of St. Louis*, 6:1895, pp. 161-181.

39. Porteus, S. D., and Berry, R. J. A. "A Practical Method for the Early Recognition of Feeble Mindedness and Other Forms of Social Inefficiency." *Vineland, N. J., Training School Bull.*, 15:1918, pp. 81-92.

40. Reed, R. W., and Mulligan, J. H. "Relation of Cranial Capacity to Intelligence." *J. Royal Anthrop. Inst.*, 53:1923, pp. 322-332.

41. Retzius, G. *Crania suecica antiqua*. Stockholm, 1900.

42. Röse, C. "Beiträge zur Europäischen Rassenkunde." *Archiv. fur Rassen-und-Gesellschafts-biologie*, 2:1905, pp. 689-798; 3: 1906, pp. 42-134.

43. Sherman, E. B. "An Experimental Investigation Concerning Possible Correlation between Certain Head Measurements and University Grades." A. B. Thesis, 1925. University of Wisconsin. (See Hull, C. L. *Aptitude Testing*, No. 23.)

44. Simon, T. "Recherches céphalométriques sur les Enfants arriérés de la Colonie de Vaucluse." *L'Année Psych.*, 7:1900, pp. 430-489.

45. Sommerville, R. C. "Physical, Motor and Sensory Traits." *Arch. Psych.*, No. 75, 1924.

46. Sorokin, P. *Social Mobility*. New York, 1927.

47. Todd, T. W. "Cranial Capacity and Linear Dimensions in White and Negro." *Amer. J. Phys. Anthrop.*, 6:1923, pp. 97-194.

48. Todd, T. W. "Entrenched Negro Physical Features." *Human Biology*, 1:1929, pp. 57-69.

49. Todd, T. W., and Lindala, A. "Dimensions of the Body; Whites and American Negroes of Both Sexes." *Amer. J. Phys. Anthrop.*, 12:1928, pp. 35-119.

50. Virchow, R. *Menschen und Affenschädel*. Berlin, 1870.

51. Viteles, M. S. *Industrial Psychology*. New York, 1932.

Chapter V

DEVELOPMENTAL DIFFERENCES

The Problem

A NECESSARY preliminary to a comparison of the abilities of two races is a consideration of their growth curves. If one race matures more quickly than another, a ten-year-old child of that race may be at a relatively more advanced stage of development, and an apparent superiority over a child of another race may be temporary and spurious. It has been suggested, for example, that the better showing of Jewish children in intelligence tests may be explained by such a difference in the rate of maturation. (Ruppin, 35.) If Italian or south European children mature more quickly than Scandinavian or north European, it may be that a comparison of children of the same age in the two groups will be unfair to the latter.

Briffault (10) points to the obvious fact that the rate of individual development becomes slower as we rise in the scale of biological organization, and that in higher forms the young are brought into the world in a condition of greater immaturity. Prolonged infancy and slow development are most pronounced in human beings. Briffault goes on to suggest that there is the same relative difference in rapidity of maturation between the higher and lower human races. Savage children develop more quickly and are far more precocious than Europeans; they complete their development sooner, and they have less capacity for further modification and progress.

This difficult problem is complicated by the social and

cultural factors which may enter into the picture. The fact that among the Malays or the Australians young children are like grown men in their conversation and behavior, and appear to be treated by the adults as equals, may clearly be due as much to a different attitude toward children as to a difference in rate of biological maturity. Similarly, education rather than physiology may be responsible for the fact that Omaha Indian children of ten know all about hunting and war; and the same may be said for the remainder of Briffault's examples. The statement is frequently made that Negro children also reach their psychological maturity somewhat earlier than Whites, and some of the results obtained by means of intelligence testing seem to bear out this notion, but here again there are other factors which must be considered. King[1] found in his study of West Virginia Negroes that boys and girls tended to drop out of school at just about the age of puberty. When he asked them why they wished to leave school, he was frequently told that they saw no reason to stay on since they would never be permitted to do the kind of work for which a more advanced education would fit them. As they came to realize that they could never be anything but laborers or quarrymen or house servants, it seemed to them a waste of time to continue with their education. It is not too far-fetched to suggest that this attitude may play a part in the apparent cessation of mental development at this age.

This general problem is best approached in two stages. It is in the first place important to discover whether there is any relationship between the development of intelligence and the physiological signs of maturation. If there is such a relationship, it becomes necessary in the second place to de-

---

[1] L. E. King, Unpublished Ph.D. Dissertation, Dept. of Anthropology, Columbia University.

termine whether races differ in the period at which these physiological signs appear. The first is a preliminary, the second a more direct attack upon the problem of racial differences in growth and maturation.

MENTAL AND PHYSICAL GROWTH

In the studies of the relation between mental and physical growth the criterion of mental development has usually been the intelligence test, although in the earlier investigations use was made also of school grade and scholastic standing. When an intelligence test was given, the results could be stated in terms of mental age. By analogy, there have been many attempts to develop a satisfactory criterion of "physiological age" to serve as an index of physiological development. For this purpose measures have been taken of height, weight, development of the secondary teeth, and stage of ossification of the bones in the wrist (the carpal area), this last usually determined by X-ray. These various measures have never been combined into a scale comparable, for example, to the Binet scale of intelligence, but they have been used singly and more or less interchangeably. The problem has usually been to determine the degree of correspondence between these measures of physiological age and tests of mental age, when chronological age is held constant. (Note: Chronological age is "held constant" either by testing subjects of the same age, or by ruling out the effect of age by the statistical method of partial correlation.)

It is occasionally stated that there is a tendency for mental precocity to be accompanied by physical retardation, and one of the earliest investigators (West, 51) concluded that precocity bears an inverse ratio to bodily development. This view is exceptional in scientific literature. Porter (33), also one of the pioneers in this field, compared the age-grade location of 33,500 boys and girls in St. Louis with measures of their height and weight, and concluded that the brighter the child, the taller and heavier he tends to be. Since the days of the first intelligence tests there have been a large number of studies indicating that the higher I.Q. groups had a slightly greater height and weight than the average, and that mental defectives tended to be somewhat shorter and lighter. Terman's (45) results with children of very high I.Q. also showed this tendency. In general, however, the differences are small and the overlapping is very great.

When correlations are used, they are with rare exceptions too low to be of real significance. Murdock and Sullivan (28) obtained a correlation of +.16 between weight and I.Q., and +.14 between height and I.Q. Paterson (30) calculated the coefficient of correlation for Porter's (33) results and found it to be only +.06 for weight and school grade. The only really high correlation in this field was obtained by Baldwin (3), who found the relation between height and mental age, with chronological age held constant, to equal +.53. Unfortunately, the correlation between weight and mental age for the same subjects was —.15, and Baldwin's conclusion that "mental age has a direct relation to physiological age as shown by height and weight" is hardly justified. After a survey of all the available material, Paterson (30) concludes that "a slight positive correlation seems to exist between stature or weight and intelligence"; the relation is positive, but "physical status and mental status are to a great extent independent" (pp. 51-52).

With the other measures of physiological age the results are somewhat similar. Rotch (34) suggested a close relationship between anatomical age as measured by X-ray of the carpal bones, and mental development; he stated that where there is delayed mental development there is delayed skeletal development as well. Baldwin and Stecher (4), however, found the relationship to be much less close than Rotch had suggested. The study by Gates (18) showed a correlation of only $+.11$ between carpal development and mental age. It should be pointed out in this connection that the stage of ossification of the wrist cannot be simply determined by the measurement of the ossified area. Children who are naturally larger may have a correspondingly larger ossified carpal area, though relatively they may be no further advanced. As a result, Prescott (32a) made use of an "anatomic index," derived by dividing the total carpal area by a definite constant rectangle; it is this index which has been used in the more recent studies.

A study by Cattell (11) found no definite correspondence between mental ability and stage of dentition. Perkins (31) suggests that extreme cases of delayed dentition are accompanied by retardation in mental development, but that in normal cases the relation is not close; in general, dentition shows a closer relationship with chronological than with mental age.

In summary, it may be said that the use of physiological age, advocated by Foster (16) and Baldwin (3) as an important aid in school grading and school promotion, has so far not been justified to any marked degree. One reason for this, as Scammon (36) has pointed out, is the difficulty of finding a unit which may properly be used as a criterion of growth. The various measures of physiological age do not always correlate very highly with one another, and it has so far not been determined which measure is the most satisfactory. Even if they are combined, however, as was done by Gates (18), the multiple correlation of all physical measurements (including ossification, height, weight, chest girth, lung capacity, grip and nutritional status) with mental age was only +.21, so that at best the relation is a slight one.

It is probable, however, that there has been altogether too much reliance upon the correlation coefficient in this field. This is not the place for a technical discussion of statistical techniques; but it should be noted that the Pearson r assumes a linear relation between two variables, so that if the relationship is non-linear it will not be revealed by the use of that method.

There are other difficulties. Suppose there are two boys, A and B, exactly twelve years old; A is five feet, two inches in height, and B, five feet. This may mean that A is more mature than B; but if A is destined to reach a height of six feet, and B, of five feet, four, then B may actually be closer to his final stature than A. If we take the total growth curve into consideration, B is really the more mature of the two. It is quite possible that the relation between mental and physical growth is of such a nature that the point reached on the mental growth curve may correspond to that reached on the physical growth curve, but a relation of this kind would be hidden by the usual correlational techniques. The only adequate way to uncover such a relationship would be to study the whole life cycle of the individual, and to have continued and repeated measures of both types of development. Until that has been done, the problem will remain obscure.

There are a number of important studies which indicate that the whole physical life cycle may be significantly interconnected. Boas (7), for example, has shown that the changes characteristic of puberty are accompanied by a marked increase in stature, the so-called adolescent growth spurt. At a later age level, Bernstein (6) has indicated that there is a correspondence between the amount of presbyopia, or flattening of the lens of the eye, and the age at which death occurs from arteriosclerosis. This suggests that degenerative changes may be related to one another in the same way as changes characteristic of growth or maturation. The exact relation to mental growth and decay still remains to be studied.

A final caution is required. These growth studies have not always taken into consideration the marked influence exerted upon growth by social and economic status. Sorokin (40) summarizes the material bearing upon this point and gives ample evidence to indicate the more rapid growth as well as the greater final stature of individuals living in a more favorable environment. Schallmayer (38) reports an experiment in which the children of workmen were placed under particularly good living conditions, and as a result surpassed wealthy children in both height and weight. Bakwin (2) has obtained similar results in the case of infants. This material indicates that the positive relation between growth and intelligence may be due partly to the fact that both are favorably influenced by a good environment; and any study in this field must consider that possibility. It is pointed out by Paterson (30), however, that the correlation remains even when the study is made upon a group which is socially homogeneous. The whole problem is a complicated one, and will probably not be solved until it is possible to have many consecutive observations of the same individuals, with careful consideration of all the social and environmental factors which may have an effect on the growth curve. (For a summary of studies bearing upon mental and physical growth, see Paterson, 30, and Wellman, 50.)

RACIAL DIFFERENCES IN GROWTH

A study by Herskovits (22) indicates that colored boys grow faster than white boys in height and weight up to the sixteenth year, but that after that time the latter show a somewhat greater stature. Both groups show the adolescent growth spurt, but it occurs about a year earlier in the case of the Negro group. Boas (7) has obtained a similar result for Hebrew boys, who exceed the non-Hebrew group in stature up to the thirteenth year and thereafter lag behind. There appears to be a difference in the growth curve, although since the Jewish group is not a genetic or racial entity, this difference is difficult to understand. Factors of diet and activity may play an important part.

Suk (44) has made a study of the eruption and decay of the permanent teeth in various races, and finds the colored races more precocious than the Whites. He states that Filipinos and Zulus have a full set of permanent teeth between the ages of eighteen and twenty, whereas among the Whites the third molar is usually lacking at that age. The number of cases in this study is small, and the finding has not been corroborated.

Another growth feature which has received special consideration in connection with racial comparisons is the time of closure of the fontanelles and sutures of the skull. Gratiolet (21) was probably the first to suggest that the earlier closure in the Negro skull is responsible for an earlier cessation of brain development. Vogt (48) accepted this notion and believed it to be the key to the earlier maturation and lower intelligence of the so-called primitive peoples. As far as the Negro is concerned, however, a study by Todd (46) has shown no racial peculiarity whatsoever. The closure occurs at almost exactly the same period in Negroes and Whites.

PUBERTY AND INTELLIGENCE

The appearance of puberty, especially in the case of girls, marks a definite change which may be regarded as an index of physiological development. Many attempts have been made to determine whether this change is accompanied by any corresponding psychological effect. The occasional occurrence of cases of puberty precox, or very early maturation, has made possible one approach to this problem. Gesell (19) studied three such cases and obtained results so conflicting that he concluded that there was no relation between puberty and the mental growth curve. He believed that social development and personality might, however, be affected. A more extensive study of 62 cases by Stone and Doe-Kulman (42) found slightly more cases below than above the average in intelligence, and also concluded that there was no specific relationship. It may be questioned whether a study of pathological cases, accompanied by general glandular disturbance, can throw light on the usual relationship found in normal cases.

A study of the relationship between puberty and mental development among normal girls was made by Crampton (12), who found post-pubescents to be superior to pre-pubescents of the same age in height, weight, strength and scholastic standing. Here, as elsewhere in this field, social and economic status may be of importance, as will be noted in greater detail below; it may be that superior status is responsible for all the factors concerned—greater height, weight and strength, earlier puberty and higher scholarship. Even if the increase in height and weight is a direct response to the metabolic changes occurring at puberty, it is still highly probable that the onset of puberty is in part a function of favorable living conditions. A recent study by Franzblau (17) compared post- and pre-pubescents of the same age by means of the International Intelligence Tests after equating them as nearly as possible for socio-economic background, and found no difference between the two groups.

Another approach to this same problem has been made by Viteles (47), who was interested in discovering whether the age at puberty had any measurable relationship to adult mental development. His subjects had all matured, but they had matured at different ages, the median lapse of time since the first menstruation being four years. He found no consistent differences in intelligence or academic grade between those of early and those of late pubescence.

The material at present available seems to offer no indication of a direct relationship between intelligence and the time of the first menstruation. In individual instances there may be such a relation, and Dearborn[1] has indicated the presence of an "adolescent spurt" in intelligence analogous to the spurt studied by Boas in the case of physical growth. Here also a great deal more will have to be done by means of follow-up studies of the same individuals over a period of years. For our purposes, however, the more essential problem is whether individuals or groups who differ in the time of puberty also differ correspondingly in the rate or level of their mental development. Since the relationship is meanwhile unproved, racial or national differences in the time of puberty, if such exist, will be no indication that the groups differ psychologically. It is of interest, however, to turn more directly to a consideration of the manner and extent of these differences.

RACIAL AND NATIONAL DIFFERENCES IN TIME OF PUBERTY

In an early discussion of this topic by Marro (26), race is mentioned as one of several factors affecting the onset of puberty. Neurath (29) also regards race as playing an important part, pointing out in addition that the effect of climate, health, physical environment, occupation and in-

---

[1] W. F. Dearborn, unpublished.

dividual constitution also requires to be considered. Schröder (39) is somewhat more conservative, and after examining the evidence concludes that "it seems probable that race plays a part." As we shall see, the effect of non-racial factors may be so marked that it would seem advisable to exercise even more caution than did Schröder before stating with certainty that there are true racial differences.

Table 12, which is modified from Schröder, will serve as a convenient starting point:

TABLE 12: GROUP DIFFERENCES IN TIME OF PUBERTY (SCHRÖDER)

Country	Investigator	Number of Cases	Average Age
United States of America	Engelmann	10,531	13.9
Italy	Rossi Doria	31,659	14.3
Finland (Helsingfors)	Engström	3,500	14.4
France	Several studies	4,377	14.6
Russia (Moscow)	Bensenger	5,611	14.8
Japan	Yamasaki	4,861	14.1
England (London)	Several studies	5,334	15.0
Poland (Warsaw)	Lebrun	15,083	15.1
Finland	Waren	10,500	15.2
Sweden	Essen-Möller	5,000	15.2
Hungary (Budapest)	Doctor	9,600	15.4
England (Manchester)	Whitehead	4,000	15.6
Germany (Berlin)	Meyer-Krieger	4,800	15.6
" "	Schäffer	11,550	15.7
Russia	Grusdeff	10,000	15.7
Finland (Helsingfors)	Heinricius	3,500	15.8
Germany (Bavaria)	Schlichting	10,522	15.9
" (Königsberg)	Sullies	3,000	16.0
Russia (Leningrad)	Rodsewitch	12,439	16.1
Denmark (Copenhagen)	Rawn	3,840	16.9

A detailed consideration of this table makes it clear that both racial and national differences are so inconsistent as to warrant great scepticism as to their significance. For example, the three studies from Finland show exceedingly marked variations; the group from Sweden differs very clearly from the Danish one, and the figures for Moscow are almost at the opposite extreme from those for Leningrad. The United States, with a population obviously European in origin, shows a figure lower than that of any of the European groups in the table. It is clear that neither race nor nation can account for results of this kind, and it is necessary to see what other factors may enter.

Climate has often been referred to as exercising an important influence. Baelz (1) points out that European girls in Japan mature earlier than those in Europe, and Glogner (20) has made the same observation for Dutch girls in the Dutch East Indies. This last result has been corroborated by figures quoted by Mayer (27) from Van den Burg, in which 168 girls of unmistakable European parentage living in the Dutch East Indies were compared with 862 girls living in Holland. The results showed that 54 per cent of the East Indian group and only 21 per cent of those in Holland had their first menstruation before they had completed their fourteenth year; 93 per cent of the East Indian group and only 79 per cent of the Holland group had menstruated by the time they were eighteen. These results apparently indicate that climate may be of outstanding importance, but it must be demonstrated that the two groups are otherwise comparable and represent in general the same social and economic class; it is possible that the Dutch living in the East Indies are mainly plantation owners whose environment differs from that of the average Dutchman in Holland not only in climate, but in a large number of other essential factors. Within the United States, Engelmann (15) reports that there are no marked differences corresponding to climate, and that the figures for southern and northern cities are about the same. The only material of this kind which he presents for the South refers to Negroes in New Orleans, who show about the same average age as Negroes in Baltimore or St. Louis. Incidentally, the average age for American Negroes in his report is 14.0 years, only three months older than the average for his White Americans.

For our purposes, the most important factor to be considered in this connection is social and economic status. It is clear from the available material that the general well-being attendant upon good living conditions tends to hasten the onset of puberty. Dickinson and Pierson (14) refer, for example, to the fact that the average age of puberty for wealthy girls in Copenhagen is 14.4, and for poor girls, 16.4. Schäffer (37) in Berlin obtained an average for the upper class of 14.0, and for the lower class of 15.7. Stratz (43) found in Bavaria that the average age for the upper social class is 12.9, for the middle class, 14.4, and for the peasant class, 16.4. Bensenger (5) in Moscow and Brierre de Boismont (9) in Paris obtained similar results. Engelmann (15) also reports that in the United States girls in higher economic classes menstruate a little earlier than those of the laboring class, though his results are not quite so conclusive as those obtained in other studies.

Puberty occurs somewhat earlier in urban than in rural regions. Marro (26) reports that girls in the country districts around Turin have their puberty about a year later than those in the city; it is interesting to note that Rousseau had made the same observation in Paris. Wrethom (32) noted that when Lapp girls left the mountains and abandoned their nomadic life to live in the Swedish towns, puberty occurred much earlier, and the average age for these Lapp girls and for Swedish girls became the same. This difference between city and country may in part be due to a difference in physical well-being due to living conditions, but it is also probable that the more stimulating life of the city with its earlier introduction to sex matters may contribute.

Marro, for example, believes that conversation with the opposite sex and the "reading of passionate literature" may
bring on an early puberty, and it has been suggested that the
early menstruation of girls in India is due to child marriages and the consequent precocious sex stimulation. Engelmann's conclusion is that mentality, surroundings, education and nerve stimulation are the factors which determine
precocity; climate and race have in his opinion very little
influence.

There is a popular opinion to the effect that Jewish girls
menstruate earlier than non-Jewish. Schäffer (37) found the
average age for German Jewesses to be 13.5, and for non-
Jewesses, 14.0. In South Russia Weissenberg (49) found the
figure for Jewesses to be 14.2, and for Russians, 14.11. Joachim
(25) found also that Jewesses in Hungary menstruated
somewhat earlier than non-Jewesses. (It must not be overlooked that economic factors may play a part.) Stöber and
Tourdes (41) found no difference between the two groups
in Strasbourg, and recently Boas (7) reported a similar finding in New York; in his study both groups were students
at the Horace Mann High School, had a relatively high and
approximately equal social status, and showed exactly the
same pubertal age of 13.1. It should be pointed out, however,
that in this study the groups were divided entirely on the
basis of their surnames, and it is quite possible that a few
Jewish girls were included in the non-Jewish group.

It has also been suggested that individual constitutional
factors may be operative, and that, more particularly, darker
girls (for example, those of south European origin) mature
earlier than fairer girls. Bolk (8) reports that this view is
unfounded, and that the average age for his brunette group
was 14.4, and for his blond group, 13.8. Heyn (24) also

points out that in his collected material dark girls do not show an earlier onset of puberty.

This material has shown that a great many factors may help to determine the time of the first menstruation. Health and economic status certainly, and climate and sex stimulation in all probability, make their respective contribution. Before concluding that race also enters, we must rule out these various factors which in themselves seem to account for all the observed differences between the various groups studied. In any case, as was suggested above, the time of first menstruation has probably no great significance for the problem of racial psychology.

BIBLIOGRAPHY

1. Baelz, E. "Die Körperlichen Eigenschaften der Japaner." *Mitt. d. dtschn. Gesellschaft für Natur und Völkerkunde Ostasiens,* 3:1883; 4:1885.

2. Bakwin, H., Bakwin, R. M., and Milgram, L. "Body Build in Infants," *Amer. J. Dis. Child.,* 48:1934, pp. 1030-1040.

3. Baldwin, B. T. "Relation Between Mental and Physical Growth." *J. Educ. Psych.,* 13:1922, pp. 193-203.

4. Baldwin, B. T., and Stecher, L. I. "Mental Growth Curve of Average and Superior Children." *Univ. of Iowa Studies in Child Welfare,* 2:1922, pp. 1-61.

5. Bensenger, W. N. "Ein Beitrag zur Anthropologie der weiblichen Bevölkerung Moskaus." *Arch. f. Anthrop.,* 14:1882, pp. 287-288.

6. Bernstein, F. "Alterssichtigkeit und Lebenserwartung." *Forschungen u. Fortschritte,* 8:1932, pp. 272-273.

7. Boas, F. "Studies in Growth." *Human Biol.,* 4:1932, pp. 307-350; 5:1933, pp. 429-444.

8. Bolk, L. "Untersuchungen über die Menarche bei der niederländschen Bevölkerung." *Ztschr. f. Geburtsh. u. Gynäkol.,* 89:1925, pp. 364-380.

9. Brierre de Boismont. See Ploss and Bartels, No. 32.

10. Briffault, R. L. *The Mothers; the Matriarchal Theory of Social Origins.* New York, 1927. (3 vols.)

11. Cattell, P. "Dentition as a Measure of Maturity." *Harvard Monographs in Education,* 9:1928, pp. 1-91.

12. Crampton, C. W. "The Influence of Physiological Age upon Scholarship." *Psychol. Clinic,* 1:1907, pp. 115-120.

13. Crampton, C. W. "Anatomical or Physiological Age *vs.* Chronological Age." *Ped. Sem.,* 15:1908, pp. 230-237.

14. Dickinson, R. L., and Pierson, H. H. "The Average Sex Life of American Women." *J. Amer. Med. Assn.,* 85:1925, pp. 1113-1117.

15. Engelmann, G. J. "Age of First Menstruation on the North American Continent." *New York Med. J.,* 75:1902, pp. 221-228.

16. Foster, W. L. "Physiological Age as a Basis for the Classification of Pupils Entering High Schools." *Psych. Clinic,* 4:1910, pp. 83-88.

17. Franzblau, R. N. "Race Differences in Mental and Physical Traits." *Arch. Psych.,* No. 177:1935.

18. Gates, A. I. "The Nature and Educational Significance of Physical Status and of Mental, Physiological, Social and Emotional Maturity." *J. Educ. Psych.,* 15:1924, pp. 329-358.

19. Gesell, A. "Precocious Puberty and Mental Maturation." *27th Yearbook, Natl. Soc. for the Study of Educ.,* Pt. I:1928, pp. 398-409.

20. Glogner, M. "Ueber den Eintritt der Menstruation bei Europäerinnen in den Tropen." *Arch. f. Schiffs- und Tropen-Hygiene,* 9:1905, pp. 337-340.

21. Gratiolet, L. P. "Sur le poids et la forme du cerveau." *Mém. Soc. d'anthropol. de Paris,* 2:1861, pp. 258-275.

22. Herskovits, M. J. "Observations on the Growth of Colored Boys." *Amer. J. Phys. Anthrop.,* 7:1924, pp. 439-446.

23. Herskovits, M. J. *The Anthropometry of the American Negro.* New York, 1930.

24. Heyn, A. "Menstruation, Haarfarbe und Libido." *Ztschr. f. Geburtsh. u. Gynäkol.,* 82:1920, p. 136.

25. Joachim, H. *Ungar. Ztschr.,* 4. See Ploss and Bartels, No. 32.

26. Marro, A. *La Pubertà.* Turin, 1897.

27. Mayer, A. "Die Bedeutung der Konstitution für die Frauenheilkunde." *Veit-Stoeckel, Hndbch. der Gynäkol.,* 3:1927. (3rd Ed.)

28. Murdock, K., and Sullivan, L. R. "A Contribution to the Study of Mental and Physical Measurements in Normal Children." *Amer. Phys. Educ. Rev.,* 28:1923, pp. 209-215, 276-280, 328-330.

29. Neurath, R. "Physiologie und Pathologie der Pubertät des weiblichen Geschlechts," in *Biologie und Pathologie des Weibes,* Vol. V, Pt. 4, by Halban and Seitz. Berlin, 1928.

30. Paterson, D. G. *Physique and Intellect.* New York, 1930.

31. Perkins, F. J. "Relation of Dentition to Mental Age." *Ped. Sem.,* 33:1926, pp. 387-398.

32. Ploss, H. H., and Bartels, M. C. A. *Das Weib in der Natur-und Völkerkunde.* Berlin, 1927. Vol. I. (11th Edition revised by v. Reitzenstein.)

33. Porter, W. T. "The Physical Basis of Precocity and Dullness." *Transactions of the Acad. of Sci. of St. Louis,* 5:1895, pp. 161-181.

33a. Prescott, D. A. "The Determination of Anatomical Age in School Children and its Relation to Mental Development." *Harvard Mono. in Educ.,* Ser. 1, No. 5, 1923.

34. Rotch, T. M. "A Study of the Development of the Bones in Childhood by the Roentgen Method." *Transactions of the Assn. of Amer. Phys.,* 24:1909.

35. Ruppin, A. *Die Soziologie der Juden.* Berlin, 1930-1931.

36. Scammon, R. E. "The Measurement of the Body in Childhood," in *The Measurement of Man* by Harris, J. A., Jackson, C. M., Paterson, D. G., and Scammon, R. E. Minneapolis, 1930. Part IV, pp. 173-215.

37. Schäffer, R. "Ueber das Alter des Menstruationsbeginnes." *Arch. f. Gynäkol.,* 84:1908, pp. 657-686.

38. Schallmayer, W. *Vererbung und Auslese.* Jena, 1920. (4th Ed.)

39. Schröder, R. "Der mensuelle Genitalzyklus des Weibes und seine Störungen," in *Handbuch der Gynäkologie* by Veit-Stoeckel. Munich, 1928. (3rd Ed.) Vol. I, Pt. II.

40. Sorokin, P. A. *Social Mobility.* New York, 1927.

41. Stöber, V. A., and Tourdes, G. *Topographie et histoire médicale de Strasbourg.* Paris, 1864.

42. Stone, C., and Doe-Kulmann, L. "Notes on the Mental Development of Children Exhibiting the Somatic Signs of Puberty

Precox." *27th Yearbook of the Natl. Soc. for the Study of Educ.*, Pt. I:1928, pp. 388-397.

43. Stratz, C. H. *Der Körper des Kindes und seine Pflege.* Stuttgart, 1922. (9th Ed.)

44. Suk, V. "Eruption and Decay of Permanent Teeth in Whites and Negroes, with Comparative Remarks on Other Races." *Amer. J. Phys. Anthrop.*, 2:1919, pp. 351-388.

45. Terman, L. M., *et al. Genetic Studies of Genius.* Stanford Univ., 1926-1930. (3 vols.)

46. Todd, T. W. "Entrenched Negro Physical Features." *Human Biol.*, 1:1929, pp. 57-69.

47. Viteles, M. S. "The Influence of Age of Pubescence upon the Physical and Mental Status of Normal School Students." *J. Educ. Psych.*, 20:1929, pp. 360-368.

48. Vogt, C. *Vorlesungen über den Menschen.* Giessen, 1863.

49. Weissenberg, S. "Menarche und Menopause bei Jüdinnen und Russinen in Südrussland." *Zentrlbl. f. Gynäkol.*, 11:1909.

50. Wellman, B. L. "Physical Growth and Motor Development and Their Relation to Mental Development in Children," in *A Handbook of Child Psychology,* by C. Murchison. Worcester, Mass., 1931, pp. 242-277.

51. West, G. M. "Observations on the Relation of Physical Development to Intellectual Ability Made on School Children of Toronto." *Science,* new ser., 4:1896, pp. 156-159.

Chapter VI

PHYSIOLOGICAL DIFFERENCES

Introduction

THE study of possible racial differences in physiological functioning is important not only in its own right, but also as a basis for a racial psychology. The behavior of an individual cannot be adequately understood without a consideration of its organic foundations, and psychology looks to physiology for many of its principles of explanation. Particularly in the field of emotional and affective experience, the activity of the autonomic nervous system and the accompanying visceral responses play a dominant part. It seems advisable, therefore, to review the evidence dealing with group differences in this respect, in order to determine whether a racial factor is in any way responsible.

Respiration and Circulation

There are no important differences, either real or apparent, to be reported in this field. Hrdlička (28) obtained approximately the same respiratory rate for a number of American Indian groups as for Whites, but found their pulse rate to be somewhat slower, ranging from an average of 57 for Zuni males to 67 for Navajo males (the average for White males being 70-72). On the other hand, Gould (18) examined 503 Indians in 1869 and found their average pulse rate to be 76.3, while Ferris (13) reports an average rate for the Quichua Indians of 74.0, showing that there are no consistent differences between Indians and Whites. Newton's (42) study of Negritos in the Philippines gave an average pulse rate for males of 76.1, with an average respiratory rate of 18.0, almost the same as for Whites; Suk (48) reports for male Negroes of Natal and Zululand a pulse rate of 72.1 and a respiratory rate of 20.5. There appears to be relatively little variation between different racial groups.

BLOOD PRESSURE

An interesting difference in blood pressure has been reported in connection with a number of Asiatic groups, who quite consistently show lower figures than do the American controls with whom they are compared. Table 13, which is modified from Foster (15), indicates the extent of this difference.

TABLE 13: GROUP DIFFERENCES IN BLOOD PRESSURE (FOSTER)

Group	Number of Cases	Average Systolic B.P.
American males	6000	128.9
American males	1000	127.5
Chinese students (Canton)	700	101.0
" " (Szechuan)	700	111.0
" " (Hunan)	261	114.5
" adults "	278	111.0
Filipino soldiers	366	115.5
" civilians	697	115.6
Hindu	500	90–105

These differences are marked, and if taken by themselves would lend a certain amount of support to the notion that there is a racial factor operative in the determination of blood pressure. Here, as elsewhere, however, it is important to consider other possible causes. It is well known from the work of Marston (38), Landis (32), Chappell (4), Larson (34), and others that blood pressure is markedly affected by emotional disturbances, and that high blood pressure may even be taken as an indication of the presence of such a disturbance; the possibility therefore arises that permanent differences in blood pressure may be due to very marked differences in mode of life, a busy excited existence manifesting itself in a blood pressure which is chronically high. It may be that this is the key to the apparent racial differences. Tung (53), for example, after noting that the blood pressure of 1233 northern Chinese was only slightly above 100 on the average, suggests that this may be due to the slow-going life which they lead, as contrasted with the "perpetual rush" and "constant nervous tension" characterizing the life of the Occident.

There is, of course, an alternative hypothesis, namely, that this greater tranquillity of the Chinese is a reflection of a slower physiological tempo, of which the low blood pressure is one aspect, and which may be racially determined. This problem will be discussed in greater detail in connection with racial differences in basal metabolism (see below). As far as blood pressure is concerned, there is definite indication that Whites who have lived for a long time among Orientals, and who have presumably taken over their kind of life, show a lower blood pressure than do those Whites who have remained in western countries. Foster (15) reports, for example, that American soldiers in the Philippines have an average systolic blood pressure of 115-116, only very slightly higher than that of Filipino soldiers, and that 120 White foreigners in Hunan, in China, showed an average figure of 112.0, almost exactly the same as that of the Chinese in Hunan.

Foster made a more direct attack upon this problem by comparing the blood pressure of a group of Americans living in China with the blood pressure of these same persons recorded a year or more earlier in America. In this first study there were 34 subjects, both male and female; 8 showed no change, 2 showed an increase, and the remaining 24 showed decreases ranging from 10 to 40 mm. of mercury—this in spite of the fact that as an individual grows older his blood pressure usually tends to rise. In a second study, 40 members of the Peking Union Medical College staff, all foreigners, had their blood pressure recorded before and after coming to China. The average was 118 in the United States and 109 in Peking; 12 subjects showed no change, three showed an increase, and 25 a decrease in blood pressure. Foster asks: "Could it be that there is some subconscious adjustment to the unhurried life of the East that lowers the general tone"?

Tung (53) continued this latter investigation, and collected readings both at home and in Peking from 58 Westerners on the staff of the Peking Union Medical College. The average length of residence in Peking was three years. In spite of an increase in average age from 34 to 37 years, the average systolic blood pressure dropped from 118 to 109. Tung comments: "The perpetual rush, tension and excitement that characterize American life and the comparatively slower and calmer life in Peking, although the work here may be no less strenuous, may be important factors in the causation of the relative hypotension." He adds that mental stress, excitement and worry may produce and maintain a high blood pressure.

An interesting application of this theory has been made by Kilborn (30) in an attempt to explain the variations in the blood pressure of 51 students in West China, from whom readings were taken on four different occasions. The four averages were, for systolic blood pressure, 114, 108, 116 and 115. The first reading was made in April-May of 1924 near the close of the academic year; the students were training for their annual field day and were also under the strain of approaching examinations. The second was in September, 1924, shortly after the commencement of the term and

after the long summer vacation; there was no special excitement, and the students were generally in a state of relaxation.
(It will be noted that this period gave the lowest blood pressure reading.) The third was in December, 1925, just after
there had been a civil war in the province, and when the
effects of the Shanghai incidents in East China were still being felt; the student enrollment in West China had definitely
decreased. The fourth reading, in September, 1926, was also
after the summer vacation, but during a period of violent
student agitation, followed by a strike that temporarily
closed the university. Kilborn notes that the diastolic blood
pressure was the highest in this fourth period. He concludes
that "a change in the state of nervous tension on the part of
the student population, whether due to academic or political
causes, is accompanied by a change in the height of the
blood pressure."

This general problem has also been approached from the
clinical angle. It has been noted, for example, that hypertension, or high blood pressure, is very rare in China. Foster
(15) has reported that out of 4000 patients in the Hunan-
Yale Hospital there was up to 1927 only one case of essential
hypertension (high blood pressure with no apparent cause)
and not more than twenty with a blood pressure over 160.
Out of 4940 cases in the Peter Bent Brigham Hospital in
Boston, Massachusetts, in 1918-19 there were 236 cases of
essential hypertension and 146 cases of hypertension accompanying chronic nephritis (kidney disease).

Houston (27), who spent five years at the University of
Yale-in-China, also ascribed this difference to certain characteristics of Chinese psychology. He notes, for example, that
the one case of essential hypertension in the Chinese records
was that of a Chinese supervisor of nurses, trained for many
years in America, with an American quickness and alertness

of movement, and in marked contrast, as she herself pointed
out, to the easy-going Chinese. Hypertension, like angina
pectoris (a disease due to spasm of the coronary arteries)
and other forms of spasm, is under the control of the vegeta-
tive or autonomic nervous system, which is very profoundly
involved in all emotional reactions, and when these reactions are reduced to a minimum the tendency to spasm will
be similarly reduced. Clinicians have pointed out that the
best cure for hypertension is calm. The Chinese have no
"spasmogenic aptitude," no tendency to spasm; they have
an inner calm which makes them impervious to these disturbances of emotional origin. When a foreigner living in
the interior of China acquires an essential hypertension it is
generally obvious, says Houston, that the sufferer is a person
living in a state of antagonism with his environment—one
who has come to China to teach everything and learn nothing. "A Chinese expressed the fundamental distinction between Chinese and occidental psychology by saying that the
occidental when meeting with a difficulty tries to remove it,
making a change in the external environment, an external
adjustment—the Chinese finds it easier to make an internal
adjustment—to change his soul to an attitude of acceptance."
Houston makes it clear that in his opinion this is a cultural,
not a racial, difference. If we stay in China long enough,
we learn to accept things, and our blood pressure goes down;
Chinese in America learn protest and non-acceptance, and
their blood pressure goes up.

This hypothesis of the intermingling of cultural, physiological and clinical factors in the determination of blood
pressure cannot in the meantime be regarded as proved, but
it offers an interesting point of departure for a study of the
manner in which bodily functions may be under the control
of psychological conditions. In this connection it is also

worth noting that a study by Donnison (9) of blood pressure
in the African native refers to essential hypertension and arteriosclerosis (hardening of the arteries) as diseases associated
with western civilization. Incidentally, it was observed that
among the Africans, natives of Kenya in the region of Lake
Victoria Nyanza, the blood pressure was almost identical
with the European norms between the ages of fifteen and
thirty-five, but from then on the Africans showed a decrease,
and the Whites a steady increase. It would be difficult to say
whether there is a corresponding increase in the "inner
calm" of the older African natives, but it is probable that
the worries of the Whites multiply with advancing age.

Attractive as this hypothesis of the relation between culture and blood pressure may be, other possible influences
must not be overlooked. In this case also, diet, climate and
exercise are factors to be considered. There may also be
differences between city and country within our own culture,
altogether apart from the "attitude of acceptance" of which
Houston speaks. Until these variables have been eliminated,
we can hardly use blood pressure as a measure of the difference between Oriental and Occidental psychology.

BASAL METABOLISM

Basal metabolism is a measure of the rate of physiological
change. It may be defined as the heat production of an individual measured during complete mental and physical
repose. It is usually determined by measuring the consumption of oxygen or the production of carbon dioxide in a
known amount of time, and expressing it in terms of calories
per hour per square meter of body surface. The determinations must be made under so-called basal conditions—at
least twelve hours after the subject's last meal (which should
not have been too rich in protein), with a rest of thirty min-

utes, with normal body temperature, during complete mental and physical repose, and awake. Norms have been derived, taking into consideration factors of height and weight, or surface area, age and sex (the metabolism of males is about 12 per cent higher than that of females); the basal metabolism of any given subject is expressed in terms of these norms, 100 per cent being the average, with a range of 10 per cent above or below usually regarded as within the normal limits. When all of these basal conditions have been fulfilled, the metabolism may be interpreted as the rate of physiological change in the organism under resting conditions. (See Benedict, 2; Du Bois, 10; Wang and Hawks, 55.)

The basal metabolism is largely, though by no means exclusively, under the control of the thyroid gland; a high basal metabolism usually means an overactive, and a low basal metabolism, an underactive thyroid. Studies of racial differences in basal metabolism have a special significance, therefore, in connection with the endocrine theory of race proposed by Sir Arthur Keith, and discussed in an earlier chapter (Chapter III). In addition, since clinicians have reported marked personality changes accompanying thyroid disturbances, and since a number of experimental studies have suggested a rather intimate relation between basal metabolism and a number of mental factors, it becomes of special importance for our purposes to see how strong a case can be made for a racial difference in basal metabolism.

Certain of the earlier studies in this field reported that Orientals had a low basal metabolism. MacLeod, Crofts and Benedict (36) studied the basal metabolism of seven Chinese and two Japanese women students averaging 24 years of age. They found very little difference in blood pressure, pulse rate and respiratory rate, but they noted a very low vital capacity and a basal metabolism on the average 10.4 per cent below the prediction standard. The deficiency held for every one of the nine subjects, the range being from —3.9 to — 16.5 per cent. They concluded that there is a specifically low cell metabolism characteristic of the Orientals. Takahira (50) studied 120 subjects in Japan and found them to be —5 to — 7 per cent below the White norms. Earle (11) obtained a similar result in China, and in his first report suggested a possible relationship between this measure of physiological speed and the tempo of Oriental life. "We hope to publish detailed results later, but from the fifty or so observations already made on the normal Chinese student, making all allowances for stature, weight, sex and age, it would appear that the metabolic pace is set at a lower level than that of western subjects, and the question arises how far this can be correlated with other differences between the eastern and western peoples. Has the rush of western civilization produced a higher metabolic rate? Is the low metabolic rate of the Chinese a physiological expression of their more philosophical outlook on life?" (P. 85.)

Granting that the average Chinese or Japanese has a basal metabolism below that of the average American, there is here as in the case of blood pressure the interesting possibility of a connection between physiology and civilization. Before it can be determined, however, whether race plays a part in this connection it is important to know what non-racial factors may enter. The same questions arise as with reference to apparent racial differences in the onset of puberty or in the comparison of blood pressures; the non-racial factors must first be considered.

The most obvious factor entering into the metabolic rate at any particular time is physical activity or muscular work. Theoretically, determinations of basal metabolism are made during complete muscular repose, but it is probable that the degree of relaxation is conditioned by the amount of work habitually performed by the organism. In an important study by Takahira (50) it was noted that day laborers had an average basal metabolism of + 5.8 per cent; policemen, + 3.3 per cent; and school teachers and tradesmen, — 3 to — 7 per cent. The same point is made by Wardlaw and Horsley (56) in their study of the basal metabolism of eight aborigines on a government reservation in the warmer part of Australia. These natives worked very little, lived wastefully, and received ample rations once a week, so that a brief period of plenty was followed by a period of want until the next rations arrived. They spent most of their time in lounging and sleeping. Their basal metabolism was exceedingly low, averaging — 30.7 per cent. One of them, however, a half-caste who was muscular and a hard worker, was slightly above the White standard. This latter study is complicated by the fact that race may enter, but there is no doubt that muscular activity plays an important part in basal metabolism.

The effect of climate has been reported in a number of investigations. Hafkesbring and Borgstrom (21) state that the basal metabolism is 14-18 per cent lower in the warm environment of New Orleans than in the northern American cities. Tilt (51) found the basal metabolism of college women in Florida to be on the average — 10 per cent. Hindmarsh (24) obtained an average figure of — 9 per cent for White students in Australia. The majority of studies in this field corroborate these findings as to the importance of climate, although there are one or two exceptions. (For example, Coro [5] did not find a lower metabolism in the case of student nurses in Havana.)

Another approach has been made to this question by Gustafson and Benedict (20), who were interested in seasonal variations in the basal metabolism of the same subjects. They made determinations on twenty Wellesley College students once each month; their results suggest that the basal metabolism tends to be low in winter and to rise to a higher level in spring and summer. No determinations seem to have been made during the very hot weather, so that these results may not have any importance in connection with marked climatic differences. It is also possible that the variations may be due in part to differences in activity. These authors in their review of the pertinent literature state that there is no agreement as to the effect of seasonal variations, but with reference to climatic conditions the consensus of opinion seems to regard tropical and subtropical climates as having a depressing effect on the basal metabolism.

The effect of diet is not very clear. Du Bois (10) is of the opinion that a change in the amount of protein in the diet has little effect, whereas Benedict (2) gives as one of the necessary conditions for the determination of basal metabolism that the previously ingested meal should not have been rich in protein. The study of the Eskimo by Heinbrecker (22) showed them to have a very high rate, $+ 33$ per cent, which the investigator is inclined to attribute to the effect of climate, but it is quite probable that the large amount of protein in the Eskimo diet may have a considerable influence.

Mental factors are also of importance, emotional disturbance tending to raise the BMR[1] very markedly. Benedict (2) tells of the case of an assistant who had an unusually high BMR one morning and reported upon questioning that he had been thrown down the stairs the evening before. Hitchcock and Wardwell (25) found a noticeable rise in a medical student after his first exciting day in the hospital. Landis

---

[1] Basal metabolic rate.

(32) obtained no consistent change resulting from a variety of emotional stimuli, but in some cases he was able to demonstrate a tremendous rise; the inhibition of laughter in one subject raised the metabolism 76 per cent, and "anger" in another raised it 63 per cent. The fact that there was so much inconsistency in the results (anger sometimes showing an increase, sometimes a decrease) led Landis to conclude that "changes in metabolic rate cannot be considered as direct measures of emotional disturbance or cumulative emotional upset"; but even in his material it seems apparent that emotional disturbance usually increases the BMR. On the other hand, Goldwyn (17) was able to lower the BMR about 4 per cent by suggesting to the subject under hypnosis that he should be mentally and physically in a state of complete relaxation.

This factor of relaxation is of particular importance. It has been noted that Whites show a definitely lower metabolism when asleep. Among the Chinese, however, the difference between waking and sleeping metabolism is very small. Their lower basal metabolism may therefore be due to their greater degree of relaxation under basal "waking" conditions. (See Necheles and Loo, 41.)

Several studies have recently appeared dealing with a possible relation between basal metabolism and personality. The work of Miles (41) suggests that a high and low heat production may be accompanied by different types of temperamental reactions, but the investigation has not been carried far enough to warrant any definite conclusion. Lanier (33) has reported a positive relation between a high basal metabolism and a tendency to work very rapidly at certain simple psychological tasks, but a carefully controlled study by Steinberg (46) has failed to show any such relationship. If we keep these various factors in mind, the case for a racial influence in basal metabolism becomes considerably weaker. The high BMR of the Eskimo, referred to above, can be explained by diet or climate, or both. The low BMR of the Australian natives may be due to a difference in living conditions. A similar interpretation can be made in the case of many other studies in this field. There have been, for example, three studies of the BMR of Maya Indians in Yucatan by Benedict and his co-workers (43, 44, 57). These studies yielded averages of + 5.2, + 5.8 and + 8.4 per cent, respectively, the number of subjects varying from 26 to 32. The subjects were males only, all of them workers in the excavations at Chichen Itza, and described as placid and unexcitable in disposition, slow sure workers, not "snappy" except under stress, but capable of sustained effort. They were doing manual labor, pick and shovel work, lifting and pulling. Since it is known from the work of Takahira and others that the type of occupation affects BMR considerably, and since these Maya Indians were all in the hard manual labor class, it may very well be that their slightly higher rate is entirely due to the kind of work they were doing. Until this has been satisfactorily checked, these results cannot be used as a definite indication of a racial difference.

Another study by Steggerda and Benedict (45) on Jamaica Negroes illustrates a similar point. The average BMR of 37 brown (mixed-blood) men was — 5.4 per cent; but the authors note that the majority of them were students who lived a much more sedentary life than the average White American student, and whose diet was much less rich in protein. These factors may account for the slight difference. A group of eight full-blooded male blacks had an average BMR of — 2 per cent, just about at the norm.

Mason and Benedict (39) studied the BMR of 54 South

Indian women aged 17 to 31, and found it to be on the average — 16 per cent. They mention as possible causes, besides race, a low protein intake, the tropical conditions of the climate and a greater state of relaxation. These same factors are also pertinent to the finding by Turner and Aboushadid (54) that 28 young Syrian women in Syria had an average BMR of — 13.3 per cent, which they explain as probably due to the quieter mode of life.

One rather obvious way of determining whether the observed differences between groups are due to race or to living conditions is to study the basal metabolism of members of one race in contrasting environments. In an old study by De Almeida (8) in Brazil it was noted that Whites in a tropical climate have an average BMR of — 24 per cent. Earle (12) studied 72 Westerners (British) in China, and found them to be slightly below the White norms, though not quite so low as the Chinese in China; on the other hand, a small group of Orientals living in London had an average BMR of — 6.5 per cent. Earle concludes that the racial difference persists even when the environment has been changed, though he points out that these differences are very small and within the normal limits, and that more work is needed in this field. A recent study by Benedict and Meyer (2c) of 18 American-born Chinese women in Boston, aged 12 to 22 years, shows an average BMR of — 9.2 per cent, which leads the authors to the conclusion that basal metabolism is definitely affected by race.

An important caution is needed with reference to the kind of life led, for example, by the foreign members of any particular community. It may be questioned whether Britishers in China live and work and eat exactly as do the Chinese, or whether Orientals in America have become completely Americanized. There may still be differences in manner of living to account for the small differences in basal metabolism. Turner and Aboushadid report that American and European women in Syria showed an average BMR of — 6 per cent, whereas the Syrian women had a BMR of — 13.3 per cent, but they point out that the Syrian women live a much quieter life which may be responsible for the difference. Du Bois' (10b) conclusion is that "one gets the impression that the racial differences are so slight that they are almost entirely obscured by the factors of repose, physical training and nutrition."

There is one further complication in this field. Many of the norms used in determining racial deviations above and below the standard are based upon surface area, which in turn is derived from the figures for height and weight. The formulæ used depend upon the usual or typical bodily configuration found among the Whites whose measurements have furnished the standards. Among racial groups whose bodily configuration is very different—for example, the Chinese, short in limb and relatively long in trunk, and certain Negroes, long in limb and relatively short in trunk— the formulæ derived from the Whites may yield a totally misleading picture. A study of 40 Australian aborigines by Hicks, Matters and Mitchell (23) showed an average BMR of — 11 per cent for females and — 13 per cent for males, with deviations occasionally as high as — 36 per cent. The authors point out that this may be due largely to a different bodily configuration and that "it is considered doubtful as to whether European standards for computing basal metabolism are applicable in these cases." Stevenson (47) has made the same point with reference to the Chinese, and Lefrou (35) in his study of African natives insists that the indices used are in many cases inapplicable because of the different relation between standing and sitting height. This factor has been largely neglected in the study of racial differences in BMR and it may exert a considerable influence.

It must again be concluded that more work is needed, and that the non-racial factors must be better controlled before any final decision as to racial differences in BMR may be reached.

VITAL CAPACITY

Approximately the same situation exists with regard to vital capacity, the total amount of air which can be exhaled at any one time. A study by Wilson and Edwards (58) of 38 colored children showed a subnormal vital capacity, and suggested that a racial factor might be operative. Foster (15) and Foster and Hsieh (16) measured the vital capacity of 500 healthy Chinese girls in China and found it to be about 30 per cent below the American standard, and Bhatia (3) obtained a similar result in India. A recent study by Krishnan and Vareed (31) on 103 medical students in South India found them also to be far below the standard; but the opinion of the investigators is that the low vital capacity is due not to race or nationality, but to the warm climate, smaller amount of exercise, low metabolism and poor chest expansion. They point out that with increased metabolism and oxygen consumption, whatever the cause, there is increased pulmonary ventilation. Constant physical exercise results in increased depth of the inspiratory excursions, and consequently in a larger vital capacity. Those of their subjects who had a good physique and good chest expansion as a result of physical training had also a vital capacity equal to western standards.

This result is reminiscent of the statement formerly made about the Jews, that they were racially flat-chested and had a very poor chest expansion. With the improvement in the

living conditions of the Jews and with their gradual participation in athletics and other forms of active exercise, this
apparent "racial" characteristic seems to have been entirely
. removed. (Fishberg, 14.)

SPEED OF NERVE CONDUCTION

An attempt has been made by Davis (7) to compare
Negroes and Whites in their speed of nerve conduction, as
measured by the latent time of the Achilles reflex, or the
time which elapses between the tap on the heel tendon and
the response of the gastrocnemius muscle. The earlier work
of Travis (52a) on the patellar reflex (knee-jerk) had suggested that there might be a relation between speed of nerve
conduction and mental ability, and Davis was interested in
seeing whether this could supply a physiological basis for
psychological race differences. Eight different groups of subjects were tested, White and Negro students, White and
Negro city children, White and Negro feeble-minded, White
country children and mountain White children. After taking
into account differences in stature, as well as the different
body proportions of Negroes and Whites, Davis reported
that the groups with the greatest speed of nerve conduction
were the White students and the White city children; then
came the Negro students, the Negro city children and the
White country children, and finally the mountain children
and the White and Negro feeble-minded. Davis is of the
opinion that these results coincide rather closely with the
relative ratings on the intelligence tests, and states that "with
regard to the fundamental abilities of social groups, it may
be concluded that biological differences have been shown
to play some part in the determination of their intellectual
level." (p. 110).

These findings are interesting, but their interpretation is

by no means simple. There is here, as in the case of so many other group comparisons, a great deal of overlapping, even between groups so far removed intellectually as the students and the feeble-minded. In addition, there are so many factors which may enter into reflex latent time that any direct relation to intelligence is hardly to be expected. It is known that speed of nerve conduction depends not only on the actual rate of transmission in the nerve fiber, but also upon the inhibiting effect of the higher nervous centers. A slow rate of conduction may mean either that the nerve fiber is itself not conducting quickly, or that there is a great deal of cortical control; conversely, a fast rate may mean that the nerve fiber is very efficient, or that the cortical control is weak or absent. Travis (52b) has shown that under conditions of alcoholic narcosis, when this control has presumably been reduced to a minimum, the latent time may be greatly decreased, and an impression given of very rapid nerve conduction. On the basis of Davis' theory we might therefore have to regard as a criterion of intelligence, a physiological measure which shows a drunken man to be superior to a sober one! Until the relative influence of central and peripheral factors in reflex time has been determined, the interpretation of these results will remain obscure.

RACIAL ODORS

There is no doubt of the existence of a body odor characteristic of each individual; even though most of us are by no means conscious of it in the majority of cases, its presence can easily be demonstrated by the ease with which dogs are able to follow a trail. There seem also to be group differences in body odors; and the question arises as to whether these are to be explained as racial peculiarities, or as the result of a combination of external factors, including diet, clothing and cleanliness.

Whatever the cause, it is certain that members of any one group often find the odor of a strange group disagreeable; this has frequently been regarded as an insurmountable barrier to free racial intermingling, for example, between Negroes and Whites. Since miscegenation between all racial groups has been going on since the beginning of history, it is not necessary to attach much significance to this notion. What may happen, however, is that after a first reaction of unpleasantness, a certain amount of adaptation (which occurs most rapidly in the case of the olfactory sense) takes place, so that the odor is no longer observed. This occurs normally between members of the same group, and there is no reason why a similar process of adaptation should not extend to others.

The reaction of unpleasantness is not necessarily one-sided, that is to say, the body odor of Whites may be just as disagreeable to members of other racial groups. Daudet (6) reports that Negroes find the odor of White women to resemble that of cadavers. Adachi (1), a Japanese who spent considerable time in Europe, writes that when first coming to the West he found the odor very strong—rancid, sometimes sweetish, sometimes bitter. Although he found it unpleasant at the beginning, he later became used to it, and still later found it sexually stimulating.

Hudson (29) tells a very illuminating story in this connection. A young English physician stationed in Bombay was in the habit of having his Hindu servant call him from church on Sunday mornings to impress the congregation with his importance as a medical man. It happened one evening that he went to a large political gathering of Hindus, but came out after a short while and said to his servant,

"What a relief to get out! In another ten minutes I should have collapsed. The smell!" To his great surprise the Hindu replied, "Ah, Sahib, *now* you will understand what I suffer every Sunday when I have to go right to the middle of the church to call you out!" (P. 87.)

A great deal was written during the Middle Ages about a specific Jewish odor. Fortunatus was entirely convinced of its existence, but believed it could be removed by baptism. Schopenhauer also believed that the Jews had a special odor. Recently this notion has been revived, particularly by Günther (19), who studied the odor supposedly characteristic of Jews by eating in a Jewish restaurant. It is hardly necessary to point out that this would give him only the odor of Jewish food, and that it cannot be considered a scientific way of studying the odor of the Jews themselves.

The characteristic body odor appears to come mostly from the skin secretions, that is to say, from the sweat glands and from the sebaceous glands, particularly in the regions where there is hair; and it is therefore much more noticeable after the body has been perspiring freely and before it has been washed. Hooton (26) asked a Japanese student at Harvard whether he detected any odor as a distinguishing feature of Whites. The reply was that he did most decidedly, and found it very unpleasant. He went on to say, however, that it was particularly disagreeable whenever he entered the Harvard gymnasium. Since Hooton had himself noticed it under these same conditions, this could hardly be regarded as an indication of a peculiar racial odor.

An experimental attempt to throw a little further light on this question was made in an unpublished study by Lawrence, who collected in test tubes a little of the perspiration of White and Colored students who had just been exercising violently in the gymnasium. These test tubes were then given to a number of White subjects with instructions to rank them in order of pleasantness. The results showed no consistent preference for the White samples; the test tube considered the most pleasant and the one considered the most unpleasant were both taken from Whites.

There may be racial differences in body odors, but it is important first to rule out the factors referred to above, particularly the factor of diet, before a final conclusion is reached. It is obvious that cleanliness is also of importance. In any case, the phenomenon of adaptation enters to remove any special unpleasantness arising from the presence of a strange group.

CONCLUSION

There are interesting and significant group differences in physiological activity, but there is no adequate proof that these are determined by heredity. The studies of blood pressure and basal metabolism in particular show the extent to which these organic functions may be affected by cultural and environmental factors, and they throw considerable doubt upon a racial interpretation. Further research is needed, preferably upon members of different races living as far as possible under the same conditions, and members of the same race living under conditions that differ widely. The available material suggests, though it does not prove, that group differences in physiological activity can be adequately explained without recourse to the racial hypothesis.

BIBLIOGRAPHY

1. Adachi, B. "Der Geruch der Europäer." *Globus*, 83:1903.
2a. Benedict, F. G. "Basal Metabolism." *Sci. Month.*, 27:1928, pp. 5-27.
2b. Benedict, F. G. "The Racial Element in Human Metabolism." *Amer. J. Phys. Anthrop.*, 16:1932, pp. 463-473.

2c. Benedict, F. G., and Meyer, M. H. "Basal Metabolism of American-born Chinese Girls." *Chinese J. Physiol.*, 7:1933, pp. 45-59.

3. Bhatia, S. L. *Proceedings Indian Science Congress 1929.* (See Krishnan and Vareed, No. 31.)

4. Chappell, M. N. "Blood Pressure Changes in Deception." *Arch. Psych.*, No. 105:1929. New York.

5. Coro, A. J. "Contribución al estudio del metabolismo basal en los países tropicales," *Arch. Soc. estud. clin.*, 27:1927, pp. 7-20.

6. Daudet, L. *La Mélancholie. Section: La domaine de l'olfactif.* Paris, 1928.

7. Davis, R. C. *Ability in Social and Racial Classes. Some Physiological Correlates.* New York, 1932.

8. De Almeida, A. O. "Le Métabolisme Minimum et le Métabolisme Basal de l'Homme Tropical de Race Blanche." *J. de Physiol. et de Path. gén.*, 18:1920, pp. 712-730, 958-964.

9. Donnison, C. P. "Blood Pressure in the African Native." *Lancet*, 1:1929, pp. 6-8.

10a. Du Bois, E. F. *Basal Metabolism in Health and Disease.* Philadelphia, 1927. (2nd Ed.)

10b. Du Bois, E. F. "Recent Advances in the Study of Basal Metabolism." *J. Nutrition*, 3:1930, pp. 217-228.

11. Earle, H. G. "Basal Metabolism." *The Caduceus*, 1:1922, 81-85.

12. Earle, H. G. "Basal Metabolism of Chinese and Westerners." *Chinese J. Physiol.*, 1:1928, pp. 59-92.

13. Ferris, H. B. "Anthropological Studies on the Quichua and Machiganga Indians." *Transactions, Connecticut Academy of Arts & Sciences*, 25:1921, pp. 1-92.

14. Fishberg, M. *The Jews: A Study of Race and Environment.* London, 1911.

15. Foster, J. H. "Blood Pressure of Foreigners in China." *Arch. Int. Med.*, 40:1927, pp. 38-45.

16. Foster, J. H., and Hsieh, P. L. "Vital Capacity of Chinese; An Occupational Study." *Arch. Int. Med.*, 32:1923, pp. 335-342.

17. Goldwyn, J. "Effect of Hypnosis on Basal Metabolism." *Arch. Int. Med.*, 45:1930, pp. 109-114.

18. Gould, B. A. *Investigations in the Military and Anthropological Statistics of American Soldiers.* New York, 1869.

19. Günther, H. F. K. "Der rasseeigene Geruch der Hautausdün-stung." *Ztschr. f. Rassenphysiologie,* 2:1929, p. 94.

20. Gustafson, F. L., and Benedict, F. G. "The Seasonal Variation in Basal Metabolism." *Amer. J. Physiol.,* 86:1928, p. 43.

21. Hafkesbring, R., and Borgstrom, P. "Studies of Basal Metabolism in New Orleans." *Amer. J. Physiol.,* 79:1926, pp. 221-228.

22. Heinbrecker, P. "Studies on Metabolism in Eskimos." *J. Biol. Chem.,* 80:1928, pp. 461-475.

23. Hicks, C. S., Matters, R. F., and Mitchell, M. L. "Standard Metabolism of Australian Aboriginals." *Austral. J. Exp. Biol. and Med. Sci.,* 8:1931, pp. 69-82.

24. Hindmarsh, E. M. "Basal Metabolic Rate of Students in Sydney, N.S.W., with Discussion on Methods of Determining Basal Metabolism." *Austral. J. Exp. Biol. & Med. Sci.,* 4:1927, pp. 225-268.

25. Hitchcock, F. A., and Wardwell, F. R. "Cyclic Variations in the Basal Metabolic Rate of Women." *J. Nutrition,* 2:1929, pp. 203-215.

26. Hooton, E. A. *Up from the Ape.* New York, 1931.

27. Houston, W. R. "The Spasmogenic Aptitude." *Med. Clin. N. Amer.,* 12:1929, p. 1285.

28. Hrdlička, A. "Physiological and Medical Observations Among the Indians of Southwestern United States and Northern Mexico." *Bur. of Amer. Ethnol. Bull.,* 34:1908.

29. Hudson, W. H. *A Hind in Richmond Park.* London, 1922.

30. Kilborn, L. G. "The Variability of Blood Pressure in Normal Persons." *China Med. J.,* 44:1930, pp. 533-540.

31. Krishnan, B. T., and Vareed, C. "Vital Capacity of 103 Male Medical Students in South India." *Indian J. Med. Res.,* 19:1931-1932, pp. 1165-1183.

32a. Landis, C. "Studies of Emotional Reactions, IV. Metabolic Rate." *Amer. J. Physiol.,* 74:1925, pp. 188-203.

32b. Landis, C., and Slight, D. "Studies of Emotional Reactions, VI. Cardiac Responses." *J. Gen. Psych.,* 2:1929, pp. 413-420.

33. Lanier, L. H., and Leedy, J. L. "Speed of Reaction in Relation to Basal Metabolism and Blood Pressure," *Psych. Bull.,* 30:1933, pp. 609-610.

34. Larson, J. A. "The Cardio-pneumo-psychogram and Its Use in the Study of the Emotions, with Practical Application." *J. Exper. Psych.*, 5:1922, pp. 323-329.

35. Lefrou, G. "Un nouvel indice de robusticité chez les noirs." *Bull. de la Soc. de Pathol. Exotique,* 34:1931.

36. MacLeod, G., Crofts, E. E., and Benedict, F. G. "The Basal Metabolism of Some Orientals." *Amer. J. Physiol.*, 73:1925, pp. 449-462.

37. Marston, W. M. "A Theory of Emotions and Affection Based upon Systolic Blood Pressure Studies." *Amer. J. Psych.*, 35:1924, pp. 469-506.

38. Marston, W. M. *Emotions of Normal People.* New York, 1928.

39. Mason, E. D., and Benedict, F. G. "The Basal Metabolism of South Indian Women." *Ind. J. Med. Res.*, 19:1931, pp. 75-98.

40. Miles, C. C., and Miles, W. R. "Personality Type and Metabolic Rate." *Proceedings Amer. Psych. Assn. Abstr.*, Sept., 1933.

41. Necheles, H., and Loo, C. T. "Über den Stoffwechsel der Chinesen." *Chinese J. Physiol.*, 6:1932, 129-224.

42. Newton, P. "Negritos of the Philippine Islands." *Amer. J. Phys. Anthrop.*, 3:1920, pp. 1-24.

43. Shattuck, G. C., and Benedict, F. G. "Further Studies on the Basal Metabolism of Maya Indians in Yucatan." *Amer. J. Physiol.*, 96:1931, pp. 518-528.

44. Steggerda, M., and Benedict, F. G. "Metabolism in Yucatan: A Study of the Maya Indian." *Amer. J. Physiol.*, 100:1932, pp. 274-284.

45. Steggerda, M., and Benedict, F. G. "The Basal Metabolism of Some Browns and Blacks in Jamaica." *Amer. J. Physiol.*, 85:1928, pp. 621-633.

46. Steinberg, Janet. "The Relation Between Basal Metabolism and Mental Speed." *Arch. Psych.* No. 172:1934.

47. Stevenson, P. H. "Calculation of Body-surface Area of Chinese." *Chinese J. Physiol.*, 1:1928, pp. 13-24.

48. Suk, V. "Anthropological and Physiological Observations on the Negroes of Natal and Zululand." *Amer. J. Phys. Anthrop.*, 10:1927, p. 31.

49. Sundstroem, E. S. "Contributions to Tropical Physiology with Special Reference to the Adaptation of the White Man to

the Climate of North Queensland." *Univ. Calif. Pub. Physiol.*, 6:1926, p. 320; *Phys. Rev.*, 7:1927, pp. 320-362.

50. Takahira and Kitagawa. "Studies of Japanese Basal Metabolism." *Report of Nutrition Inst. of Tokio,* No. 88:1924.

51. Tilt, J. "Basal Metabolism of Young College Women in Florida." *J. Biol. Chem.*, 86:1930, pp. 635-641.

52a. Travis, L. E., and Hunter, T. A. "The Relation Between Intelligence and Reflex Conduction Rate." *J. Exp. Psych.*, 11:1928, p. 342.

52b. Travis, L. E., and Dorsey, J. M. "Effects of Alcohol on the Patellar Tendon Reflex Time." *Arch. Neurol. and Psychiat.*, 21:1929, pp. 613-624.

53. Tung, C. L. "Relative Hypotension of Foreigners in China." *Arch. Int. Med.*, 40:1927, pp. 153-158.

54. Turner, E. L., and Aboushadid, E. "Basal Metabolism and Vital Capacity of Syrian Women." *Amer. J. Physiol.*, 92:1930, pp. 189-195.

55. Wang, C. C., and Hawks, J. E. "Recent Advancement in the Study of Basal Metabolism in Health and Disease." *J. Amer. Diet. Assn.*, 5:1929, pp. 87-101.

56. Wardlaw, H. S. H., and Horsley, C. H. "Basal Metabolism of Some Australian Aborigines." *Austral. J. Exp. Biol. & Med. Sci.*, 5:1928, pp. 263-272.

57. Williams, G. D., and Benedict, F. G. "The Basal Metabolism of Mayas in Yucatan." *Amer. J. Physiol.*, 85:1928, pp. 634-649.

58. Wilson, M. G., and Edwards, D. J. "Vital Capacity of Lungs and Its Relation to Exercise Tolerance in Children with Heart Disease." *Amer. J. Dis. of Children,* 22:1921, p. 443.

PART II

THE PSYCHOLOGICAL APPROACH

Chapter VII

THE SIMPLER PSYCHOLOGICAL FUNCTIONS

INTRODUCTION

THE studies reviewed in this chapter deal with possible racial differences in sense perception and in speed of reaction. These functions may not actually be "simpler," but the term is here used to indicate that they are closer to the physiological level than those to be discussed in later chapters. They have a special interest for us because of the popular belief that people at a more primitive level are superior in these sensory-motor activities, and that the development of the intellect has occurred at the expense of the simpler forms of psychological activity. The alleged ability of "natives" to perform extraordinary feats of sense perception which are quite impossible for White men has therefore paradoxically been regarded as a sign of their inferiority. There are a number of significant investigations touching upon this and related questions.

REACTION TIME

One of the early studies in this field is by Bache (1), who measured the reaction time of a small number of Whites, American Indians and Negroes. His results are summarized in Table 14, which gives the time in milli-seconds.

TABLE 14: GROUP DIFFERENCES IN REACTION TIME (BACHE)

Group	Number of Cases	Auditory R.T.	Visual R.T.	Electrical R.T.
Whites	12	146.9	164.8	136.3
Indians	11	116.3	135.7	114.6
Negroes	11	130.0	152.9	122.9

It is apparent that the Whites are the slowest of the three groups, and Bache finds it necessary to explain why a presumably superior group should do so poorly in this test. He states that it is the lower, not the higher man, who is more responsive to stimuli of the sort which are related to secondary reflex action; men, in proportion to their intellectuality, tend less and less to quickness of response in the automatic sphere; the reflective man is the slower being.

Lapicque (13) tested the visual reaction time of 28 Europeans, 18 Andamanese and 7 Hindus. Unlike Bache, he found the Europeans to be the quickest; but there was so much variation among them, corresponding to differences in social level, that he was inclined to believe that race is of little importance.

A similar point is made by Myers (19) who studied reaction time as part of the work of the Cambridge expedition to Torres Straits in 1899. He gave tests to natives of Murray Island and Sarawak, and compared the results with those obtained in England. The results are given in Table 15.

TABLE 15: GROUP DIFFERENCES IN REACTION TIME (MYERS)

Group	Auditory Reaction		Visual Reaction	
	Number	Time	Number	Time
Murray Island.........	17	135.7	11	243.8
England..............	24	141.6	21	222.3
Sarawak..............	18	120.7	9	208.0

In simple reaction time there was not a great deal of difference between the Murray Islanders and the English group, each being superior in one of the experiments. The natives of Sarawak, however, were faster in both. In choice-visual reaction time the Murray Islanders were inferior to the Englishmen; but Myers points out that the English were all of the well-educated class, and that a fairer comparison would have been between the Murray Islanders and English villagers. There is no doubt that here, as in the more complicated psychological measures, social and economic factors must be considered in all racial comparisons.

A recent study has been made in Hawaii by Livesay and Louttit (15), who tested 253 university students of different racial and national origin. Their results are presented in Table 16.

TABLE 16: GROUP DIFFERENCES IN REACTION TIME (LIVESAY AND LOUTTIT)

Group	Number	Visual R.T.	Auditory R.T.	Choice R.T.
Caucasian males...........	14	250	181	411
Chinese males.............	29	295	205	397
Japanese males.............	69	288	205	397
Part-Hawaiian males.......	15	272	182	366
Caucasian females..........	45	297	217	449
Chinese females............	42	300	222	449
Japanese females...........	41	345	244	469
Part-Hawaiian females.....	31	300	231	446

The authors point out that race differences in reaction time are small and insignificant, and do not consistently favor any one group over any other. The sex differences though also small are larger and more consistent than the race differences and favor the male subjects.

VISUAL SENSITIVITY

Travelers have frequently reported great visual ability among so-called primitive peoples, but they usually fail to distinguish between visual acuity as such, and powers of observation developed by experience. Rivers (21), in connection with the Cambridge expedition referred to above, tested the visual acuity of Papuan natives in Murray Island, Mabuiag and Kiwai, and found them to be only slightly superior to Whites, this superiority being explained as due to their relative lack of eye defects. Their visual powers are, however, extraordinary; they can distinguish birds amid the foliage of trees, they can tell at a tremendous distance that a boat is approaching, etc. Ranke (20) gives an instance of African natives who could tell the sex of a deer a long way off by noticing the gait; although it seemed to him almost miraculous at first, he himself was able to do it after learning what to look for. Damoglou (6) tells of Negro camel drivers who can recognize by the footprint whether the person who has passed is young or old, male or female, whether carrying a load or not, whether a young woman or a mother. Not visual acuity, but long-continued practice in attending to minute details, is responsible for this ability.

Rivers noted among the Todas the curious fact that they were not nearly so susceptible as Whites to the Müller-Lyer illusion, in which two equal lines are made to appear of different lengths by the addition of arrowhead lines at their extremities. He suggests that the savage attends more directly to the two lines which are to be compared, whereas civilized man allows the figures as a whole to affect him. It was mentioned to the writer by Dr. Reo Fortune that many Melanesian groups (it is not certain whether this would apply also to the Todas) make use of two kinds of spears, one for fighting, and one for spearing fish, shaped like the two different figures used in the illusion; it may be that this furnishes the necessary corrective.

There has been considerable discussion of the color sense of primitive peoples, and of a possible evolution of the power of color discrimination. Gladstone (9) was perhaps the first to raise the question of a relationship between the color sense and the names used to characterize the various colors; he made a careful study of the color epithets used by Homer, and came to the conclusion that at that time the color sense was hardly developed and little more could be distinguished than differences in brightness. Geiger (8) made a similar study of ancient Greek literature, of the Indian Vedas, the Zendavesta, the Norse Eddas, and ancient Chinese and Semitic writings, and advanced the view that there had been an evolution in the color sense of man, red being distinguished first, and the other colors following in the order of the spectrum, with blue and violet last. Magnus (16) studied a number of the languages of primitive peoples and also found a marked poverty in the names for blue.

Kepner (11) noted that the Visayans of Leyte Island in the Philippines had no native terms to distinguish green from blue, and that a number of his subjects confused these two colors. Rivers (22) suggested that among the Todas in southern India the defective nomenclature for blue which is so generally found among races of low culture is associated with a certain degree of defective sensibility for this color. The Torres Straits Islanders (21) use the same word for green and blue, and show a marked tendency to confuse blue with a number of other colors like green and violet and, to a lesser extent, yellow. Rivers believed that there might be some degree of insensitiveness to blue. Virchow (23) had earlier pointed out, however, that it is very dangerous to infer that a defective color nomenclature necessarily means a lack of the power to discriminate colors. He examined a number of Nubians in Germany in 1877 and found that although they used the same word for blue as for black and for other dark colors, they were able to sort colored papers and wools correctly.

It is important to note that the technique used in most of these experiments, namely, having the subjects match wools of the same color, is by no means satisfactory as a measure of color sensitivity. The matching may be determined by the names used, rather than by an objective relationship. Many American Indian tribes (Zuñi, Apache, Huichol) use the same word for light green and light blue, and a different word for both dark green and dark blue, so that when they are asked to match colors it is natural for them to group them in this manner. This is no more peculiar than that we should use the same word, *blue*, to designate such widely different sensory experiences as those presented by baby blue, Alice blue, powder blue, turquoise, peacock, cobalt, Prussian, royal, midnight and navy blue. We have made our classification entirely on the basis of hue, with no regard for intensity or saturation. Other groups have chosen to make their classification differently. Even with regard to hue alone, any division must to some extent be artificial; the spectrum is continuous, with no sharp line between one color and the next, and a great many ways of dividing it are equally possible. Before we can assume that primitive groups lack the power of color discrimination, we must make certain that they understand the principle on which our identification is based.

Some of the studies of color blindness among racial groups have yielded interesting results. Rivers (22) found a high percentage of color blindness among the Todas (43 out of 503 had red-green blindness) and also among the people on the island of Lifu (out of 8 individuals examined 3 were color-blind). The method of wool matching which Rivers used is not, however, very dependable. Recent studies of racial differences have been made with the much more satisfactory Ishihara test by Clements (4) and Garth (7). The following table, which compares Whites, American Indians and Negroes, is taken from Clements:

TABLE 17: GROUP DIFFERENCES IN INCIDENCE OF COLOR BLINDNESS (CLEMENTS)

Group	Investigator	Number of Cases	Number Color-Blind	Per Cent Color-Blind
Whites...............	Von Planta	2000	159	7.95
Whites...............	Miles	1286	106	8.20
Whites...............	Haupt	448	35	7.80
American Indians.....	Clements	624	12	1.90
American Negroes....	Clements	323	12	3.70

Garth tested 390 Indians in the Southwest, and found 1.79 per cent of them to be color-blind to red and green. There appears to be a very definite difference between American Indians, and to a lesser extent also between American Negroes, and Whites, which in the meantime remains unexplained.

Rivers had the impression that the relative insensitivity to blue which he noted in the Torres Straits might be regarded as a form of color blindness, due to the manner in which the color sense developed genetically. Interestingly enough, however, the genetic color theory which has been most widely accepted, namely, that of Ladd-Franklin (12), regards blue and yellow as appearing early in the scale of development, with red and green as a later stage. If it is true, as Rivers and others have suggested, that there may be groups with a well-developed red and green sense and an inability to recognize blue, this would be an important argument against the Ladd-Franklin theory. On the other hand, if the theory should turn out to be well founded, the probability would be that the insensitivity of primitive peoples to blue is apparent, rather than real.

THE SKIN SENSES

McDougall (17) tested the skin sensitivity of the Torres Straits Islanders by determining the two-point threshold (the smallest portion of skin which can yield simultaneously two distinct cutaneous sensations), and he found the Murray Islanders to have about twice the power of tactile discrimination of Englishmen. Rivers (22) tested the Todas in the same fashion, finding them not to differ very greatly from the English standards.

McDougall also tested the pain sensitivity of the Murray Islanders by means of Cattell's algometer, which records in kilograms the pressure exerted upon the skin when the subject first shows he is suffering pain. The onset of pain is usually detected by a slight, presumably involuntary flinching. McDougall found by this method that the susceptibility to pain among the Murray Islanders was only half as great as among Englishmen; Rivers found the Todas also to have a higher pain threshold than his English subjects. He points out, however, that the Todas regarded this experiment as a test of their power to endure pain, and were therefore a little less ready to admit that they were being hurt. Damoglou (6), who notes the ability of Soudanese Negroes to bear tremendous pain without flinching, believes that this has a psychological, rather than a physiological, basis. A young man who could not bear pain would have no standing in the community, would be unacceptable as a mate in marriage; and thus it becomes a matter of pride with him not to show that he is suffering.

This point reappears in connection with a study made by means of a pain test devised by Libman (14). He noticed in his medical practice that a number of patients who showed all the signs and symptoms of angina pectoris failed to complain of the terrific pain in the chest region characteristic of this disease. Libman applied to them his pain test, which consists of pressing with the two thumbs on either side of the head over the branch of the facial nerve between the mastoid process and the mandible, and found these patients to be hyposensitive as compared with the normal controls. He found a group of prize-fighters also to be hyposensitive, and the same was true of a large number of Indians in the Southwest. Libman believed that this might offer a physiological explanation of the proverbial stoicism of the American Indian. It is important, however, to keep in mind the contributing cultural factors. In the first place, these Indians would be very reluctant to admit that a White man, usually regarded as an inferior, could hurt them with his bare fingers. More important than that, however, is the tradition that it is absolutely essential to be able to bear pain without flinching. In many American Indian tribes the little boy had to learn this very early in life, and found it impossible to join in the play of the older boys until he had proved his endurance. Torture, self-inflicted or administered by others, was frequently welcomed as an opportunity to display this ability. Under these culturally determined conditions it is not surprising that American Indians should have a higher threshold for pain than Whites, altogether apart from a fundamental physiological difference.

In studies of this kind it must not be overlooked that pain may depend to a large extent upon subjective factors. It is well-known that suggestion or hypnosis can increase or decrease the subject's sensitivity to pain stimuli; even self-induced hypnosis may have this effect, as in the case of the dervishes and the Hindu fakirs, who capitalize on their ability to ignore what to others would mean excruciating torture. It is probably impossible ever to arrive at a measure of pain sensitivity independent of such subjective attitudes.

AUDITORY SENSITIVITY

Myers (19) tested the auditory acuity of the Murray Islanders by noting the distance from which they could hear the ticking of a clock; he found that the White experimenters heard it rather better than the Islanders, and concluded that the latter had inferior auditory acuity. It is by no means unlikely, however, that relative familiarity with the kind of sound made by a clock might have something to do with these results. The measurement of the upper limit of pitch by means of the Galton whistle showed very little difference from the controls tested in Scotland.

A more extensive study of racial differences in hearing was made by Bruner (3), who tested a number of racial groups represented at the St. Louis exposition in 1904. For auditory acuity he used an apparatus something like the Seashore audiometer, in which a number of clicks are sounded through a telephone receiver, and the subject repeats what he has heard. The relative standing of the various groups was as follows: Whites, Cocopa Indians, school Indians, Pygmies, Patagonian Indians, Vancouver Island Indians, Ainu, Filipinos. Bruner estimated the relative keenness of hearing of the two extreme groups, Whites and Filipinos, to be in the ratio of 24:5.

Bruner's study of the upper limit of pitch by means of the Galton whistle yielded a somewhat different order. The most successful group (when the right ear was used) was the Pygmies; then came the Whites, Cocopa Indians, school Indians, Patagonians, Filipinos, Ainu, Vancouver Island Indians.

No experimental work has been done on racial differences in the preference for special consonances or dissonances, but indirectly an interesting question is raised by the variations reported by students of primitive music. Consonance in western music has been explained by Helmholtz (10) as due to an identity in the overtones of certain notes; the greater this identity, the greater the resulting experience of consonance.

Moore (18) has suggested, however, that to a very large extent consonance is simply the result of habit; and in an experiment he was able by repetition to change certain combinations of tones from dissonances to consonances, subjectively considered. The material from non-western peoples substantiates Moore's, rather than Helmholtz's, theory. Much of the music of the South African natives, for example, would be regarded by us as extremely dissonant; Herzog (private communication) has noted that in two-part singing the voices may be separated by sevenths, an apparently agreeable combination. Consonance in this case can hardly be due to an identity of overtones.

THE SENSE OF SMELL

It has often been remarked by travelers among primitive peoples that they appear to use the sense of smell much more effectively than do Whites. Damoglou (6) tells of Soudanese Negro camel drivers who find their way about the desert in this manner; they can also smell their way to water in the midst of miles of sand, by scenting the presence of camels two or three hours' journey away. Myers (19) subjected this notion to experimental study by presenting to the Torres Straits Islanders variously diluted solutions of odorous substances, asking them to report which of these were stronger. He found them on the whole to have a slightly higher olfactory acuity than the Scotch controls. On the other hand, Rivers (22) found the Todas to be slightly inferior in this respect.

Myers also conducted an experiment in smell preferences to determine whether the people of the Torres Straits had the same likes and dislikes as the Whites. He noted that violet, musk and thyme were the favorite odors, civet the most repulsive, and that asafetida and valerianic acid were usually disliked. There were, however, a number of exceptions, although there was generally substantial agreement with the White preferences. It has been pointed out by Daly and White (5) that valerian, now considered highly unpleasant, once had considerable vogue. In the sixteenth century its roots were placed among clothes as perfume, and it is still so used in India today. There is probably more variability in olfactory preferences than is usually recognized, between both individuals and groups.

CONCLUSION

With reference to sense perception in general, it may be concluded with Rivers that there is no difference in sense acuity as such, but that the differences depend entirely upon the training of powers of observation.

BIBLIOGRAPHY

1. Bache, R. M. "Reaction Time with Reference to Race." *Psych. Rev.*, 2:1895, pp. 475-486.
2. Boas, F. *The Mind of Primitive Man*. New York, 1911.
3. Bruner, F. G. "The Hearing of Primitive Peoples." *Arch. Psych.*, No. 11:1908.
4. Clements, F. "Racial Differences in Color Blindness." *Amer. J. Phys. Anthrop.*, 14:1930, pp. 417-432.
5. Daly, C. D., and White, R. S. "Psychic Reactions to Olfactory Stimuli." *Brit. J. Med. Psych.*, 10, Pt. I:1930, pp. 70-87.
6. Damoglou, C. "Hyperacuité olfactive et visuelle et impassibilité à la douleur chez les nègres soudanais." *Rev. de l'Hypnot*, 17:1902, pp. 20-21.
7. Garth, T. R. "The Color-Blindness of Indians." *Sci.*, 71:1930, p. 462.
8. Geiger, L. *Contributions to the History of the Development of the Human Race*. London, 1880. (Trans.)
9. Gladstone, W. E. *Studies on Homer and the Homeric Age*. Oxford, 1858. (3 vols.)
10. Helmholtz, H. L. F. *On the Sensations of Tone as a Physiologi-*

cal Basis for the Theory of Music. London, 1912. (4th Ed. Trans.)

11. Kepner, W. A. "Observations on Color Perception Among the Visayans of Leyte Island, P. I." *Science,* new ser., 22:1905, pp. 680-683.

12. Ladd-Franklin, C. L. *Colour and Colour Theories.* New York, 1929.

13. Lapicque, L. "Sur le Temps de Réaction Suivant les Races ou les Conditions Sociales." *C. R. Acad. d. Sci.,* 132:1901, pp. 1509-1511.

14. Libman, E. "Observations on Sensitiveness to Pain." *Transactions of the Assn. of Amer. Physicians,* 41:1926, pp. 305-308.

15. Livesay, T. M., and Louttit, C. M. "Reaction Time Experiments with Certain Racial Groups." *J. App. Psych.,* 14: 1930, pp. 557-565.

16a. Magnus, H. *Die geschichtliche Entwicklung des Farbensinnes.* Leipzig, 1877.

16b. Magnus, H. *Ueber ethnologische Untersuchungen des Farbensinnes.* Berlin, 1883.

17. McDougall, W. *Report of the Cambridge Anthropological Expedition to Torres Straits.* Vol. II, 1901.

18. Moore, H. T. "The Genetic Aspect of Consonance and Dissonance." *Psych. Monog.,* 17, No. 73:1914.

19. Myers, C. S. *Report of the Cambridge Anthropological Expedition to Torres Straits.* Vol. II, 1901.

20. Ranke, K. E. "Einige Beobachtungen über die Sehschärfe bei südamerikanischen Indianern." *Corr. Bl. Anthrop. Ges.,* 28:1897, pp. 113-119.

21. Rivers, W. H. R. *Report of the Cambridge Anthropological Expedition to Torres Straits.* Vol. II, 1901.

22. Rivers, W. H. R. "Observations on the Senses of the Todas." *Brit. J. Psych.,* 1:1905, pp. 321-396.

23. Virchow, R. "Ueber die Nubier." *Ztschr. f. Ethnol.,* 10:1878, Pt. II, pp. 333-356; 11:1879, Pt. II, pp. 449-456.

Chapter VIII

INTELLIGENCE TESTING—THE FACTORS
INVOLVED

INTRODUCTION

IN THE field of racial psychology no other problem has attracted so much attention as the question of the inherent intellectual superiority of certain races over others. This problem, as we have already noted (Chapter I), has been approached in a great many different ways, but usually with so much obvious bias as to make the scientifically minded student very sceptical of the conclusions. With the development of the first intelligence scales by Binet (6) and their use in the quantitative measurement of individual differences, it was felt that perhaps an instrument had finally been devised which would make it possible to study with complete objectivity the relative ability of various races. Terman (48), one of the early authorities in this field, expressed the opinion that the Binet scale was a true test of native intelligence, relatively free of the disturbing influences of nurture and background. If this were so, the difficult problem of racial differences in intelligence might be solved as soon as a sufficiently large body of data could be accumulated.

The data are now available. The number of studies in this field has multiplied rapidly, especially under the impetus of the testing undertaken during the World War, and the relevant bibliography is extensive. The largest proportion of these investigations has been made in America, and the results have shown that racial and national groups differ markedly from one another.

Negroes in general appear to do poorly. Pintner (39) estimates that in the various studies of Negro children by means
of the Binet, the I.Q. ranges from 83 to 99, with an average
around 90. With group tests Negroes rank still lower, with a
range in I.Q. from 58 to 92, and an average of only 76.
Negro recruits during the war were definitely inferior; their
average mental age was calculated to be 10.4 years, as compared with 13.1 years for the White draft.

In the case of the American Indian, the I.Q.'s are also
low, the majority being between 70 and 90. Mexicans do
only slightly better. Chinese and Japanese, on the other
hand, show relatively little inferiority to the Whites, the
I.Q.'s ranging from 85 to 114, with an average only slightly
below 100.

Among European immigrant groups, Italians have in general made a poor showing. In a series of studies their I.Q.'s
ranged from 76 to 100, with an average about 87. Poles do
equally poorly and in the Army tests were even slightly below the Italians. Immigrants from northwestern Europe
have in general been more successful, and the demonstration by the Army psychologists that in the test results the
immigrants from Great Britain, Holland, Germany and the
Scandinavian countries were superior to others has been
corroborated by more recent studies. (See Pintner, 39.)

If we had absolute faith in tests of intelligence, we should
have to regard this evidence of racial differences as conclusive. In recent years, however, more work has been done
on the tests themselves, and little by little the conviction has
grown that Terman's statement was an exaggeration, and
that environmental factors cannot be ignored in any valid
interpretation of these results. There may still be some controversy as to the extent to which these factors enter, but material has accumulated which leaves no doubt that they play

an important part. (See below.) In a recent critical survey, Garrett and Schneck (21) write that "the examiner must always remember that comparisons are permissible only when environmental differences are absent, or at least negligible" (Pt. II, p. 24).

For that reason no attempt will be made here to give a detailed summary of all the studies of racial differences made by means of intelligence tests. The reader who is interested will find a convenient account in the book by Garth (22), as well as in several briefer reviews by the same author. This chapter will rather be concerned with a critical discussion of some of the environmental, or non-racial, factors affecting the results, and individual studies will be cited only where they help to clarify the argument.

One preliminary caution is necessary. The problem of heredity versus environment, nature versus nurture, as it is here being considered, does not refer to individual, but to group, differences. This needs to be kept clearly in mind. It may be decided, for example, that heredity does not account for the observed intellectual differences between Negroes and Whites, and that the conditions of the environment are alone responsible. It would not follow that heredity did not enter into individual differences. There would still be room for wide variability within the Negro or within the White group, part of which at least could be explained only by the superiority or inferiority of individual or family germ plasm. The fact that persons living in almost the same environmental conditions will still differ widely from one another in intelligence, and the fact that identical twins living in very different environments will yet resemble each other closely, argue strongly in favor of an hereditary basis for part of the differences in intelligence between individuals and family lines. The problem of group differences, however, cannot be so easily dismissed, and it is to that problem that we now turn. (The reader who is interested in the studies pertinent to hereditary and environmental factors in individual differences will find an excellent account in Schwesinger, 44.)

MOTIVATION

One of the essentials in all group comparisons is that the members of both groups should be equally interested in the tests, and that they should be competing with equal eagerness for the best possible results. Peterson, Lanier and Walker (38) have pointed out that it cannot always be assumed that Negroes are motivated as strongly as Whites. Among the Dakota Indians the writer learned that it is considered bad form to answer a question in the presence of someone else who does not know the answer; it is regarded as a kind of showing-off, and consequently the teachers find it exceedingly difficult to persuade the children to recite in class. These children also learn that they must not reply to a question unless they are absolutely sure of the answer; and investigators who have gone among them with the Binet have observed their long silences, in striking contrast to the tendency of White children to try out an answer in the hope that it may possibly be correct. In Australia, Porteus had difficulty in inducing the native to solve a problem (in this case a performance test) by his own efforts. These aborigines are used to concerted thinking, every problem in tribal life being debated and settled by a council of elders, the discussion continuing until a unanimous decision is reached. On many occasions the subject was evidently most puzzled by the fact that Porteus would give him no assistance, even when, as with one tribe he was testing, he had just been made a tribal member (41).

The importance of motivation is illustrated in a study by Baldwin (4), who compared Negro and White girls in a reformatory school in Pennsylvania. He noted that whereas the White girls showed sustained attention, the Negro girls were much slower to warm up and much readier to drop back and lose interest. "They are suspicious as to the value of the task" (p. 327). It need hardly be pointed out that an attitude of this kind would affect the results adversely.

RAPPORT

The relation between the experimenter and the subject may also be very important, particularly where these two belong to different races. It has frequently been noted that when a White tester enters a Negro school in the South to make an investigation, he has to face an attitude of fear and suspicion which is certain to interfere with the performance of an intellectual task. The same is probably true in the case of American Indian subjects, and to a lesser extent also with the foreign-born.

That the importance of rapport is not always recognized can be illustrated by an example from Porteus (41), who in his study of the intelligence of Australian aborigines included among his subjects one convicted murderer whose test performance was complicated by the presence of a chain on his leg and a police constable standing over him with a gun. Even when one is conscious of the necessity for establishing the proper rapport, it is not always possible to know whether one has succeeded. In an investigation in Italy the writer learned quite by accident that his foreignness was causing much more of a disturbance among his subjects than he had any reason to anticipate. After the writer had spent a day working in a country school near Turin, the teacher showed him what his first subject that morning had written as his daily theme. "Today a foreign doctor came to the school and the teacher told me to go alone with him into another room. I was terribly afraid and commended myself to the Holy Virgin. As I left the classroom I asked Pietro to say an Ave Maria for me. But the doctor only wanted me to do some puzzles for him."

The effect of the relationship between subject and tester appeared clearly in a study of the comparative suggestibility of Negro and White children by Ogeloff (unpublished dissertation for the M.A. degree at Columbia University). The tests were of two kinds, those depending on the prestige of the experimenter, and those described as ideo-motor, in which the personality of the experimenter plays no part. (See Aveling and Hargreaves, 3.) In the prestige tests, the Negroes showed themselves to be definitely less suggestible than the Whites, and the investigator comments that they seemed also less friendly, and, in some cases, even resentful. It is safe to infer that a similar attitude may enter into other tests of Negroes by Whites.

CULTURE

Culture, in the sense in which it is here used, refers to those attitudes and experiences which an individual receives from the society of which he is a member. Cultural differences may have a definite effect on test performance. It is obviously necessary for a subject to be familiar with the actual materials entering into a test, but in addition it may be that these materials and the test situation in general have for him a different meaning from that presupposed. Fitzgerald and Ludeman (16) give an example of the reaction of Plains Indian children to one of the tests in the National Intelligence Test, Scale A, Form I. Test 3, Exercise 17, reads: "Crowd (closeness, danger, dust, excitement, number)." The task of the subject is to underline the two words in the parentheses which tell what a crowd always has. A great many of the Indian children underlined "danger" and "dust," and in some cases also "excitement," instead of the expected "closeness" and "number"; the authors point out that the experience of the children with crowds on the prairie made this answer logical for them.

Similar examples might easily be multiplied. Another test in the N.I.T. Scale gives the following sentence to be completed: "——— should prevail in churches and libraries." The missing word is of course "silence"; but clearly most southern Negro children would be taught by their acquaintance with churches that silence is neither expected nor desired, and they would therefore not be so likely as White children to answer correctly. One of the tests in the Army Alpha, Form 6, calls for a reaction to the question: "Why should all parents be made to send their children to school?" The expected answer is that "school prepares the child for his later life"; but the unfortunate experience of many American Indians has been that their schooling has unfitted them for the life they are later required to lead on the reservations. One item in the Binet asks, "What is the thing for you to do if a playmate hits you without meaning to do it?" The crux of this question is of course the fact that the injury was not intended; but there are many peoples, including a large number of American Indian tribes, who make no distinction in the punishment of a deliberate or an accidental injury.

The non-linguistic, or performance, tests present similar difficulties. The Goodenough test of "drawing a man" is based upon the concept of a fully clothed man as seen in our society. When Porteus gave this test to the Australians, he found that they would almost invariably draw the man naked and so lose those points given for correct drawing of the clothes. This test also assumes that a man is the figure most frequently drawn by children; the writer found that among the Dakotas (Sioux) the horse was much more popular. The Army Beta contains a picture-completion test, in which the task is to draw in the missing portions. One of the pictures is of a house lacking a chimney; Boas (private communication) tells of a Sicilian child who drew in its place a crucifix. His particular experience had taught him that no house was complete without one.

The large majority of tests of intelligence depend at least to some extent upon speed. Even the Binet, in which the time factor is of relatively less importance, contains some items in which it enters very definitely, for example, the "naming words" test. In the case of the group tests the scores are markedly affected by the rate at which the questions are answered. The attitude toward speed varies greatly in different cultures, and not all peoples will work on the tests with equal interest in getting them done in the shortest time possible. Peterson and his associates (38) have noted this relative indifference to speed among Negroes, and the writer found that the injunction to "do this as quickly as you can" seemed to make no impression whatsoever on the American Indian children on the Yakima Reservation in the State of Washington (31). Porteus (41) makes the same point in the case of his Australian subjects.

It is safe to say that this indifference to speed is cultural, and not innate. Our review of the material bearing upon basal metabolism and other fundamental organic functions revealed no consistent physiological basis for a racial difference in speed of reaction. The further fact that American Indian children who have lived a long time among Whites, or who attend a busy and progressive school, show a definite tendency to approximate White behavior in this respect, also points in the same direction (31).

Speed is regarded as a value in western, and particularly in American, civilization. Children learn very rapidly that the "race is to the swift," and they will tend to work quickly at their tasks, even when there is no special instruction to hurry. In other communities, for example, among the American Indians, children may be specifically taught to think carefully before they act, and not to answer before they are sure of what to say. In the study referred to above, in which White and Indian children were compared by means of a series of performance tests in the Pintner-Paterson scale, there was a very striking qualitative difference in the way the two groups worked. Typically, the White child jumped at the task, tried out a piece quickly in a succession of positions until he had hit upon the right one, finished the test rapidly, but with a relatively large number of errors. The Indian child, though he received the same instructions, looked at the problem very carefully, slowly and cautiously picked up one of the pieces, put it in the right place, and slowly and cautiously went on to the next. He usually took much longer than the White child, but he made fewer errors (31).

Speed is not always at a premium. When the Australian native hunts the wallaby, or small kangaroo, he needs, in Porteus' words (41), "sustained muscular control, an undivided attention, an extreme sensory wariness, inexhaustible patience and concentration of purpose" (p. 64). The White man is usually unsuccessful, largely because he cannot keep still long enough. This raises the whole question as to whether our particular criterion of intelligence is applicable to groups with a different background. The Dakota Indians regarded the woman who could do the best beadwork as the most important in the community. For the Eskimo, fishing ability; for the Plains Indians, prowess in war; for the Australians, the ability to follow a track in the bush, might be considered a measure of excellence.

This relativity in the concept of intelligence has suggested the possibility of devising new tests based upon cultural criteria differing from our own. Schwesinger (44) suggests that in this way the problem of equating the background of the two groups which are being compared might be successfully overcome. If we have two groups, A and B, let us also have two tests, x and y, x being a satisfactory test for group A, and y for B. Let us now give x to B and y to A. If A shows up better in B's test than B in A's, then we should have the right to say that A is superior. This ingenious suggestion is not, however, practicable. Before we can make any reasonable interpretation of the results, we should have to know that the test x is just as closely or as distantly related to the culture of B, as y is to that of A. This we have no way of discovering.

It is, however, relatively easy to devise a test in which members of an apparently inferior group make an excellent showing. Porteus was very much impressed by the tracking skill of the Australian natives and he made photographs of a number of footprints, the task being to match two photographs of the same foot. This was of course an artificial problem, even for the Australians, who were accustomed to dealing with footprints and not with photographs; but in spite of that fact they did just as well as a group of presumably superior White students in Hawaii with whom they were compared. "Allowing for their unfamiliarity with photographs we may say, then, that with test material with which they are familiar the aborigines' ability to discriminate form and spacial relationships is at least equal to that of Whites of high school standards of education and of better than average social standing." (Porteus, 41, p. 401.)

Among the Dakota Indians a "beadwork test" was devised to illustrate the same point. The subjects, American Indian and White girls, were all taught how to do beadwork on a loom; they were then shown a small sample of beadwork designed by Miss Ella Deloria, who was assisting the writer in this study; the samples were taken away after four minutes, and the task was to reproduce the pattern on the loom as closely as possible. It should be noted that the sample was not familiar to any of the subjects; yet the Indian girls definitely surpassed the Whites, presumably because of their greater familiarity with beadwork in general. This proves nothing about the relative ability of the two groups, but it does show the unfairness of taking a test arising from one culture and applying it to another, as we have been in the habit of doing.

Social and Economic Status

Many studies testify to the close correspondence between standing in the tests and the social and economic status of the groups tested. This was revealed in the study made by the Army testers, and it has been amply verified by subsequent investigations in England, France, Germany and Japan, as well as in the United States. There are marked differences, not only between adults in various occupational levels, but also between their children, the professional and moneyed classes ranking higher than skilled and unskilled laborers. The studies by Goodenough (24), Collins (11), Duff and Thomson (14), Bridges and Coler (7), Fukuda (19), Freeman (18), Haggerty and Nash (25), Arlitt (1), and others all give this same general result. (See Pintner 39, for a review of these studies.)

The obvious difficulty in the interpretation of these findings is the question as to what is cause and what is effect; whether people are in the upper economic levels because they are more intelligent, or whether they do better on the tests because of their superior opportunities. The answer to this question is of great significance in the problem of racial differences. Most of the groups who rank low in the tests, for example, the Negro, the Mexican, the Italian, come largely from the lowest economic levels; if economic status affects test scores to any extent, they are very definitely handicapped in a comparative study.

Intelligence may be regarded as the cause of economic status only if opportunities are equal and competition is entirely free. Even within a relatively homogeneous, native-born White American population, this is not altogether true; the handicaps are not evenly distributed. In the case of the Negro, however, the difficulties in his way are so great that any inference from industrial status to intelligence is completely unwarranted. The kind of competition the Negro has to face in his search for a job has been carefully described by Johnson (27), Feldman (15) and Spero and Harris (47), who leave no doubt as to the additional handicaps he must overcome. The same is true, though not to so great an extent, of some foreign-born White groups, who tend to enter the occupations at the lowest economic level, emerging from these only after a generation. That their economic inferiority is only temporary is made clear by a report of the U. S. Immigration Commission (49), which indicates that although at the start the immigrants have much lower occupations than the native-born, in the second generation the majority rise to the average native-born level. Until we can be certain that the same opportunities have been given to the Negro and the Italian as to the native-born White, any direct comparison of average test scores will be meaningless.

A more direct analysis of the influence of social and economic level upon intelligence has been made in important recent studies of foster children who were placed in more favorable environments. Freeman, Holzinger and Mitchell (18) found that children in good foster homes made an average gain of 5.3 points in their intelligence quotient after a period of four years; when a comparison was made between siblings in better and in poorer homes, the former had an I.Q. about 9 points higher. The authors believe that these results show clearly the influence of the improved environment; but the possibility must not be ignored that a form of selection may have taken place, the more intelligent children having been adopted into the more intelligent homes.

Burks (9) attacked the problem somewhat differently. In her study a comparison was made between foster children and true children in homes which had been matched for socio-economic level, education of the parents, and other environmental factors. The average I.Q. of the foster children was 107, and of the true children 115. This suggested that heredity entered very significantly into the results. The further fact that foster children resembled foster parents in intelligence much less than true children did their own parents, although the environments were presumably identical in the two cases, also pointed in the same direction. In this connection the relative importance of heredity and environment does not concern us so much as Burks' demonstration of a definite gain in intelligence due to a shift in environment; she estimates that in the change from a poor to an exceptionally good home the improvement may be as much as 20 points in I.Q.

Although these two studies differ somewhat in interpretation and emphasis, they agree in their demonstration that an improvement in the economic level of children who have been adopted into foster homes definitely improves their intelligence test performance. It may be added that a further study of orphan children by Lithauer and Klineberg (33) also noted a rise of six points in the I.Q. as the result of a similar change. There seems to be no doubt about the improvement, although its extent may still be a matter of controversy. In any case these studies make it clear that economic status is at least in part responsible for the level of test performance.

One additional study may be mentioned in this connection. It is clearly of interest to know how early in life the occupational differences in intelligence manifest themselves. Goodenough (24) showed that they hold for pre-school children; but during those early years it is already possible for the environment to have left its mark, and the differences can therefore not be attributed entirely to heredity. Furfey (20) went one step further, and gave to 277 infants, aged one to twelve months, the series of "Babytests" contained in the Linfert-Hierholzer Scale (32) in order to see whether there were differences corresponding to socio-economic status before the environment had had time to exercise much influence. As a measure of environment he used the Chapman-Sims score (10), correlating this with the scores on the tests. All the correlations were negligible. If we could be certain that these tests measured the same thing as those in more general use, this result would be of very great importance. There is the additional complication that many children who are inherently superior may not show this superiority until after a certain degree of maturation.

McGraw (35) made a study of Negro and White infants

in Tallahassee, Florida, by means of the Bühler "Babytests," and found the White babies superior. The White babies also showed superiority, however, in height and weight. This physical difference may mean that the pre-natal as well as the post-natal environments of the Negroes were inferior, and it is quite probable that the poorer physical condition will be reflected in the behavior of the infant, upon which the mental ratings depend. Here again economic factors may be of primary importance.

It has sometimes been suggested that in order to obviate the difficulty introduced into racial comparisons by these economic factors, a better procedure would be to equate the two racial groups—for example, the Negro and the White—for these factors, and then see which is superior. It is hard to do this with any exactness; but even if it were possible, it would by no means be conclusive. If we picked a particularly good group of Negroes, economically and socially speaking, it might be argued that they were exceptions, and could not be taken as typical of their race; if we took a relatively poor group of Whites, the same objection could be made. This factor of sampling or selection, which will be discussed later in greater detail, enters into this type of comparison to an undeterminable extent, and makes the result meaningless.

With all these complications, it remains true that an improvement in status usually means an improvement in test score, and that social and economic factors cannot be disregarded in racial comparisons.

LANGUAGE

The effect of relative familiarity with the language in which the test is administered is of obvious importance, and was recognized very early in the history of testing. This resulted in the construction and use of a large number of performance tests in which language does not appreciably enter, but the feeling seems to have persisted that language tests are somehow superior. In spite of criticism, most studies of racial differences have been made by means of linguistic tests.

Many of the groups tested—for example, the American Indians, the Mexicans, the Italians and other European immigrants—have been bilingual, retaining their own language to some extent while in the process of learning English. A number of investigations have shown that bilingualism adversely affects intelligence test performance. Smith (45) and Saer (42) have both demonstrated that Welsh children speaking only one language do consistently better on the Binet than those speaking both Welsh and English. Yoshioka (53) has shown that Japanese children in California who attend Japanese part-time schools after regular school hours to learn the language of their parents, are definitely inferior in their N.I.T. scores to both the American and the Japanese norms. Mead (36) and N. Klineberg (unpublished master's dissertation in Columbia University Library) have obtained similar results in the case of Italian children, those who still speak Italian in their homes being inferior to those speaking only English. Jamieson and Sandiford (26) found monoglot Indians in southern Ontario to be superior to the polyglot group in all the linguistic tests. Decroly (13) noted that the Walloon children in Belgium, who spoke only French, obtained better scores than the Flemish children, who spoke two languages. In the case of the Jewish children, the studies of Schiller (43) and Halpern (unpublished master's dissertation in Columbia University Library) have revealed no important differences of this kind.

It is not probable that bilingualism results in a definite or permanent intellectual inferiority. There may be some confusion in the minds of the children until the two languages have been completely mastered; there may also be a handicap arising from a relatively lesser knowledge of either language. The actual vocabulary of the child may enter directly into the test, and it is clear that if he has to learn words in two languages he will not know so many in either one. It follows that the ability of an Indian or Italian child to speak and understand English does not justify the use of an English language test in comparing him with one who has spoken that language all his life.

In the interpretation of these studies it is important to bear in mind the possibility that there are other differences between monoglot and polyglot children. It has been suggested that in many cases they come from different levels of their society, the wealthier and more "progressive" families tending to a more complete assimilation of the new culture. This may be partly true, but it must not be overemphasized, as there are in many groups cultural loyalties and traditions which keep the old language alive, and which by no means point to an inferiority. In any case, the newcomers, however intelligent, can hardly be expected to speak a perfect English immediately.

The case of the American Negro is somewhat different. His native tongue is English; it is usually the only language he speaks. In many cases, however, he speaks it so badly that he is placed at a great disadvantage in intelligence tests involving anything like a precise discrimination of the meaning of terms. The absolute or relative illiteracy of the southern Negro recruits in the American Army during the World War made their scores on the Army Alpha of little significance; and even the use of the Army Beta, the non-language test, had its disadvantages, as the Negroes could not understand the necessity for the pantomimic instructions when, according to their lights, there was nothing the matter with their English. This language difficulty was impressed upon the writer most clearly during an investigation among West Virginia rural Negroes when he experimented with one of the forms of the Otis Self-administering Examination, in this case given orally. When Negro children were asked to give the opposite of a simple word like "strong" or "pretty," in a great many cases they did not know the meaning of the word "opposite." Usually when the concept was made clear to them, not without difficulty, the correct answer would be given. If they were required to take the Otis test as a written examination, in the usual manner, they would naturally make a zero score on all the "opposite" items.

There is another method which may be used to determine the importance of the language factor. A number of racial groups have been tested with both linguistic and non-linguistic tests; and if it could be assumed that these are identical except for the factor of language (see below, p. 172), it would be of interest to see whether the performance improves when this factor does not enter. This technique was used in a study of immigrant groups by Pintner and Keller (40), who found that most of the inferiority disappeared when the comparison was made by means of performance tests.

If we compare the studies of various racial groups by these two types of tests, it becomes clear that the linguistic tests place many of them at a disadvantage. In the following tables the attempt has been made to collect those results which can be stated in terms of the intelligence quotient, so that the findings of different investigators may be compared in terms of the same criterion. There are a number of objections to this procedure, the most important being that an I.Q. obtained by one psychologist through the use of one test may not be comparable to an I.Q. obtained under other conditions. Another objection is that averaging the averages gives equal weight to studies which may differ markedly in their significance. The results may still be of interest.

TABLE 18: INTELLIGENCE QUOTIENTS OF ITALIANS

Linguistic Tests			Performance Tests		
Investigator	Test	I.Q.	Investigator	Test	I.Q.
Arlitt	Binet	85	Goodenough	Goodenough	89
Bere	"	85	Young	Army Beta	96
Brown	"	78			
Colvin and Allen	"	91			
" "	N.I.T.	76			
Graham	Binet	85			
Hirsch	Pintner-Cunningham	86			
Kempf and Collins	Binet	87			
Kirkpatrick	Illinois	83			
Madsen	Binet	79			
Pintner and Keller	"	84			
Rigg	N.I.T.	91			
Young	Army Alpha	88			
	Average	84.5		Average	92.5

Unfortunately, in the case of this group, there were only two investigations by means of performance tests which could be included in this table. The results do show, however, that the inferiority of the Italians is much more marked in the case of the linguistic tests. Incidentally, it is interesting to note the wide variability among the Italian samples, the range being from 76 to 96 and illustrating the importance of a possible "sampling error" which may enter into racial comparisons.

The following table presents results for Chinese and Japanese, who are for our purposes being considered together. (The studies on the two groups are distinguished from each other by the initial preceding the name of the investigator.)

TABLE 19: INTELLIGENCE QUOTIENTS OF CHINESE AND JAPANESE

Linguistic Tests			Performance Tests		
Investigator	Test	I.Q.	Investigator	Test	I.Q.
(J) Darsie	Binet	90	(J) Darsie	Army Beta	100
(J) Fukuda	Binet	97	(C) Goodenough	Goodenough	104
(C) Graham	Binet	87	(J) Goodenough	Goodenough	102
(C) Graham	Binet	91	(C) Murdoch	Army Beta	100
(C) Hoag	N.I.T.	87	(C) Porteus,	Porteus	
(J) Hoag	N.I.T.	81	Babcock	Fm. Bd.	98
(C) Porteus, Babcock	Binet	87	(J) Porteus,	Porteus	
(J) Porteus, Babcock	Binet	85	Babcock	Fm. Bd.	101
(C) Yeung	Binet	97	(C) Porteus,		
			Babcock	Porteus Maze	92
			(J) Porteus,		
			Babcock	Porteus Maze	99
			(C) Sandiford,	Pintner-	
			Kerr	Paterson	107
			(J) Sandiford,	Pintner-	
			Kerr	Paterson	114
			(C) Symonds	Pintner	99
Average		89.1	Average		101.5

In this case the discrepancy between the two groups of tests is very marked, the difference being more than 12 points in the I.Q. It will again be noticed that there is great variation, the I.Q.'s ranging from 81 to 114 (33 points); on the Binet alone, the range is 12 points, from 85 to 97. The Oriental groups are superior to the Italian, but this superiority is not so great as is usually believed; part of it is undoubtedly due to the fact that the Orientals have more frequently been examined by means of performance tests.

The studies of the American Indians show this same discrepancy. See Table 20.

TABLE 20: INTELLIGENCE QUOTIENTS OF AMERICAN INDIANS

Linguistic Tests			*Performance Tests*		
Investigator	Test	I.Q.	Investigator	Test	I.Q.
Garth	N.I.T.	69	Goodenough	Goodenough	86
"		76	Jamieson,		
"	Otis	70	Sandiford	Pintner	97
Garth, Garrett	N.I.T.	69.6	Jamieson,	Pintner-	
" "	"	72.5	Sandiford	Paterson	92
Fitzgerald,					
Ludeman	"	87.5			
Jamieson,					
Sandiford	"	80			
Jamieson,	Pintner-				
Sandiford	Cunningham	78			
	Average	75.3		Average	91.7

In this case there is a difference of 16.4 points in the I.Q. obtained by the two groups of tests; the range is from 69 to 97 (28 points).

Finally, the same difference may be demonstrated in the case of the Mexicans, as can be seen in Table 21.

TABLE 21: INTELLIGENCE QUOTIENTS OF MEXICANS

Linguistic Tests			*Performance Tests*		
Investigator	Test	I.Q.	Investigator	Test	I.Q.
Dickson	Binet	78	Goodenough	Goodenough	88.5
Garth	N.I.T.	78	Young	Army Beta	96
"	"	83			
Heilman	"	79			
Sheldon	Binet	89			
Young	Army Alpha	87			
	Average	82.3		Average	92.3

Here the difference is exactly ten points in I.Q., and the range is 78 to 96, 18 points.

As was noted above, this type of comparison assumes that linguistic and non-linguistic tests measure the same kind of intelligence and measure it in the same way. When the performance tests were first introduced, this assumption was made; Army Beta was regarded as the equivalent of Army

Alpha, except that it could be used with illiterates; the Pintner-Paterson Scale was supposed to be substantially equal to the Binet, but especially applicable to deaf-mutes and to the foreign-born. It was soon noted, however, that the correlations between the two types of tests were not usually very high. They ran in the neighborhood of + .50 (see Garrett and Schneck, 21), which indicated that there were a number of factors differentiating the two types, as well as a number which they had in common. With the introduction of factor analysis, this point became even clearer. A distinct linguistic factor was recognized, entering significantly in the Binet and similar tests, and distinct from numerical and spatial factors which played a more important part in other types of tests. The statistical controversy as to the "general intelligence," or G of Spearman (46), has not been settled, but there is now substantial agreement to the effect that it does not enter equally into all tests of intelligence, and that these can therefore not be directly equated. The tables presented above must as a consequence not be regarded as conclusive, or as an entirely justifiable comparison of the results of the two types of tests. They do, however, suggest the extent of the language handicap which may enter in the case of certain groups, and they show very directly how the results may be affected by the particular test chosen by the investigator, as well as by the accident of sampling.

It was noted above that Jewish children do not appear to be markedly influenced by a language disability. In their case there is little or no relationship between the amount of English spoken in their homes and their standing in the linguistic tests. They appear, in spite of their frequent bilingualism, to make a much poorer showing on the performance tests than, for example, on the Binet. A study by Florence Halpern (unpublished M.A. thesis) on a group of

Jewish children from the New York East Side reports a Stanford-Binet I.Q. of 96.2 and a Pintner-Paterson I.Q. of only 81.5. This finding illustrates the importance of knowing something about the cultural factors entering into the life of a group before attempting to interpret their performance. There is among Jewish families such a marked emphasis upon schooling and upon "abstract" intelligence, to the almost total disregard of manual dexterity and "mechanical" intelligence, that this result was really to be expected. It would be interesting to make a similar comparison among Jewish children among whom mechanical and scientific toys have become more popular.

SCHOOLING

The factor of school training raises many problems similar to those already discussed. There is no doubt of the rather close correspondence between amount of education and standing in the tests. This was first demonstrated clearly by the Army testers (52), whose results are summarized in Table 22.

TABLE 22: ALPHA SCORES AND SCHOOL GRADE COMPLETED (ARMY RESULTS)

Group	0–4	5–8	High School	College	Beyond College
White officers	112.5	107.0	131.1	143.2	143.5
" native-born	22.0	51.1	92.1	117.8	145.9
" foreign-born	21.4	47.2	72.4	91.9	92.5
Colored, north	17.0	37.2	71.2	90.5	
" south	7.2	16.3	45.7	63.8	

A number of studies followed with similar results. Garth, Lovelady and Smith (23) found a correlation of + .847 for intelligence and school grade in the case of American Indians, and + .845 for intelligence and educational achievement. Davis (12) also demonstrated a close relation between the intelligence quotients of students in a private Negro high school and the number of months they had been in school. It is estimated by Kelley (28) that some ninety percent of a general intelligence test and an all-around achievement (i.e., scholastic) test measure the same thing.

It has sometimes been urged that amount of education is an effect, rather than a cause, of intelligence, the more intelligent children staying longer at school and doing better in their school work. This is certainly true in part, but there is no doubt that opportunity, as determined mainly by economic status, also enters. In addition, there is direct evidence that schooling is important in determining the level of the I.Q. In one study Barrett and Koch (5) demonstrated a very marked increase in I.Q. resulting from the nursery school training of orphanage children; the experimental group improved from 91.7 to 112.6 I.Q. points, whereas the control group which received no such training showed a gain of only five points, from 92.6 to 97.7. Wellman (50) reported a similar rise in the case of children who attended summer sessions at the University of Iowa Elementary School. An earlier study by Woolley (51) gave the same result. Very recently Lowry (34) was able to bring about an average rise of 11.76 points in the intelligence quotient of 50 elementary school children in Latrobe, Pennsylvania, by a three-months' drill in reading. It seems reasonable to suppose that if such short periods of training can produce this marked effect, a long-continued consistent superiority in schooling will also be effective.

These studies make it clear that merely equating two groups for school grade and assuming that therefore their training has been substantially identical can hardly be justified. Four years of schooling in a southern rural Negro school are certainly not equivalent to four years in a White school in New York or Chicago. It would be difficult to overemphasize the frequent discrepancy in per capita expenditures, in equipment and facilities, in the training of the teachers and in the length of the school term. (See Johnson, 27.) In spite of this, many of the comparisons upon which the conclusions regarding racial differences are based involve groups whose schooling is equally disparate. The study by Foreman (17) has demonstrated a close correspondence between scores on achievement tests and expenditures for the schooling of Negro children in a number of southern rural communities. It would be interesting to repeat this study with tests of intelligence. In any case, there seems to be little doubt that the inadequate schooling of the average southern Negro child may also be regarded as playing an important part in test performance.

SAMPLING

The final factor to be considered in this connection is the question of the degree to which any particular group can be taken as representative of the whole race or nation to which it belongs. This enters as a complication in a great many studies. Since almost all the racial comparisons have been made in the United States on groups that have migrated from other countries, the results cannot be extended to the parent populations until we know what kind of selection or sampling has been operative. The superiority of the Chinese over the Italians in America may mean simply that those Chinese who have come to the United States are a particularly intelligent group, as compared with these Italians. This point has frequently been made in connection with the Army results (52), which demonstrated an apparent superiority of northern over southern Europeans in America, but which Brigham (8) and others attempted to generalize to include similar groups in Europe. What little we know of the German and the Italian migrant, for example, suggests strongly that they do not come from comparable social and economic strata of their respective countries. We need a number of careful studies of the conditions of migration in each group, and of the forces operative in the stimulation or discouragement of migration in each case, before we can know the degree to which the various samples are representative. The same problem arises when we compare different samples of the same population, for example, rural and urban groups in America, or northern and southern American Negroes. The whole question of sampling or selection will be discussed at length in the following chapter.

Conclusion

The factors we have discussed as playing a part in racial comparisons make clear at least some of the difficulties in the way of basing a racial psychology upon tests of intelligence. Until and unless these factors are adequately controlled, such comparisons will have little meaning. It should be added that although *no one* of these factors accounts by itself for the observed racial differences, the combination of *all* of them, acting in different ways and to a variable extent depending upon specific circumstances, may very well be responsible.

The writer wishes to emphasize again his view that these various factors do not explain away *individual* differences in mental test performance. This discussion concerns group differences alone, and the evidence on the "constancy of the I.Q.," and, in general, on individual and family differences in intelligence, is irrelevant to this issue.

BIBLIOGRAPHY

1. Arlitt, A. H. "Further Data on the Influence of Race and Social Status on the I. Q." *Psych. Bull.,* 18:1921, pp. 95-96.
2. Arlitt, A. H. "On the Need for Caution in Establishing Race Norms." *J. App. Psych.,* 5:1921, pp. 179-183.
3. Aveling, F., and Hargreaves, H. L. "Suggestibility with and without Prestige in Children." *Brit. J. Psych.,* 12:1921, pp. 53-75.
4. Baldwin, B. T. "The Learning of Delinquent Adolescent Girls as Shown by Substitution Tests." *J. Educ. Psych.,* 4:1913, pp. 317-332.
5. Barrett, H. E., and Koch, H. L. "The Effect of Nursery-School Training upon the Mental-Test Performance of a Group of Orphanage Children." *J. Genet. Psych.,* 37:1930, pp. 102-122.
6. Binet, A. See *L'Année Psychologique,* Vols. I-XVII, 1895-1911, for Binet's work.
7. Bridges, J. W., and Coler, L. E. "Intelligence and Social Status." *Psych. Rev.,* 24:1917, pp. 1-31.
8. Brigham, C. C. *A Study of American Intelligence.* Princeton, 1923.
9. Burks, B. S. "The Relative Influence of Nature and Nurture upon Mental Development, etc." *27th Yearbook, Nat. Soc. Study Educ.,* Pt. I:1928, pp. 219-316.
10. Chapman, J. C., and Sims, V. M. "The Quantitative Measurement of Certain Aspects of Socio-economic Status." *J. Educ. Psych.,* 16:1925, pp. 380-390.
11. Collins, J. E. "The Intelligence of School Children and Parental Occupation." *J. Ed. Res.,* 17:1928, pp. 157-169.
12. Davis, R. A., Jr. "Some Relations between Amount of School Training and Intelligence among Negroes." *J. Educ. Psych.,* 19:1928, pp. 127-130.
13. Decroly, O. "Essai d'Application du Test de Ballard dans les Écoles Belges." *Année Psych.,* 27:1926, pp. 57-93.
14. Duff, J. F., and Thomson, G. H. "The Social and Geographical Distribution of Intelligence in Northumberland." *Brit. J. Psych.,* 14, Pt. II:1923, pp. 192-198.

15. Feldman, H. *Racial Factors in American Industry.* New York, 1931.

16. Fitzgerald, J. A., and Ludeman, W. W. "The Intelligence of Indian Children." *J. Comp. Psych.*, 6:1926, pp. 319-328.

17. Foreman, C. *Environmental Factors in Negro Elementary Education.* New York, 1932.

18. Freeman, F. N., *et al.* "The Influence of Environment on the Intelligence, School Achievement and Conduct of Foster Children." *27th Yearbook, Nat. Soc. Study Educ.*, Pt. I: 1928, pp. 103-317.

19. Fukuda, T. "A Survey of the Intelligence and Environment of School Children." *Amer. J. Psych.*, 36:1925, pp. 124-139.

20. Furfey, P. H. "The Relation between Socio-economic Status and Intelligence of Young Infants as Measured by the Linfert-Hierholzer Scale." *J. Genet. Psych.*, 35:1928, pp. 478-480.

21. Garrett, H. E., and Schneck, M. R. *Psychological Tests, Methods and Results.* New York, 1933.

22. Garth, T. R. *Race Psychology: A Study of Racial Mental Differences.* New York, 1931.

23. Garth, T. R., Lovelady, B. E., and Smith, H. W. "The Intelligence and Achievement of Southern Negro Children." *Sch. and Soc.*, 32:1930, pp. 431-434.

24. Goodenough, F. L. "The Relation of the Intelligence of Pre-School Children to the Occupation of Their Fathers." *Amer. J. Psych.*, 40:1928, pp. 284-294.

25. Haggerty, M. E., and Nash, H. B. "Mental Capacity of Children and Parental Occupation." *J. Educ. Psych.*, 15:1924, pp. 559-572.

26. Jamieson, E., and Sandiford, C. "The Mental Capacity of Southern Ontario Indians." *J. Educ. Psych.*, 19:1928, pp. 536-551.

27. Johnson, C. S. *The Negro in American Civilization.* New York, 1930.

28. Kelley, T. L. *Interpretation of Educational Measurements.* Chicago, 1927.

29. Kelley, T. L. *The Influence of Nurture upon Native Differences.* New York, 1926.

30. Klineberg, O. *Negro Intelligence and Selective Migration.* New York, 1935.

31. Klineberg, O. "An Experimental Study of Speed and Other Factors in 'Racial' Differences." *Arch. Psych.*, No. 93: 1928.

32. Linfert, H. E., and Hierholzer, H. M. *A Scale for Measuring the Mental Development of Infants during the First Year of Life.* Baltimore, 1928.

33. Lithauer, D. B., and Klineberg, O. "A Study of the Variation in I. Q. of a Group of Dependent Children in Institution and Foster Home." *J. Genet. Psych.*, 42:1933, pp. 236-242.

34. Lowry, E. "Increasing the I. Q." *Sch. and Soc.*, 35:1932, pp. 179-180.

35. McGraw, M. B. "A Comparative Study of a Group of Southern White and Negro Infants." *Genet. Psych. Mono.*, 10:1931, pp. 1-105.

36. Mead, M. "Group Intelligence Tests and Linguistic Disability among Italian Children." *Sch. and Soc.*, 25, No. 642:1927, pp. 465-468.

37. Peterson, J., and Lanier, L. H. "Studies in the Comparative Abilities of Whites and Negroes." *Ment. Meas. Mono.*, 5, 1929.

38. Peterson, J., Lanier, L. H., and Walker, H. M. "Comparisons of White and Negro Children in Certain Ingenuity and Speed Tests." *J. Comp. Psych.*, 5:1925, pp. 271-283.

39. Pintner, R. *Intelligence Testing: Methods and Results.* New York, 1931. (New ed.).

40. Pintner, R., and Keller, R. "Intelligence Tests of Foreign Children." *J. Educ. Psych.*, 13:1922, pp. 214-222.

41. Porteus, S. D. *The Psychology of a Primitive People; a Study of the Australian Aborigine.* New York, 1931.

42. Saer, D. J. "The Effect of Bilingualism on Intelligence." *Brit. J. Psych.*, 14: 1923-1924, pp. 25-38.

43. Schiller, B. "Verbal, Numerical and Spatial Abilities of Young Children." *Arch. Psych.*, No. 161: 1934.

44. Schwesinger, G. C. *Heredity and Environment.* New York, 1933.

45. Smith, F. "Bilingualism and Mental Development." *Brit. J. Psych.*, 13:1922-1923, pp. 271-283.

46. Spearman, C. *The Nature of "Intelligence" and the Principles of Cognition.* London, 1923.

47. Spero, S. D., and Harris, A. L. *The Black Worker; the Negro and the Labor Movement.* New York, 1931.

48. Terman, L. M. *The Measurement of Intelligence.* Boston, 1916.
49. U. S. Immigration Commission. *Occupations of the First and Second Generations of Immigrants in the United States.* Washington, 1911.
50. Wellman, B. L. "The Effect of Pre-School Attendance upon the I. Q." *J. Exper. Educ.,* 1:1932, pp. 48-69.
50a. Witty, P. A., and Lehman, H. C. "Racial Differences: the Dogma of Superiority." *J. Soc. Psych.,* 1:1930, pp. 394-418.
51. Woolley, H. T. "The Validity of Standards of Mental Measurement in Young Childhood." *Sch. and Soc.,* 21:1925, pp. 476-482.
52. Yerkes, R. M. (Ed.) "Psychological Examining in the U. S. Army." *Mem. Nat. Acad. Sci.,* 15:1921.
53. Yoshioka, J. G. "A Study of Bilingualism." *J. Genet. Psych.,* 36:1929, pp. 473-479.

Chapter IX

INTELLIGENCE TESTING—THE PROBLEM OF SELECTION

THE NEGRO

ALTHOUGH it is true, as was mentioned in the preceding chapter, that Negroes rank below Whites in most intelligence test studies, it must also be kept in mind that Negro groups·may differ markedly from one another, and that they are by no means invariably inferior. It is well known, for example, that during the war the Army testers found Negro recruits from the North far superior to Negroes from the South, and, in the case of certain of the northern states, superior also to southern Whites (24). This is shown in Table 23.

TABLE 23: SOUTHERN WHITES AND NORTHERN NEGROES, BY STATES, ARMY RECRUITS

Whites		Negroes	
State	Median Score	State	Median Score
Mississippi	41.25	Pennsylvania	42.00
Kentucky	41.50	New York	45.02
Arkansas	41.55	Illinois	47.35
Georgia	42.12	Ohio	49.50

It was suggested at the time that one of two factors might account for these results: 1, the superior environment of the northern Negro, or 2, a selective migration of the more intelligent Negroes from South to North. The Army testers did not decide between these alternatives.

More recent studies, for the most part conducted upon children rather than upon adults, have in general corroborated these findings. There is on the average a difference of about seven points in the I.Q. of northern and southern Negro children (Klineberg, 13). Usually the northern Negroes are still below the White norm, but in some studies they show no inferiority whatsoever. Clark (3), for example, gave the National Intelligence Test to 500 Negro elementary school children in five schools in Los Angeles, and obtained a median I.Q. of 104.7, which is slightly above that of the White children with whom they were compared. Peterson and Lanier (19) gave a series of tests to twelve-year-old White and Negro boys in three different cities, Nashville, Chicago and New York. They found in general that whereas in Nashville there was a marked superiority of White over Negro boys, in Chicago this was not nearly so great, and in New York it disappeared altogether. Their conclusion was that these results could best be explained on the theory that there had been a selective migration northward, and that New York in particular had attracted an especially intelligent class of Negro migrants. Incidentally, they interpreted Clark's results in Los Angeles in a like manner.

This problem of selective migration appears to the writer to be crucial in the present status of Negro intelligence testing. If there is such a selection, the superiority of the New York and Los Angeles samples will prove nothing as to the intelligence of the average Negro; these groups will then be exceptions. If, on the other hand, there is no selective migration on the basis of intelligence, their superiority can mean only that an improved environment may raise the test scores of the Negro to the White level. In that case the whole argument for a racial difference as based on tests of intelligence will have no foundation.

A series of studies recently completed at Columbia University (see Klineberg, 13) has been directed toward a solution of this problem. In one study the attempt was made to

discover whether those Negroes who left the South for the
North showed a measurable superiority in intelligence over
those who stayed behind. For this purpose the school records
in three southern cities, Birmingham, Nashville and Charleston (South Carolina), were examined carefully to see how
the marks obtained by those children who had migrated to
the North compared with those who remained behind. The
records for 1915-1930 were studied in this manner. When it
was discovered that a particular Negro boy had left Nashville, let us say, for New York or Chicago in 1927 after
finishing the fifth grade, the records were examined to determine where he had ranked in comparison with the other
members of his class. A simple statistical formula was used
for transmuting his rank into a score based upon percentile
position in the class, so that the ranks of all the children
could be placed on a comparable basis. The destination of
the migrant was usually learned from the school authorities.
In this way over 500 cases were collected of migrants who
were known to have gone to one or another of the large
northern cities, and the results were analyzed for any indication of their superiority.

There was no evidence in favor of a selective migration.
As it happened, the migrants from Charleston were a somewhat superior group; those from Nashville were just about
average; those from Birmingham were definitely below. The
migrants as a group were almost exactly at the average of
the whole Negro school population in these three southern
cities. Whatever the selective factors in migration may be,
they appear to differ markedly for the different communities. To the extent that school marks are a measure of ability,
the use of the blanket phrase "selective migration" is obviously unwarranted, as it is by no means invariably the
superior persons who leave.

It may be that this study will be criticized on the ground that it deals with the children, whereas the adults migrate, taking their children along. It should be remembered, however, that when selective migration is used as an explanation of the superiority of Negro children in Los Angeles or New York, it is necessarily assumed that they are superior because their parents were superior. These children did not themselves migrate; they also were brought to the northern cities by their parents or grandparents. In the hypothesis of selective migration as accounting for northern superiority, there is involved the assumption of the superiority of the stock rather than of the individual, and the use of children in this study is therefore perfectly justifiable.

So far then, we have no right to assume that the superiority of northern Negroes is due to selection. On the other hand, we have very direct evidence of the degree to which the northern environment may affect the test performance of southern-born Negro children. In our series of studies over 3000 Negro school children in Harlem in New York City were tested, the measures including a number of different linguistic and performance tests—the Stanford-Binet, the National Intelligence Test, Otis Intermediate, Pintner-Paterson, Minnesota Form Board. In each study the children examined were of the same sex, the same age, attended the same or similar schools in Harlem, were all southern-born and of approximately the same social and economic status. They differed as far as could be ascertained only in one important respect, namely, the number of years during which they had been living in New York. In each case they were compared with a New-York-born group which was taken as the standard.

It was argued that if the superiority of the northern over the southern Negroes is entirely due to selective migration, the length of residence in New York City should make no appreciable difference in the test scores, since all the migrants have presumably been selected for high intelligence. If, however, the environment has an effect, this should show itself in a gradual improvement in the test scores at least roughly proportionate to the length of time during which the superior environment has had a chance to operate. It was felt, therefore, that this procedure might make it possible to choose on strictly experimental grounds between the two alternatives.

The results vary slightly in the different studies, but almost without exception they agree in showing that the lowest scores are obtained by the groups which have most recently arrived from the South. There is a close though by no means perfect relationship between test score and length of residence in New York. This is illustrated in the following two tables, the first of which presents the combined Binet I.Q.'s obtained in two studies, one on ten-year-old boys and the other on ten-year-old girls:

TABLE 24: BINET I.Q. AND LENGTH OF NEW YORK RESIDENCE (KLINEBERG)

Group	Number of Cases	Average I.Q.
Less than one year	42	81.4
One-two years	40	84.2
Two-three years	40	84.5
Three-four years	46	88.5
More than four years	47	87.4
New-York-born	99	87.3

The second table presents the combined National Intelligence Test scores obtained in three studies, two on twelve-year-old boys and the third on twelve-year-old girls.

There appears to be no doubt that an improvement in the environment, with all that that implies, can do a great deal to raise the intelligence test scores. Interestingly enough,

TABLE 25: N.I.T. SCORE AND LENGTH OF RESIDENCE (KLINEBERG)

Residence Years	Number of Cases	Average Score
One and two years....................	150	72
Three and four years..................	125	76
Five and six years.....................	136	84
Seven and eight years.................	112	90
Nine and more years..................	157	94
Northern-born........................	1017	92

this improvement seems to take place most markedly in the first five or six years; those children who have lived in New York for a longer period seem to show little further advancement. The subjects in these studies were all ten- and twelve-year-old children; and the results probably mean that when the school years have been spent entirely in New York City, the environmental opportunities may be said to have been equalized. It should be added that with the performance tests this result is not so clear, and that the environmental effect appears largely to be restricted, as far as these studies go, to tests with a definite linguistic component.

Two further checks were applied to this material. In one of the studies, anthropometric measurements were taken in order to determine whether the various migrating groups differed from one another in their possession of Negroid characteristics. It was found that the New-York-born group was a little less Negroid than those born in the South, but there was no difference between the groups corresponding to their length of residence in New York. This factor therefore can obviously not account for the observed differences in intelligence. In the second place, the question was asked whether there was any indication that the quality of the migrants was deteriorating, and that this fact rather than the change in the environment might account for the better showing of the earlier migrants. This was studied by comparing in two successive years two groups of twelve-year-old boys who had lived in New York the same length of time. The results showed that almost invariably the later migrants were superior. There is therefore no indication of a deterioration in the quality of the more recent migrants, and the correspondence between test score and length of residence in New York seems to be due to the influence of the better environment.

This finding is in agreement with the results obtained by Long (15) and McAlpin (18). Long studied third- and fifth-grade Negro migrant children in the city of Washington, and found a similar rise proportionate to length of residence. McAlpin used the Kuhlmann-Anderson test on Negro school children in Washington and found a difference of about six I.Q. points between those born in the city and those who had migrated from the South. Peterson and Lanier (19) in their important study also found New-York-born Negro children to be superior to those born elsewhere (although the difference was not entirely reliable statistically).

Even in the northern cities the Negro children are usually below the White norms, although Clark's study in Los Angeles and Peterson's and Lanier's in New York showed no such inferiority. The real test of Negro-White equality as far as intelligence tests are concerned can be met only by a study in a region in which Negroes suffer no discrimination whatsoever and enjoy exactly the same educational and economic opportunities. Such a region is difficult to find, although there may be an approximation to it in Martinique or Brazil. Davenport and Steggerda (4) describe their Negro group in Jamaica as living on substantially the same plane as the Whites. From that point of view it is interesting to note that the differences between the two groups in Army Alpha were much smaller than in most other studies. There are eight sub-tests in Army Alpha; in four of these the Whites were superior, and in four they were surpassed by the Blacks. The total score for the Whites was 10.23, and for the Blacks, 9.64, a difference which is not statistically significant. It is safe to say that as the environment of the Negro approximates more and more closely that of the White, his inferiority tends to disappear.

It is the writer's opinion that this is where the problem of Negro intelligence now stands. The direct comparison between Negroes and Whites will always remain a doubtful procedure because of the impossibility of controlling the various factors which may influence the results. Intelligence tests may therefore not be used as measures of group differences in native ability, though they may be used profitably as measures of accomplishment. When comparisons are made within the same race or group, it can be demonstrated that there are very marked differences depending upon variations in background. These differences may be satisfactorily explained, therefore, without recourse to the hypothesis of innate racial differences in mental ability.

NORDIC, ALPINE AND MEDITERRANEAN

It was mentioned in the preceding chapter that most tests of European groups in America show a definite superiority of north Europeans over immigrants from central and southern Europe. The results of the Army testing program (24) are too well known to require more than passing comment; they showed the groups from the British Isles, Germany, Holland and the Scandinavian countries to rank well above those from Greece, Russia, Italy and Poland. Subsequent studies in this country, for the most part of children of immigrants, gave much the same rank order; the investigations of Goodenough (8) and Hirsch (11a) may be taken as representative.

Two important inferences were drawn from these findings and presented in considerable detail by Brigham (2a). The first was that the various European groups from which these samples came differed in much the same way as did their representatives in America; the second, that there were also innate differences between the racial stocks—Nordic, Alpine and Mediterranean—of which the European nations were composed. The first of these inferences has been legitimately challenged because of the possibility that the various groups of immigrants are not equally representative. As Hankins (9) writes, "our immigrants are not fair samples of their respective nationalities" (p. 326). The only fair comparison is between the European groups in Europe, and even in that case it is no easy matter to find unselected and perfectly typical samples.

The second inference is a little more complicated. What Brigham did, was to give tentative estimates of the proportion of Nordic, Alpine and Mediterranean blood in each of the European countries from which the immigrants came. For example, Germany is estimated as being 40 per cent Nordic and 60 per cent Alpine; Italy is 5 per cent Nordic, 25 per cent Alpine and 70 per cent Mediterranean; Sweden is 100 per cent Nordic; Russia is 5 per cent Nordic and 95 per cent Alpine, etc. In order to obtain an estimate of the intelligence of the three European races, the distributions of the intelligence test scores were divided according to these proportions and recombined into Nordic, Alpine and Mediterranean groups. That is to say, since the Germans were assumed to be 40 per cent Nordic and 60 per cent Alpine, 40 per cent of the German subjects were listed with the Nordics, and were each assumed to have obtained the average

German score; the remaining 60 per cent were similarly listed with the Alpines. The same was done with all the other nationalities. The results showed a definite and reliable superiority of the Nordic over the other two groups.

Most of the criticism of this procedure came from the anthropologists. The brief review given in Chapter II of the racial composition of European nations and of the intricate relation between race and nation has shown the difficulty of inferring from one to the other. As Lowie (17) writes: "With a given Italian we do not know the proportion of Alpine and Mediterranean and possibly Nordic, blood" (p. 29). It is quite impossible to assume, as Brigham does, that the German sample in America is 60 per cent Alpine and 40 per cent Nordic without knowing much more than we do about the physical characteristics and the exact geographical origin of the American sample. In any case the procedure of dividing the German score proportionately between the Alpine and Nordic components is really inconsistent with the view that there are racial differences in intelligence, since these differences should also hold between the various racial components of one and the same nation. The whole relation between test score, immigrant sample, nation and race is too complex to be treated in this fashion. It should be noted that Brigham himself no longer accepts the conclusions drawn in his earlier study (2b).

At least two studies have been conducted in this country in an attempt to answer these anthropological criticisms. Estabrooks (5a) used cephalic index as a criterion of race, and calculated the coefficients of correlation between this index and the results of the intelligence tests. As the correlation was negligible, he concluded that race and intelligence are not related. This procedure unfortunately does not distinguish between Nordics and Mediterraneans, who are both long-headed; and as the most important apparent differences are between these two groups, the method can hardly be justified. Hirsch (11a) subdivided his various national and "natio-racial" groups into blond, mixed and brunette types, on the basis of hair and eye coloration. He argued that if the Nordics were really superior, the blond type within any nation should excel the mixed and brunette types within that same nation. He found no such superiority, and concluded that there were no racial differences. This technique is much better, but it remains doubtful whether a dark German and a dark Italian can be so simply equated. Boas (1) writes: "Individuals of the same bodily appearance, if sprung from populations of distinct type, are functionally not the same. For this reason it is quite unjustifiable to select from a population a certain type and claim that it is identical with the corresponding type of another population. Each individual must be studied as a member of the group from which he has sprung" (pp. 29-30).

For these reasons the investigation which is now to be reported (Klineberg, 14) attempted to obtain as pure samples as possible of the three European races in Europe. Three countries were chosen for this study—France, Germany and Italy—because each one of these is made up of at least two of the three races (France, of all three), so that comparisons might be made between different racial groups within the same nation, as well as between different samples of the same race. All the racial comparisons were made between rural groups, because in the large cities the mixture of types is so great as to obscure the nature of the constituent elements; samples were also taken in the cities, however, in order to make possible a comparison between rural and urban groups. The subjects were all boys from ten to twelve years of age.

In the rural districts a relative purity of racial sampling was obtained by choosing the subjects according to three distinct criteria used in combination. In the first place, those geographical areas were visited in which, according to the maps of the distribution of various traits, the physical characteristics of the race being studied were to be found with the least intermixture; secondly, only those subjects were chosen for the study who themselves as well as their parents had been born in that particular area; thirdly, every subject had to possess the physical characteristics regarded as typical of that particular race. Altogether seven rural groups were chosen: a German Nordic group in the Province of Hanover; a French Nordic in French Flanders; a German Alpine in Baden; a French Alpine in the Massif Central (Auvergne and Velay); an Italian Alpine in Piedmont; a French Mediterranean in the eastern Pyrenees; and an Italian Mediterranean in Sicily. The three city groups were taken from Paris, Rome and Hamburg. The tests were a group of six tests in the Pintner-Paterson Performance Scale. In all, 1000 boys were tested, ten groups with exactly 100 subjects in each.

For every subject the scores obtained on the six tests were combined on the basis of the Pintner-Paterson Point Scale (21, p. 176), in which the total number of points is used as a measure of intelligence. Table 26 gives the principal results for the ten groups:

TABLE 26: TEST SCORES OF EUROPEAN GROUPS (KLINEBERG)

Group	Average	Median	Range	S.D.	S.D. Av.	No.
Paris	219.0	218.9	100–302	46.2	4.62	100
Hamburg	216.4	218.3	105–322	45.6	4.56	100
Rome	211.8	213.6	109–313	42.6	4.26	100
German Nordic	198.2	197.6	69–289	49.0	4.90	100
French Mediterranean	197.4	204.4	71–271	45.6	4.56	100
German Alpine	193.6	199.0	80–311	48.0	4.80	100
Italian Alpine	188.8	186.3	69–306	48.4	4.84	100
French Alpine	180.2	185.3	72–296	46.6	4.66	100
French Nordic	178.8	183.3	63–314	56.4	5.64	100
Italian Mediterranean	173.0	172.7	69–308	54.2	5.42	100

These results indicate a definite, consistent and statistically reliable superiority of the city over the country groups. The differences among the three racial groups are small and unreliable. There are in addition marked variations between samples of the same race; the German Nordic group is a particularly good one, but the French Nordic is among the poorest; the Italian Mediterranean makes the lowest score, but the French Mediterranean has the best median score of all. This makes it impossible to attach any real significance to the concept of race as an explanation of the observed differences. The results offer no support to the theory of a definite racial hierarchy.

A very recent study by Franzblau (6) of Danish and Italian girls in Europe and America has also demonstrated the importance of sampling in connection with group differences. The investigation made use of the International Intelligence Test; and the results showed that whereas in the United States the Danish girls (tested in Racine, Wisconsin) were markedly superior to the Italian girls (in New York City), there was no difference between Danish girls tested in Copenhagen and Italian girls tested in Rome. This indicates that the immigrant groups in the United States do not adequately represent the parent European populations, and that the comparisons made in this country may therefore give no true information as to national or racial differences.

CITY AND COUNTRY

The superiority of the city groups irrespective of race or nationality suggests that environmental factors are by far the more important. There is, however, the possibility that selective migration from country to city is responsible. This problem also has definite importance in the whole field of racial differences and requires special consideration at this point.

A large number of studies agree in their demonstration that urban are superior to rural children in tests of intelligence. There has been a rather widespread tendency to explain this difference in terms of selection. In his summary of this material, Pintner (20) writes: "In general . . . it would appear as if the urban districts rate higher in intelligence than rural districts and that this is due to the migration of superior intelligence to the cities" (p. 253).

There is very little objective evidence in favor of this hypothesis. It is usually argued on purely logical grounds, that it takes energy and initiative to leave one's home in order to start all over again elsewhere; further, that the intelligent are more keenly aware of the limitations imposed upon them by rural life, and more alive to the richer possibilities of the city. Estabrook (5) writes, "energetic individuals will not in general remain in areas that do not afford opportunity for development" (p. 112). He believes that the blood of good stocks will seek a good environment. Hornell Hart (10) also argues that migration is a selective process, picking out the energetic individuals and those who are potentially distinguished in intellectual pursuits, and leaving behind the feebly motivated and the inferior. Similarly, Hirsch (11b) appeals to selective migration as accounting in part for the low general intelligence of the east Kentucky mountaineers, and Pyle and Collins (22) point to the better stock in the cities as one explanation of the retardation of rural children.

On purely logical grounds, however, almost as good a case may be made on the other side. It may be urged that those who are unsuccessful, and therefore presumably less intelligent, would be more likely to leave than those who have property and friends and standing in their community. For example, Zimmerman's (25) study of farm families in Minnesota has shown that the more successful stay on the farm more frequently than others, and that it is the unsuccessful or their children who migrate to the city to become wage earners.

Zimmerman suggests that the cities attract the extremes of intelligence, whereas the farms retain those who are average. Gillette (7) similarly believes that the cities are accumulating a disproportionate share of educated leaders on the one hand, and of pathological and subnormal classes on the other, but that the level of inherent talent is not disturbed by rural-urban migration. It seems clear that the question may be argued in many different ways, and that more objective methods are required to reach a solution.

In connection with intelligence test differences the investigation by Shimberg (23) is of interest. She found that although city children were superior to country children on the ordinary type of information test, this may be regarded as a function of the test, rather than as an indication of a true difference. If the information test is first standardized on rural children and then given to children in the city, the latter may actually prove to be inferior. Jones, Conrad and Blanchard (12) have also referred to the environmental handicaps faced by rural children, and after a careful analysis of the test items, have concluded that "a rural child moving to the city would increase his intelligence test scores, merely as a result of changed environmental conditions."

An indirect demonstration of this change was made in the case of rural Negro children migrating to New Orleans, Nashville and Atlanta. This was part of the general study of selective migration among Negroes referred to above, and the same technique was used as in the case of southern

Negro migrants to the North. The subjects, all of them twelve-year-old boys, the majority of whom were born in rural districts, were divided according to their length of residence in the city. Their scores on the N.I.T. improved very definitely in proportion to the number of years they had lived in the better environment. The figures are presented in Table 27.

TABLE 27: N.I.T. SCORE AND CITY RESIDENCE (KLINEBERG)

Residence Years	Average Score	Number of Cases
One year	38.3	39
Two	43.2	25
Three	44.7	36
Four	62.5	47
Five	56.2	52
Six	62.2	53
Seven and more	68.7	165
City-born	74.6	359

Very recently, the technique was also employed of studying the school records made by White rural children in New York, New Jersey and Connecticut, before they migrated to the large cities. In a first study it was possible to use only school acceleration or retardation as a rough measure of ability, as neither school grades nor intelligence quotients were available. In a second study, however, a number of counties were located in which intelligence tests had been used for the last few years, and where as a consequence a large number of migrants were found for whom test scores were on record. In both cases the migrants showed no superiority over those who stayed behind. Selective migration from country to city remains an unproved assumption.

This result has a definite implication for the question of racial differences. If there is no selective migration to the city, and if there are still such marked differences between rural and urban White children of the same race and pre-

sumably of the same hereditary constitution, it can be only
the difference in environment which is responsible. It is a
safe inference, therefore, that the environment may be similarly important in racial comparisons.

The material pertinent to selective migration has been
analyzed by Lorimer and Osborn (16), who conclude tentatively that "among large regional groups, in the United
States, differences in economic and other environmental
factors, such as climate, education, and so forth, may be
sufficient to explain cultural-intellectual differences without
recourse to genetic explanation" (p. 216).

Bibliography

1. Boas, F. *Anthropology and Modern Life.* New York, 1928.
2a. Brigham, C. C. *A Study of American Intelligence.* Princeton, 1923.
2b. Brigham, C. C. "Intelligence Tests of Immigrant Groups." *Psych. Rev.,* 137:1930, pp. 158-165.
3. Clark, W. W. "Los Angeles Negro Children." *Educ. Res. Bull.,* Los Angeles City Schools, 1923.
4. Davenport, C. B., and Steggerda, M. *Race Crossing in Jamaica.* Washington, 1929.
5. Estabrook, A. H. "Blood Seeks Environment." *Eugenical News,* 11:1926, pp. 106-114.
5a. Estabrooks, G. H. "A Proposed Technique for the Investigation of Racial Differences in Intelligence." *Amer. Natural.,* 62:1928, pp. 76-87.
6. Franzblau, R. N. "Race Differences in Mental and Physical Traits: Studied in Different Environments." *Arch. Psych.,* No. 177:1935.
7. Gillette, J. M. "Urban Influence and Selection." *Publ. Amer. Sociol. Soc.,* 23:1928, pp. 1-14.
8. Goodenough, F. L. "Racial Differences in the Intelligence of School Children." *J. of Exp. Psych.,* 9:1926, pp. 388-397.
9. Hankins, F. H. *The Racial Basis of Civilization: A Critique of the Nordic Doctrine.* New York, 1926.
10. Hart, H. N. "Selective Migration as a Factor in Child Welfare

in the U. S., with Special Reference to Iowa." *U. of Iowa Studies*, No. 7, Vol. I. Iowa City, 1921.

11a. Hirsch, N. D. M. "A Study of Natio-racial Mental Differences." *Genet. Psych. Mono.*, 1:1926, pp. 239-406.

11b. Hirsch, N. D. M. "An Experimental Study of the East Kentucky Mountaineers." *Genet. Psych. Mono.*, 3:1928, pp. 183-244.

12. Jones, H. E., Conrad, H. S., and Blanchard, M. B. "Environmental Handicap in Mental Test Performance." *U. of Calif. Publ. in Psych.*, 5, No. 3:1923, pp. 63-99.

13. Klineberg, O. *Negro Intelligence and Selective Migration*. New York, 1935.

14. Klineberg, O. "A Study of Psychological Differences Between 'Racial' and National Groups in Europe." *Arch. Psych.*, No. 132:1931.

15. Long, H. H. "The Intelligence of Colored Elementary Pupils in Washington, D. C." *J. Negro Educ.*, 3:1934, pp. 205-222.

16. Lorimer, F., and Osborn, F. *Dynamics of Population*. New York, 1934.

17. Lowie, R. H. *Are We Civilized? Human Culture in Perspective*. New York, 1929.

18. McAlpin, A. S. "Changes in Intelligence Quotient of Negro Children." *J. Negro Educ.*, 1:1932, pp. 44-48.

19. Peterson, J., and Lanier, L. H. "Studies in the Comparative Abilities of Whites and Negroes." *Ment. Meas. Mono.*, 5: 1929.

20. Pintner, R. *Intelligence Testing: Methods and Results*. New York, 1931.

21. Pintner, R., and Paterson, D. G. *A Scale of Performance Tests*. New York, 1917.

22. Pyle, W. H., and Collins, P. E. "The Mental and Physical Development of Rural Children." *Sch. and Soc.*, 8:1918, pp. 534-539.

23. Shimberg, M. E. "An Investigation into the Validity of Norms with Special Reference to Urban and Rural Groups." *Arch. Psych.*, No. 104:1929.

24. Yerkes, R. M. (Ed.) "Psychological Examining in the U. S. Army." *Mem. Nat. Acad. Sci.*, 15:1921.

25. Zimmerman, C. C. "The Migration to Towns and Cities." *Amer J. Sociol.*, 32:1926, pp. 450-455; 33:1927, pp. 105-109.

Chapter X

THE MEASUREMENT OF NON-INTELLECTUAL TRAITS

The Problem

RACIAL and national groups have been described as differing in personality as well as in intellectual ability. (See Chapter I.) Kretschmer (18), for example, speaks of the "childlike cruelty" of the Mediterraneans; Lenz (22), of the Nordic "sense of honor"; McDougall (24), of Nordic "introversion." These characterizations, important as they may be for a racial psychology, are made without adequate evidence, and clearly depend on a more or less accidental personal impression. There have been significant attempts to give a more adequate foundation to possible differences in personality, by basing them on the nature of the endocrines or of the total bodily constitution (Chapter III), but these have so far not been conclusive. The question arises as to the possibility of attacking the problem more directly, by an objective measurement of the "non-intellectual" traits, that is to say, traits other than those which can be studied by means of tests of intelligence.

The Difficulties

With the development in recent years of tests of personality and of special aptitudes and abilities, a number of attempts have been made to apply these methods to the study of racial differences. Unfortunately, the difficulties in this field are at least as great as in the case of intelligence testing. There are all of the same complications, and others besides.

Obviously if we wish to compare two racial groups for innate differences in personality, we have to make certain that these differences are not due to environmental factors. Social and economic background may have just as marked an effect upon the nature and degree of emotional expression, upon honesty, upon suggestibility, as upon the ability to solve linguistic problems. Motivation, rapport, culture in its widest sense, are just as important in both cases, and just as hard to control.

There are added difficulties in this field, arising out of the nature of the tests. There are two criteria which a test must satisfy if its use is to be justified. In the first place, a test must be *reliable*, that is to say, it must give consistent results if repeated on two different occasions. If the test cannot be repeated, the criterion of reliability may also be satisfied, in the case of a long test with many items, if one half of the test gives results very similar to the other half. In the second place, a test must be *valid*, that is, its results must agree with some independent criterion of the function which is being measured. In the case of the Binet, for example, the validity has been checked by measuring the correspondence of its results with school records, teachers' estimates, the diagnosis of a physician (in the case of the feeble-minded) —which are all accepted criteria of intelligence.

The tests used in connection with personality have usually failed to satisfy one or both of these criteria. The Downey Will-Temperament Test (6), for example, has been challenged on both these grounds; the Seashore tests of musical ability (33) have been criticized by Moss (26a) on the ground that there exists no constant relation between test results and musical endowment; Scudder and Raubenheimer (32) have made a careful study of several mechanical aptitude tests, and have shown that though they supposedly measure the same things, the correlation coefficients between them are very low. Hartshorne and May (12) obtained similar results in the case of their honesty tests, as did also Warner Brown (2) in connection with tests of suggestibility. These results do not necessarily mean that the tests are invalid, since they may each be measuring separate, highly specific functions. This very specificity, however, makes it difficult to use them as measures of so-called traits of personality. It is not unfair to say that the testing of non-intellectual traits has not progressed far enough to be of real value in the field of racial differences. As Daniel (5) writes: "Interpretation of test results cannot be more valid than the instruments used in securing the data. . . . Race comparisons are meaningless in investigations utilizing measures of non-intellectual traits and special abilities of uncertain reliability and validity" (p. 423).

It may be of interest, however, in spite of these complications, to refer for purposes of illustration to a few of the studies in this field.

PERSONALITY AND TEMPERAMENT

One of the best-known tests in this field is Downey's Will-Temperament Test, which depends largely upon changes in handwriting under varying conditions. It has been used in a number of racial comparisons, but Peterson and Lanier (29) report that it was found unsuitable as a test of racial differences, and that no significant results were obtained by its use. In the case of the Negro a number of investigations arrive at conflicting conclusions; those of Sunne (37), Peterson and Lanier (29), McFadden and Dashiell (25) and Hurlock (14) may be mentioned. Garth's (9a) study of Whites and Indians concluded that the former had "stronger personalities"; but just what that means it is difficult to say.

Crane's (4) study of race differences in inhibition has attracted considerable attention. Unfortunately his bias appears rather clearly in the initial question which he set himself to answer. "What is the psychological explanation of the impulsiveness, improvidence and immorality which the Negro everywhere manifests (p. 10)?" He believed it to be largely due to defective inhibition, and he constructed an apparatus by which he hoped to measure it. This consisted of a sort of guillotine in which a heavy block of wood was made to drop from a height toward the hand of the subject which was held on a platform below; he was told that the block would stop before it hit him, and that he was not to move his hand. At the same time, the subject was given a slight shock to create the illusion that the block had actually hit him. All movements of the hand were recorded on a kymograph. The results showed that both racial groups gave an almost equal number of withdrawals; the Whites gave a lesser reaction on the first drop, but required more trials before they were able to keep their hands motionless. The Negroes responded more violently on the first or second drop, but then gave a perfect performance. Crane concludes that in an elevator accident the colored man would at first be terrifically disturbed, and then comparatively calm, whereas the White might exhibit more control at the outset, but would remain disturbed much longer! Even this relatively unimportant conclusion may be questioned, as such an inference from the laboratory to the outside world requires further proof.

In the Pressey X-O Test (30), in which the subject is required to cross out those words which represent something that he fears or dislikes, Bond (1) noted that the total affectivity scores—the total number of cross-outs—was considerably greater in White than in Negro subjects. As far as these results go, they do not substantiate the notion that Negroes are more emotional. Sunne (37) used the same test on New Orleans school children, and found that the Negroes underlined more words representing what they thought to be *wrong*, and the Whites, more words for those things in which they were *interested*.

Sumner and Sumner (36) gave to 193 Negro students at Howard University the House Mental Hygiene Inventory (13), which is a modification of the Woodworth Personal Data Sheet. They found no reliable differences in percentage of neurotic traits between their Negro group and the White group tested by House.

The Allport Ascendance-Submission Test was given by Cooper (3) to a small group of Negro college students; their scores did not differ significantly from the White norms supplied by the Allports.

Kellogg and Eagleson (16) studied "social perception" in Negro children as measured by the ability to interpret the facial expression of a White woman in six different emotional poses. They found that in comparison with the data obtained by Gates (10) on White children, "a striking similarity was evidenced year by year in the data for the two racial groups." They conclude that the growth of social perception in Negro children is the same in all major respects as that which Gates found for White subjects. Staiman[1] tested White and Negro adults for their ability to judge emotional expression as posed by both a White and a Negro woman, and found no important differences.

Young (41) studied differences between Negro and White children in suggestibility by means of a test, the first part of which established "an alternating yes-no attitude in the child," that is to say, the first question was answered by

[1] Martin Staiman, Unpublished Master's Essay, Columbia University.

"yes," the second by "no," the third by "yes," and so forth; the second part measured the tendency of this alternating attitude to continue. The Negroes were found to be much more suggestible. Hurlock (14) also gave a number of tests of suggestibility to White and Negro children, and obtained a similar result. It is important to keep in mind in this connection that the attitude of the Negro toward the White examiner might have a marked effect on these reactions. It is probable that with certain Negro subjects and certain White experimenters the suggestibility might be heightened; with others it might be decreased. In the study by Ogeloff reported in Chapter VIII it was found that the Negro children tested in Brooklyn were rather negativistic in those tests which depended upon the prestige of the experimenter. There is probably no type of test in which the question of rapport plays a more important part.

The inconsistency of the results in this field can be illustrated by the results of two studies of "self-ratings" by Chinese subjects. In both cases Chinese students were asked to rate themselves on a five-point scale with reference to six desirable traits, and then to rate all other students with whom they were intimately acquainted. In the first study, made by Trow and Pu (39) in the United States, the great majority of subjects underrated themselves as compared with the standing assigned to them by their associates, and there seemed to be some evidence for a distinct racial or cultural trait. In a second study, however, made in China by Luh and Sailer (23), there was no such tendency to underestimation. These authors believe that the earlier finding might have been due to feelings of inferiority resulting from the presence of the Chinese in a foreign country.

An interesting study has been made by Lehman and Witty (20) of what they call "the Negro child's index of social participation." They find the Negro child much more likely to engage in play activities in a group, rather than as an individual. The Negroes have a higher index of social participation than the Whites. Donald Young (40) refers to the Negro as being an individualist; this can be only partly true, as there appears to be no doubt of his feeling of solidarity with his group, and his desire and need for companionship.

Lehman and Witty also advance the suggestion that many of the play activities of Negro children as well as the activities of adults serve as escape mechanisms from feelings of inferiority. A similar view is held in another connection by Guy Johnson,[1] whose careful study of the Negro press has revealed many tendencies of a ˙ compensatory character, to be explained only as a reaction to the Negro's inferior status. He feels a constant need to prove that he is really the equal of the White and he will seize upon every news item which enhances the prestige of his race. This is a fruitful concept, but it may easily be carried too far. Recent history is not lacking in examples of similar mechanisms among racial and national groups whose feeling of inferiority is not especially conspicuous.

MUSICAL ABILITY

It has often been suggested that the Negro has special endowments in the field of music. Moss (26), for example, writes: "The Negro possesses an innate sense of rhythm which appears in his songs and dances" (p. 95). "With the Negro, rhythm seems to be an innate quality, and he can extract music from any sort of instrument" (p. 104). Negroes themselves have often questioned statements of this sort. They have frequently suggested that the greater musical interest of the Negro, and the apparently greater ability pro-

[1] Unpublished.

ceeding from it, can best be explained on cultural grounds. It is true that in many Negro communities, especially in the deep South, music is an important part of life, but this is by no means universal. In the larger cities there are whole groups of Negroes to whom music means just about as much or as little as to the average White. In rural West Virginia, where the writer spent several months, he found very little interest in music, and that little was concerned not with spirituals, but with modern American popular songs.

The studies of Negroes and Whites by means of the Seashore Test of Musical Ability show very conflicting results. Even in the case of rhythm, which has sometimes been regarded as a Negro specialty, the differences are not consistent. Peterson and Lanier (29), Johnson (15) and Streep (35) found that the Negroes were superior in this respect, but Gray and Bingham (11) showed them to be inferior. Garth (9b) compared Negroes with American Indians, who are not usually regarded as particularly gifted in rhythm, and found the Indians to be superior. The same contradictions are found in the other tests of the Seashore battery. In the study by Peterson and Lanier (29), the Whites excelled the Negroes in the test for consonance, whereas Gray and Bingham (11) found that consonance was the only test in which the Negroes did better than the Whites. Garth's (9b) summary of part of this material concludes with the statement that there are no satisfactory group differences, and certainly no clear-cut differences between the races.

CONCLUSION

This review is far from complete, but it is doubtful whether even a more exhaustive survey would reveal any significant racial differences. The problem is of especial importance, but there are in the meantime no satisfactory methods for its solution. It is a hopeful sign that so much attention has recently been directed toward the improvement of techniques in this field, and that new methods are continually being suggested (see Murphy and Murphy, 27; Symonds, 38). There is no doubt that tests of personality require a great deal of improvement before they may be applied with profit to the problem of racial psychology.

BIBLIOGRAPHY

1. Bond, H. M. "An Investigation of the Non-Intellectual Traits of a Group of Negro Adults." *J. Abn. & Soc. Psych.*, 21:1926, pp. 267-276.

2. Brown, W. "Individual and Sex Differences in Suggestibility." *U. of Calif. Publ. in Psych.*, 2, No. 6:1916, pp. 291-430.

3. Cooper, P. "Notes on Psychological Race Differences." *Social Forces*, 8:1930, pp. 425-426.

4. Crane, A. L. "Race Differences in Inhibition." *Arch. Psych.*, No. 63:1923.

5. Daniel, R. P. "Negro-White Differences in Non-Intellectual Traits, and in Special Aptitudes." *J. Negro Educ. Yearbook*, III:1934, pp. 411-423.

6. Downey, J. *The Will-Temperament and Its Testing*. Yonkers-on-Hudson, 1923.

7. Frazier, E. F. *The Negro Family in Chicago*. Chicago, 1932.

8. Garrett, H. E. "Jews and Others: Some Group Differences in Personality, Intelligence, and College Achievement." *Person. J.*, 7:1929, pp. 341-348.

9a. Garth, T. R., and Barnard, M. A. "The Will-Temperament of Indians." *J. App. Psych.*, 11:1927, pp. 512-518.

9b. Garth, T. R. *Race Psychology*. New York, 1931.

10. Gates, G. S. "An Experimental Study of the Growth of Social Perception." *J. Educ. Psych.*, 14:1923, pp. 449-462.

11. Gray, C. T., and Bingham, C. W. "A Comparison of Certain Phases of Musical Ability of Colored and White Public School Pupils." *J. Educ. Psych.*, 20:1929, pp. 501-506.

12. Hartshorne, H., and May, M. A. *Studies in the Nature of Character. Studies in Deceit,* Vol. I, New York, 1928.

13. House, S. D. "A Mental Hygiene Inventory." *Arch. Psych.*, 14, No. 88:1927, pp. 1-112.

14. Hurlock, E. B. "Will-Temperament of White and Negro Children." *J. Genet. Psych.*, 38:1930, pp. 91-100.

15. Johnson, G. B. "A Summary of Negro Scores on the Seashore Music Talent Tests." *J. Comp. Psych.*, 11:1931, pp. 383-393.

16. Kellogg, W. W., and Eagleson, B. M. "The Growth of Social Perception in Different Racial Groups." *J. Educ. Psych.*, 22: 1931, pp. 367-375.

17a. Klineberg, O. "An Experimental Study of Speed and Other Factors in 'Racial' Differences." *Arch. Psych.*, No. 93:1928.

17b. Klineberg, O. "A Study of Psychological Differences between 'Racial' and National Groups in Europe." *Arch Psych.*, No. 132:1931.

18. Kretschmer, E. *The Psychology of Men of Genius*. New York, 1931. (Trans.)

19. Lambeth, M., and Lanier, L. H. "Race Differences in Speed of Reaction." *J. Genet. Psych.*, 42:1933, pp. 255-297.

20. Lehman, H. C., and Witty, P. A. "The Negro Child's Index of More Social Participation." *J. App. Psych.*, 10:1926, pp. 462-469.

21. Lehman, H. C., and Witty, P. A. "Some Compensatory Mechanisms of the Negro." *J. Abn. and Soc. Psych.*, 23:1928, pp. 28-37.

22. Lenz, F. "Psychological Differences between the Leading Races of Mankind." Chapter XV in Baur, Fischer and Lenz, *Human Heredity*, New York, 1931, pp. 623-700.

23. Luh, C. W., and Sailer, R. C. "The Self-Estimation of Chinese Students." *J. Soc. Psych.*, 4:1933, pp. 245-249.

24. McDougall, W. *Is America Safe for Democracy?* New York, 1921.

25. McFadden, J. H., and Dashiell, J. F. "Racial Differences as Measured by the Downey Will-Temperament Test." *J. App. Psych.*, 7:1923, pp. 30-53.

26. Moss, F. A. *Your Mind in Action: Applications of Psychology.* Cambridge, Mass., 1929.

26a. Moss, J. C. "The Yardstick Applied to Musical Talent." *The Mus. Quart.*, 16:1930, pp. 236-262.

27. Murphy, G., and Murphy, L. B. *Experimental Social Psychology.* New York, 1931.

28. Peterson, J. *The Comparative Abilities of White and Negro Children.* Baltimore, 1923.

29. Peterson, J., and Lanier, L. H. "Studies in the Comparative Abilities of Whites and Negroes." *Ment. Meas. Mono.,* 5: 1929.

30. Pressey, S. L. "A Group Scale for Investigating Emotions." *J. Abn. Psych.,* 16:1921, pp. 55-64.

31. Roback, A. A. "Have the Jews an Inferiority Complex?" *B'nai Brith Mag.,* 39:1925, p. 339.

32. Scudder, C. R., and Raubenheimer, A. S. "Are Standardized Mechanical Aptitude Tests Valid?" *J. Juv. Res.,* 14:1930, pp. 120-123.

33. Seashore, C. E. *The Measurement of Musical Talent.* New York, 1915.

34. Seashore, C. E. "Three New Approaches to the Study of Negro Music." *Annals Amer. Acad. Pol. and Soc. Sci.,* 140:1928, pp. 191-192.

35. Streep, R. "A Comparison of White and Negro Children in Rhythm and Consonance." *J. App. Psych.,* 15:1931, pp. 53-71.

36. Sumner, F. C., and Sumner, F. H. "Mental Health of White and Negro College Students." *J. Abn. & Soc. Psych.,* 26: 1931, pp. 28-36.

37. Sunne, D. "Personality Tests: White and Negro Adolescents." *J. App. Psych.,* 9:1925, pp. 256-280.

38. Symonds, P. M. *Diagnosing Personality and Conduct.* New York, 1931.

39. Trow, W. C., and Pu, S. T. "Self-ratings of the Chinese." *Sch. and Soc.,* 26, No. 659:1927, pp. 213-216.

40. Young, D. *American Minority Peoples.* New York, 1932.

41. Young, P. C. "Intelligence and Suggestibility in Whites and Negroes." *J. Comp. Psych.,* 9:1929, pp. 339-359.

Chapter XI

RACE MIXTURE

The Problem

THE problem of race mixture, or miscegenation, has important points of contact with the whole field of racial differences. In the minds of most people the decision as to the relative superiority and inferiority of various races must necessarily precede their attitude toward the crossing of races. Those who oppose the mixing of another group with their own usually do so on the ground that the other group is inferior, and that the crossing will therefore necessarily reduce the quality of their own pure race.

Since the larger portion of this book is concerned with the question of race differences, there is no need of its further discussion at this point. Those who agree that there is no scientific foundation for the doctrine of racial superiority may be less concerned about race purity, and they may possibly develop a more favorable attitude toward race mixture as a consequence. It should be realized, however, that the problem is not so simple, and that even in, the case of races of admitted equality, there is still a difference of opinion as to whether mixture should be encouraged.

These complications should be kept clearly in mind. Gates (12), for example, discusses various types of crossing and states that only when an advanced and a primitive stock intermarry do serious difficulties arise, and the mixture is undesirable. He writes that "the racial elements of the more primitive stock will dilute and weaken the better elements of the more progressive stock, with a retarding or degrading effect on the progressive stock as a whole. It is, therefore, clear that miscegenation between, for example, the white races and African races—which for ages have been undergoing separate evolution which must have been at very different rates, assuming that both are descendants from the same original stock—is wholly undesirable from a eugenic or any other reasonable point of view" (p. 336). It was pointed out in a previous chapter (Chapter II) that the greater primitiveness of the Negro had not as yet been demonstrated, and it is therefore not quite so unreasonable as Gates would suggest to refuse to accept his argument. Even in the case of two groups that would certainly be regarded by Gates as primitive and advanced, namely, the Hottentots and the Dutch Boers, respectively, Fischer (9) has shown that the mixture has been very successful. There are, however, other arguments against race crossing which do not depend upon the assumption of a racial hierarchy.

Alleged Disadvantages

Perhaps the most outspoken opponent of race mixture among American scientists is Davenport, who in a series of papers (3a; 3b; 3c), as well as in the book, *Race Crossing in Jamaica,* written with Steggerda (4), has described what he regards as some of its baleful consequences. Race mixture frequently results in "disharmony." "A hybridized people are a badly put-together people." When the mixed population inherits conflicting characteristics from two parent groups, the disharmony may be marked. The Scotch have a large frame and large viscera, whereas the Italians have a small frame and small viscera; in crossing, there is danger of the combination of large viscera in a small frame, which may cause crowding, or of small viscera in a large frame, resulting in inadequate support. Similarly, the mixture of two groups, one with large teeth in large jaws and the other with small teeth in small jaws, might result in offspring whose teeth and jaws were disproportionate; Davenport regards this as responsible for the extent of tooth decay in America.

In the case of Negro-White crosses there are said to be corresponding disharmonies. The arms and legs of the Negro are long in proportion to his trunk, whereas those of the Whites are relatively short. Crossing might result in an individual with the long legs of the Negro and the short arms of the White, who has "to stoop more to pick up a thing on the ground than one with the opposite combination" (4, p. 471). This does not seem to be a very serious inconvenience; but in any case it is just as probable that he would have the "opposite combination," which would put him at an advantage in picking things up from the ground!

The authors find similar disharmonies in the mental sphere. In their study of Whites, Browns and Blacks in Jamaica by means of a group of intelligence tests, they report that on the average the Browns did not do so badly, but there was among them a greater number of persons "who were muddled and wuzzle-headed." Just what these terms signify is not made very clear, nor is there any statistical evidence given for such a conclusion.

The fundamental assumptions underlying this whole point of view have been challenged in a series of publications by Castle (2a; 2b; 2c), who points out that the theory of physical disharmony is based upon the fallacy of a unit character inheritance of specific organs. In an experiment in which cross breeding occurred between two species of rabbits, one of which was four times the average weight of the other, no disharmony was observed in the offspring. The hybrids are intermediate in weight, and "all parts of the skeleton are intermediate and *suited* to each other, all being developed under a common influence, the fundamental rate of growth, which is the master controller of all general ontogenetic processes from early cleavage stages on." It is clear that the success of many animal breeding experiments testifies in the same direction.

Castle points out further that a careful study of Davenport's and Steggerda's figures for arm and leg length gives no evidence in favor of their disharmony theory. The figures are given in Table 28.

TABLE 28: RACE MIXTURE AND BODILY PROPORTIONS (DAVENPORT AND STEGGERDA)

	Black	Brown	White
Leg length in cm........	92.5 ±0.4	92.3 ±0.3	92.0 ±0.4
Arm length in cm.......	57.3 ±0.3	57.9 ±0.2	56.8 ±0.3
Total stature...........	170.6 ±0.6	170.2 ±0.5	172.7 ±0.7

The differences among the three groups are so small that it is hard to see how any disharmony could possibly result. The Brown group is no more variable—if anything slightly less so—than the other two, which also argues against a special disharmony in their case. These arguments of Castle's seem conclusive.

Mjøen (18) has studied Lapp-Norwegian crosses from this same point of view and finds among them a "want of balance" as compared with the parent groups. His evidence comes mainly from the mental and social sphere. "Prostitutes and the 'unwilling to work' are found more frequently among types showing strong race mixture than among relatively pure types." It need hardly be mentioned, however, that characteristics of this kind are largely affected by cultural and social rather than biological factors. When the hybrids suffer certain special disabilities as compared with the parent populations, as, for instance, in the case of the

Anglo-Indian mixtures in India, specific problems may arise to influence the further history of that group. Castle (2c) criticizes Mjøen for his neglect of the social factors, pointing out that human race problems are by no means exclusively biological in character.

Alleged Advantages

In favor of race crossing it has been urged that it often results in "hybrid vigor," a phenomenon by virtue of which the mixed group may be superior in many respects to the "pure" races. If we regard inbreeding as bad, it should follow that race mixture, an extreme form of outbreeding, should be correspondingly valuable. It is now widely recognized that inbreeding is dangerous not so much in itself as in the opportunity it gives for defective recessive genes to show themselves as the result of the mating of two individuals with exactly the same potential defects. If a brother and a sister have absolutely no flaws in their genetic constitution, there is no reason why they should not have perfectly normal, healthy offspring; it is because these flaws are latent that there is always a possible danger in this form of mating. The more similar the heredity of the two parents, the greater is this danger. In the case of two distinct races, the chances of defective offspring are presumably reduced, since corresponding defective genes will not so readily occur. The genetic weaknesses will be present in both parents, but they will probably be related to different characteristics, and therefore have a much better chance of remaining recessive.

Jennings (16) writes: "The union of two somewhat different parents to produce offspring has indeed many advantages. . . . Often one parent, or both, carries imperfect genes, that taken alone would result in defective offspring. The union of two is therefore a method of insurance; a device by which the frequency of getting at least one good gene to each pair is greatly increased. The mating of two slightly diverse races often gives offspring that are superior to either race. The chromosomes are not sufficiently diverse to poison each other; the structures produced are not incompatible, but instead are supplementary. The offspring therefore excel the parent in vigor and efficiency" (pp. 276-277).

Several studies of mixed-blood groups lend support to this notion of hybrid vigor. Boas' (1) anthropometric investigation of the half-blood Indian showed him to be taller than either of the parent groups (the White parents were mostly of French extraction), with more children per family than the pure-blood Indian, the averages being 7.9 and 5.9 children, respectively, in the case of mothers over forty years of age. Fischer's (9) well-known study of the Rehobother Bastaards, a mixture of Hottentots and Boers in South Africa, reports them to be vigorous mentally as well as physically, with 7.7 children per family several generations after the original crossing. Williams (24) has remarked on the vitality of the Maya-Spanish mixtures in Yucatan, and Rodenwaldt (21) makes a similar statement about the Mestizos in Kizar. It should be added in this connection that size of family is by no means a perfect indication of the amount of physical vigor.

One of the most important recent studies of race mixture has been made by Shapiro (22) in the case of the descendants of the mutineers of the *Bounty* and native Polynesian women. He reports favorably on their health and longevity, the size of their families and the excellence of their social structure. He concludes: "This study of race mixture on the whole rather definitely shows that the crossing of two fairly divergent groups leads to a physical vigor and exuberance which equals if not surpasses either parent stock. My study of the Norfolk Islanders shows that this superiority is not an ephemeral quality which disappears after the F_1 or F_2 generation, but continues even after five generations. . . . This conclusion regarding the physical vigor of the Norfolk hybrids applies also to their social structure, which on Pitcairn was not only superior to the society instituted by the Englishmen themselves, but also contained elements of successful originality and adaptability" (p. 69).

Other studies of race mixture have, however, found no very clear evidence of hybrid vigor, for example, Dunn's (6) study of Chinese-Hawaiian crosses in Hawaii, and the investigations of the American Negro by Herskovits (13c) and Day (5). In all these three studies race mixture was not found to be harmful in any way, nor, on the other hand, was it found to have any special advantages, the hybrids being intermediate between the two parent groups in most of the traits measured. Hooton's (14) comment on Day's findings is worth noting: "I cannot see that these data afford any comfort to those who contend that miscegenation between Negroes and Whites produces anthropologically inferior types."

The special interest in Herskovits' results arises from his discovery that the group of Negro-White hybrids, containing also a large intermixture of Indian blood, is inbreeding to form a type that is no more variable than the parent populations. This conflicts with the theoretical position of Jennings (16), who argues that a mixed race may be expected to be very heterogeneous; further knowledge of the hereditary principles involved is necessary before this whole question of variability can be properly interpreted.

A special case for the superiority of one mixed-blood group has been made by Reuter (20) in an attempt to account for the fact that mulattoes appear to have a greater achievement

to their credit than have full-blood Negroes. He argues that
a form of biological selection has taken place which is responsible for this difference. On the White side the ancestry
was probably not superior, but on the side of the Negro it
seems to have been the best elements of the race which entered into the mixture. Reuter argues that the White slave-
owners picked the choicer Negro girls for their mistresses,
and in this way a repeated selection occurred. In addition,
superior Black men tend to marry light girls, so that whatever talent there is in the Black group becomes a part of
the mulatto. "In the American mulatto the evolution of a
superior race may be seen in progress" (p. 163).

This argument as it stands completely overlooks the important part played by social and educational factors. It is
well known, for example, that even during slavery the light-
colored Negroes were given special opportunities, engaged
in domestic service instead of working in the fields, and were
encouraged to acquire an education. Since they were in many
cases related to their master, the proscription against teaching slaves to read and write was not enforced so far as they
were concerned, and it is not strange that they should have
far outstripped the Blacks. (See Carter Woodson, 25.) Reuter himself, in a later paper (20), appears to accept this position, and to explain the status of the mulatto entirely in
terms of superior opportunities, rather than as a form of
selection. He writes: "The chief explanation of hybrid superiority must be found in social rather than biological facts"
(p. 198).

Little can be said with any definiteness either in favor of
or against race mixture. On the biological side there seems to
be no great significance in the argument of "disharmonies in
detail," and not much more in that of "hybrid vigor." In
the case of the latter, it may be agreed that inbreeding is

frequently harmful; but it is not necessary to go outside the confines of any one race to find a mate with sufficiently diverse genetic lines to insure healthy offspring. Miscegenation as such is biologically neither good nor bad; its effects depend entirely upon the health and vigor of the individuals who enter into the mixture. The observed effects of race crossing appear to depend very much more on social than on biological factors.

A word is in place at this point concerning the widespread popular belief that a single drop of Negro blood in an otherwise lily-white family may result in the appearance of a coal-black baby several generations later. This appears to be a superstition without any foundation in fact. A small amount of Negro blood might conceivably produce slightly thicker lips or a faintly darker pigmentation, but for the combination of all the characteristics of a full-blood Negro there would be required the simultaneous effect of so many different genetic factors that for all practical purposes this may be regarded as an impossibility. It requires a relatively large amount of Negro blood to give a truly Negroid appearance. In the study by Day (5) referred to above, it is noted that one-quarter or less of Negro blood in an individual may make him unrecognizable as a Negro. In her particular subjects there was not a single quadroon who could not easily "pass for White." This may not hold in all cases, but certainly the notion of a sudden eruption of markedly Negroid characteristics out of a minimum of Negroid blood may safely be discarded.

THE INTELLIGENCE OF MIXED-BLOODS

Intelligence tests have been used in an attempt to discover whether there is any relation between degree of mixture and intelligence. Particularly in the case of the mixture of an allegedly superior group like the Whites with a supposedly inferior one like the American Indians or the Negroes, it was thought that there might be an improvement in intelligence as the proportion of White blood increased. This was the view of Ferguson (8), who gave a series of simple psychological tests to a group of Negroes, and found that when he divided his subjects on the basis of their Negroid appearance, the darker ones were inferior. This was before the days of the application of anthropometric measurements in this field, and the group was classified by inspection alone.

In the more recent studies, the procedure has been to make accurate measurements of certain Negroid traits, particularly skin color, nose width and lip thickness, and to calculate coefficients of correlation between these and standing in intelligence tests. The procedure employed is described by Herskovits (13a), who showed that in the mass these measures corresponded closely to degree of Negro blood as determined by the genealogies, although there were a great many individual exceptions. Herskovits also made a study of their relation to intelligence test performance among Howard University students and found the correlations to be insignificant, that is to say, there was no demonstrable relation of any kind between Negroid traits and intelligence. The same result was obtained by Peterson and Lanier (19a) in their study of Negro boys in New York City, and by Klineberg (17) in the case of West Virginia rural Negroes. It appears that when more refined techniques are substituted for the cruder methods of classification used by Ferguson, there is no clear indication within socially homogeneous groups that intelligence increases in proportion to the amount of White intermixture. It should be added, however, that even though no single physical Negroid trait shows any relation to intelligence, a combination of them which more truly reflected the amount of intermixture might possibly be of greater significance. In view of the advantages which mulattoes have had over pure-blood Negroes, this finding would still not prove their hereditary superiority.

The attempt has also been made to study this question in connection with mixed-blood Indians. In an early study by Garth (10) mixed-bloods were found to be regularly superior to full-blood Indians. Hunter and Sommermier (15) obtained a positive correlation of + .41 between degree of Indian blood and total score on the Otis Intelligence Test in the case of students at Haskell Institute, and they concluded that a racial difference between Whites and Indians is therefore indicated. Garth's earlier position was very similar; even though he noted the difference in schooling and school attainment between mixed and full-blood Indians, he at one time believed that an equality in this regard would not remove the observed differences. Later he pointed out that in these comparisons there was always the uncontrolled factor of the different social status of the two groups, and that the superiority of the mixed-bloods might therefore not be due to racial factors. In his most recent statement (11) he appears to reject the racial hypothesis entirely. A recent study by Eells (7) of mixed- and full-blood Alaska Indians found a rather close correspondence between the proportion of White blood and Binet score, but Telford (23) in North Dakota and Klineberg (17) among the Yakima Indians found no such relationship; in the latter study those subjects with the most and those with the least Indian blood made the lowest scores. The results therefore conflict too greatly to permit of any definite conclusion; even if the consensus of opinion argues in favor of the superiority of the mixed-bloods, there are, as Garth mentions, so many uncontrolled and uncontrollable factors operating to the advantage of the mixed group that the interpretation of the results in racial terms is not justified.

One final methodological point should be mentioned. The interpretation of the achievements of a mixed group in terms of race will always be doubtful unless we can know the exact nature of the component elements. The argument, for example, that if Whites are superior to Negroes the intelligence of the mixed-bloods should increase in proportion to their degree of White blood, depends upon the assumption that those who entered into the mixture were typical representative samples of the parent groups. If the White parents were an inferior group, or the Negroes a superior one, the reverse relation might hold; if the White parents constituted a particularly good group, the relation might hold, but it would be meaningless as far as racial differences are concerned. This is the problem of selection or sampling in a different form. It may not play any very important part; but until that is known, the results cannot be satisfactorily interpreted.

Conclusion

With reference to race mixture in general, it may be concluded that there are no proved advantages or disadvantages, as far as the hereditary make-up of the hybrids is concerned. The results of race crossing would appear to depend entirely upon the nature of the particular individuals who are concerned, and the social acceptability of the hybrids.

Bibliography

1. Boas, F. "The Half-Blood Indian." *Pop. Sci. Monthly,* 14:1894, pp. 761-770.
2a. Castle, W. E. "Race Mixture and Physical Disharmonies." *Sci.,* 71:1930, pp. 603-606.

2b. Castle, W. E. "Biological and Social Consequences of Race Crossing." *Amer. J. Phys. Anthrop.,* 9:1926, pp. 145-156.

2c. Castle, W. E. *Genetics and Eugenics.* Cambridge, Mass., 1923.

3a. Davenport, C. B. "Do Races Differ in Mental Capacity?" *Human Biol.,* 1:1929, pp. 70-89.

3b. Davenport, C. B. "The Effects of Race Intermingling." *Proceedings Amer. Phil. Soc.,* 56:1917, pp. 364-368.

3c. Davenport, C. B. *Characters in Mongrel vs. Pure-bred Individuals.* Washington, D. C., 1911.

4. Davenport, C. B., and Steggerda, M. *Race Crossing in Jamaica.* Washington, 1929.

5. Day, C. B. *Negro-White Families in the United States.* Cambridge, Mass., 1932.

6. Dunn, L. C. "Some Results of Race Mixture in Hawaii." *Eugenics in Race and State,* 2:1921, pp. 109-124.

7. Eells, W. C. "Mental Ability of the Native Races of Alaska." *J. App. Psych.,* 17:1933, pp. 417-438.

8. Ferguson, G. O. "The Psychology of the Negro." *Arch. Psych.,* No. 36:1916.

9. Fischer, E. *Die Rehobother Bastards und das Bastardierungsproblem beim Menschen.* Jena, 1913.

10a. Garth, T. R. "The Results of Some Tests on Full- and Mixed-Blood Indians." *J. App. Psych.,* 5:1921, pp. 359-372.

10b. Garth, T. R. "A Comparison of Mental Abilities of Mixed- and Full-Blood Indians on a Basis of Education." *Psych. Rev.,* 29:1922, pp. 221-236.

10c. Garth, T. R. "The Intelligence of Mixed-Blood Indians." *Psych. Bull.,* 24:1927, pp. 179-180.

11. Garth, T. R. *Race Psychology: A Study of Racial Mental Differences.* New York, 1931.

12. Gates, R. R. *Heredity in Man.* New York, 1929.

13a. Herskovits, M. J. "On the Relation between Negro-White Mixture and Standing in Intelligence Tests." *Ped. Sem.,* 33: 1926, pp. 30-42.

13b. Herskovits, M. J. "A Critical Discussion of the Mulatto Hypothesis." *J. Negro Educ.,* Yearbook III, July, 1934.

13c. Herskovits, M. J. *The American Negro.* New York, 1928.

14. Hooton, E. A. "Notes on Anthropometric Data" in *Negro-White Families* by C. B. Day. 1932.

15. Hunter, W. S., and Sommermier, E. "The Relation of Degree of Indian Blood to Score on the Otis Intelligence Test." *J. Comp. Psych.*, 2:1922, pp. 257-277.

16. Jennings, H. S. *The Biological Basis of Human Nature*. New York, 1930.

17. Klineberg, O. "An Experimental Study of Speed and Other Factors in 'Racial' Differences." *Arch. Psych.*, No. 93:1928.

18. Mjøen, J. A. "Harmonic and Disharmonic Race Crossings." *Eugenics in Race and State*, 2:1921, pp. 41-62.

19a. Peterson, J., and Lanier, L. H. "Studies in the Comparative Abilities of Whites and Negroes." *Ment. Meas. Mono.*, No. 5, Baltimore, 1929.

19b. Peterson, J., Lanier, L. H., and Walker, H. M. "Comparisons of White and Negro Children in Certain Ingenuity and Speed Tests." *J. Comp. Psych.*, 5:1925, pp. 271-283.

20. Reuter, E. B. *Race Mixture: Studies in Intermarriage and Miscegenation*. New York, 1931.

21. Rodenwaldt, E. *Die Mestizen auf Kisar*. Batavia, 1927.

22. Shapiro, H. L. "Descendants of the Mutineers of the Bounty." *Mem. of the Bishop Museum,* Honolulu, 1929. No. 1.

23. Telford, C. W. "Test Performance of Full- and Mixed-Blood North Dakota Indians." *J. Comp. Psych.*, 14:1932, pp. 123-145.

24. Williams, G. D. "Maya-Spanish Crosses in Yucatan." *Papers of the Peabody Museum,* 13:1931, pp. 1-247.

25. Woodson, C. G. *The Negro in Our History*. Washington, 1928. (5th Ed.)

Chapter XII

CRIME

INTRODUCTION

THERE have been many generalizations as to the predisposition of various races to different types of crime, as well as to crime in general. Frequently these have been made upon mere observation, and occasionally upon crime statistics; it is the purpose of this chapter to examine critically the evidence upon which the generalizations rest.

As an example of what may be found in this field and of the readiness with which race is held responsible for variations in criminality among groups, the views of Baur, Fischer, and Lenz (2) may be cited. These writers note that in the United States there is much more crime among Negroes than among Whites, and they conclude that this is "obviously due to the fact that the Negroes have less foresight, and that they have less power of resisting the impulses aroused by immediate sensuous impressions" (p. 678). They observe also that there is more crime among immigrants from southern and eastern parts of Europe than from the northwestern portions, owing to the fact that Nordics have "greater self-control, foresight, self-respect, and respect for the life and property of others" (p. 678).

As evidence of the superiority of the Nordics in this regard, a table is presented showing the amount of crime in the various provinces of Germany between the years 1882 and 1891; the figures represent the number of crimes for each 100,000 of the population.

TABLE 29: INCIDENCE OF CRIME IN GERMAN PROVINCES (BAUR, FISCHER, LENZ)

Province	Number of Crimes
Hanover, Oldenburg	711
Hesse, Nassau	729
Rhenish Prussia	746
Wurtemberg, Baden	811
Pomerania, Schleswig Holstein, Mecklenburg	822
Silesia	1060
Bavaria	1170
East and West Prussia	1570
Posen	1612
Upper Silesia	1711

These figures, which are very old, obviously require to be checked by more recent and more complete data. Even as they stand they are by no means consistent; to mention only one of the more glaring discrepancies, Wurtemberg and Baden make an excellent showing, and they are probably the least Nordic of all German provinces, with the one possible exception of Bavaria.

THE ANALYSIS OF CRIME STATISTICS

Crime statistics in general are about the most difficult to interpret accurately. If we are interested in comparing, for example, the crimes of Negroes and Whites in America, we have a great deal of available material in court and prison records. We may compare the number of convictions; but there is no way of taking into account the well-known tendency of many courts, particularly in the South, to convict Negroes more readily than Whites. We may compare the number of arrests, only to find it impossible to measure adequately the relative promptness with which a Negro is likely to be placed under suspicion. This point has recently been made by Woofter (24), who notes that "adverse impressions as to Negro criminality have prevailed, but the studies

in this field are as yet insufficient to warrant any assumption
of racial predisposition to crime, especially when it is remembered that the Negro is more likely to be arrested 'on
suspicion' or slight evidence" (pp. 582-583).

These are not the only difficulties. If we compare immigrant groups, for example, Poles and Irish in America, we
can draw no inference as to the criminal propensities of
these groups in their own countries, nor of the racial stock
to which they belong; we have to contend with the unknown
factor of sampling (discussed at length in Chapter IX),
which renders it impossible to know whether these immigrant groups are truly representative. Nor can we remove
the difficulty by comparing the figures for Poles and Irish
in their own countries, because we have no means of equating or weighing their respective methods of law enforcement and court procedure. Unless crime and criminals are
treated in exactly the same way in the two countries, no such
comparison would have any meaning. Even if we wish to
content ourselves with the figures for these two groups in
the United States alone, without making any generalizations
as to the parent countries, we should have to make the assumption that their standing before the law is identical—
which in New York City, at least, is certainly untrue, certain
groups having a distinct advantage over others in political
power.

One final danger may be mentioned—one common to almost all varieties of statistical comparison. It is always possible that the figures for one particular year or decade, or for
one particular section of the country, may be exceptional, or
at least not universally valid. It is notorious in the field of
statistics that a judicious choice of figures may prove almost
anything. A striking example is the analysis by McDougall
(16) of racial tendencies to suicide, the introvert character

of the Nordic supposedly making him more susceptible than either the Alpine or the Mediterranean to this particular solution of his difficulties. McDougall illustrates this point by reference to a not-unfamiliar form of domestic tragedy. A man learns that his wife has run off with someone else. If he is an extrovert, his anger will be directed against the external cause of his misfortune and he will commit murder; if he is an introvert, his sorrow will be turned inward upon himself and he will commit suicide. There are statistics which lend a certain amount of support to this theory; there are years in which some Nordic countries show a higher suicide rate than countries predominantly Alpine or Mediterranean. McDougall's figures follow (taken from E. Morselli's *Le Suicide*):

TABLE 30: ANNUAL SUICIDES PER MILLION POPULATION (MORSELLI)

Denmark	268	England	72	Spain	17
Scandinavia	127	Australia	90	Russia	30
N. Germany	150	Wales	52	N. Italy	46
S. Germany	165	Ireland	10	S. Italy	26

Unfortunately for this theory, Hankins (8) has collected more figures, and the additional material shows no such racial difference. Scotland, for example, a distinctly Nordic country which does not enter into McDougall's table, has one of the lowest suicide rates in the whole of Europe. Hankins' figures follow (taken from Mayo-Smith, *Statistics and Sociology*):

TABLE 31: ANNUAL SUICIDES PER MILLION POPULATION, AVERAGES 1887–1891 (MAYO-SMITH)

Saxony	340	Austria	159	Norway	66
Denmark	253	Belgium	122	Holland	58
France	218	Sweden	119	Scotland	56
Switzerland	216	Bavaria	118	Italy	52
Prussia	197	England	80	Ireland	24

Granting all these difficulties of interpretation, it is still of interest to examine some of these figures rather closely, particularly from the point of view of uncovering some of the cultural factors which may enter. These, rather than race, may make it possible to understand the observed differences. For example, Lombroso (14) has attributed to a racial difference the fact that in Italy murder and manslaughter are most frequent in those provinces with the most Mediterranean blood; Calabria, Sicily and Sardinia lead the rest of the country in homicide rate. There is no indication that this author recognized the importance of a difference in the folkways, particularly as manifested in the institution of the "vendetta" in many of the southern provinces. This institution alone would account for the fact that personal injuries and insults would be settled outside the law, in a manner determined by the particular code of honor prevailing in these communities. A person who did not react in the violent manner prescribed by this code would lose caste among his fellows. This, rather than a difference in racial type in Italy, is probably the most important single factor. However, Lombroso (13) is not always so dogmatic in his insistence upon race as a cause of crime. He has pointed out that the prevalence and type of crime in any area may be determined by geographical conditions, by climate and by economic necessity.

One of the most striking examples of a local peculiarity in the incidence of crime is found in the case of Artena in the province of Rome, known in the whole countryside as inhabited by thieves, robbers and murderers. Lombroso cites the following figures per 100,000 yearly; see Table 32.

It is unfortunately impossible to have comparable figures for other years, but Lombroso mentions that even in the Middle Ages Artena had a similar repute. It may be pointed out that Artena is not in one of the more Mediterranean

TABLE 32: INCIDENCE OF CRIME IN ARTENA (LOMBROSO)

Crime	Italy, 1875–88	Artena, 1852–88
Murder and manslaughter.....	9.38	57.0
Bodily violence...............	34.17	205.0
Highway robbery.............	3.67	113.75
Thievery....................	47.36	177.0

portions of Italy, and its criminal history argues very much more in favor of the importance of a set of local customs than of a special racial constitution.

CRIME IN THE UNITED STATES

Within the United States one of the facts to be yielded by a study of crime statistics is the large amount of crime in comparison with other countries. Gillin (5) refers to the United States as holding a leading place in world crime, noting that in 1916 Chicago, with only one-third the population of London, had 105 murderers to London's 9, and 20 more than all of England and Wales. New York City in the same year had six times as many homicides as London, and only 10 less than England and Wales together. The importance of these figures for our purposes lies in the fact that the foreign-born have so often been held responsible. Morrison (17) says that the high crime rate in America may be attributed "to the boundless hospitality of her shores." According to the 1910 census report, twice as many foreign- as native-born Whites were committed in proportion to their total numbers.

This last comparison illustrates still another statistical difficulty, as has been noted by Sutherland (21). The foreign-born are chiefly adults and consequently much more likely to figure disproportionately in the criminal records; they are also largely city dwellers, and as the city has more than its share of crime this, too, places them at a disadvantage. When a correction is made by considering only the population over fifteen years of age, the foreign-born do not contribute more than their fair proportion. The Immigration Commission of 1910 made a careful study of the criminal statistics of several cities, and concluded that the foreign-born had lower rates for arrests, convictions and commitments; the City Council Committee on Crime of the city of Chicago reached the same conclusion in 1915.

The recent careful investigation by the Wickersham Commission in 1929 (23) showed that this was true for the whole of New York State, and not only for the large cities. The number of arrests per 100,000 of the population 18 years and over was 207.8 for the foreign- and 346.7 for the native-born White. Only two groups of immigrants, the Mexican and the Greek, exceeded the figures for the native-born. Even the Italians, who are usually considered to have a high crime rate, showed slightly less than the native-born, 344.0.

There is only one item in which the foreign-born are charged more frequently, namely, for violation of the law governing the sale, possession and carrying of weapons. In this respect, the Mexicans have by far the greatest number of arrests, 240.8, as against 20.9 for the native-born. It is hardly necessary to point out that this may be explained by the "mores" of Mexico, where it is a regular custom to go armed in many rural communities. The same is probably true to a lesser extent of other immigrant groups who offend in this respect.

In crimes of violence some of the immigrant groups contribute more than a fair proportion. In homicide the native-born rate of 7.0 is exceeded by Austria with 9.4, Italy with 9.7, Lithuania with 14.3, and Greece with 116.4; in assault the native-born figure of 56.7 is surpassed by Poland with 62.0, Italy with 95.5, Greece with 232.7, and Mexico with

521.6. That this may to some extent be due to sampling is a warranted conclusion.

Changes in Criminal Tendency

Before interpreting these figures in terms of race it is important to note the interesting demonstration by Sutherland (21) of the way in which crime statistics become modified as the result of a change in culture. His analysis of commitments for murder, manslaughter and assault among criminals of Italian origin in Massachusetts in 1915 shows this very clearly. His figures follow:

TABLE 33: HOMICIDE AND ASSAULT, ITALIANS (SUTHERLAND)

Group	Commitments per 100,000
Born in Italy	192
Native-born, one or both parents born in Italy	24
Native-born of native parents	24
Native-born, one or both parents foreign, not Italian	22

The figures suggest that an apparent racial or national propensity toward a particular type of crime may entirely disappear under the modifying influence of a different environment. It becomes quite impossible, therefore, to attribute to this propensity a biological significance.

It is even more interesting to note how rapidly a change may occur in the kind of crime committed by a particular national group after the new environment has had a chance to operate. Sutherland cites the number of convictions of first- and second-generation Irish immigrants in Massachusetts in 1908 and 1909.

TABLE 34: CHANGE IN TYPE OF CRIME, IRISH (SUTHERLAND)

Offense	Irish Immigrants	Second Generation	Native Whites
Homicide	2.3	1.0	0.5
Rape	0.0	0.3	0.7
Gaming	1.2	2.7	3.6

These figures as far as they go are very striking. There appear to be fashions or folkways in crime characteristic of a particular culture and which are gradually assimilated by those who become a part of it. The Irish in America tend to lose or at least to reduce their relative readiness to commit homicide, but they adopt in proportion the apparently more American crimes of gaming and rape. Patterns in crime seem to be as much a part of culture as any other folkways.

A very recent study by Stofflet (20) in New Jersey has demonstrated a similar tendency for second-generation Italians and Poles to show fewer cases of homicide and assault than the immigrants of the same nationality, and at the same time to show an increase in predatory types of crime, that is, burglary and robbery. This is a change in the direction of the crimes committed by the standard group made up of native-born of native-born parents. A qualitative study of the conditions under which homicide was committed showed that among the immigrants it occurred usually in defense of "family honor," or to avenge a personal insult, or under the influence of drink, whereas in the second generation it almost invariably accompanied a predatory offense. There seems to be no doubt about a definite change in criminal behavior in the same national group within one generation. Giardini's (4) study of Italian convicts in Pennsylvania revealed substantially the same trend.

As far as total amount of crime is concerned, the real problem is presented not by the immigrants themselves, but by their children. Accurate figures are difficult to obtain; but Lenroot (11), Glueck (6) and others have shown that the native-born of foreign parentage make an altogether disproportionate contribution to both delinquency and crime. The very fact that this appears in the second and not in the first generation, makes it clear that it cannot have a racial or a biological basis, since this is obviously the same for both groups. The explanation is rather to be found in the mal-adaptation resulting from the conflict of cultures found in the second generation. Levy (12) has shown in his careful study of delinquents that in a great many cases they are led into difficulties with the law because of the opposition be-tween what their parents demand of them and what is per-mitted to their American friends. It is not difficult to see why this should happen. A second-generation Italian girl is strictly forbidden to attend mixed parties or to go out un-chaperoned with boys of her own age. In Italy she would not expect such freedom, but in America everyone has it, and this particular Italian girl sees no reason why she should be restricted by her old-fashioned parents; she runs away from home and ends up in the Juvenile Court. This sort of case is by no means an exception. The cause of the con-flict may vary, but something of this sort accounts for a very large amount of delinquency. Incidentally, this helps to explain its greater frequency among groups of south European origin, whose "mores" differ so markedly from those of America.

What is most needed in this field is a study of at least three generations in America of the same national or racial ancestry. The first generation is still strange, unadapted; the second is in the state of conflict; it is only in the third that assimilation has really taken place. It is therefore only in a comparison of, for example, third-generation Poles and Irish —to revert to the groups mentioned above—that we can hope for a solution of the problem of the racial factor in crime. These third generations are presumably equally adapted to American life and living under approximately equal cultural conditions. If after three generations the crime statistics still differ, either qualitatively or quantitatively, we should have evidence of a racial difference. Although in the meantime there are no such statistics, the material available for the second generation, incomplete though it is, points so clearly to the disappearance of the differences that it is reasonable to exclude the racial factor.

DELINQUENCY AREAS

The recent careful studies of those areas in large American communities in which crime or delinquency occurs with greatest frequency have given additional evidence in favor of the view that social and not racial factors are primarily responsible. One of the most important of these studies was made in Chicago by Shaw (18), who noted the number of arrests of boys 10 to 16 years of age in various parts of the city. He and his associates divided the city of Chicago into concentric circular areas with the Loop district as the center. The following table gives the number of arrests per 100 boys in 1926:

TABLE 35: DELINQUENCY AREAS (SHAW)

Community Areas	Arrests
1st mile from center	20.9
2nd " " "	10.7
3rd " " "	11.9
4th " " "	8.1
5th " " "	5.6
6th " " "	3.1
7th " " "	1.7

The interesting thing about Shaw's study from the racial point of view is that there was relatively little change in the delinquency rate, while the racial composition of the central area changed entirely. There have been successive waves of migration into this district, several groups following one another in rapid succession. Each of these groups held in turn the lowest-paid jobs and had to live in the poorest and most congested portion of the city. The group that happened to be living in this district invariably made an altogether disproportionate contribution to the city's crime and delinquency. For the time being, the race to which this group belonged might have been regarded as having a special propensity in this direction. Then the social and economic status of the group improved, enabling it to move to a better residential district, and incidentally to reduce its crime rate; its place, both in the congested area and in the city's crime records, was taken by the next group of migrants. An apparent racial tendency disappeared entirely under the influence of improved living conditions.

Similar studies have been made in other cities, and these results have been corroborated. Maller (15) has shown in New York City a high correlation between delinquency rate and a number of social factors, among which congestion is one of the most important. Burt (3) in London obtained a correlation of $+.77$ between delinquency and density of population, and of $+.67$ between delinquency and poverty. It may of course be argued that delinquency is not caused by these other factors, but that they are all the common result of the poor quality of the human beings who inhabit these areas. The recent social experiment by Shaw and his co-workers[1] has, however, shown more directly the effect of external factors. They have taken one particular area in Chicago with a high delinquency rate and have introduced into it a large number of recreational facilities—gymnasiums, playgrounds, clubs, reading rooms, etc.—so that the boys now have something to do with their leisure instead of engaging in gang activities. The delinquency rate has shown a remarkable decrease in a short space of time.

[1] Unpublished.

An Experimental Approach

Another indication of the relation between crime and so-cio-economic factors may be found indirectly in the interest·ing experimental-psychological *Studies in Deceit*, conducted by Hartshorne and May (9). These investigators were interested in the measurement of dishonesty among school children, and they used for this purpose an ingenious series of tests in which the subject was given a chance to cheat, without of course knowing the object of the experiment. A large number of children availed themselves of the opportunity. For our purposes the important result was the close correlation between the deception scores and the occupational level of the subjects. The authors show that the observed group differences are associated with social status. For example, a Jewish group of low social status cheated more frequently than the average American; a Jewish group of high status, less frequently.

The "Criminal Type"

One final problem should be mentioned. When one speaks of the relation between race and crime, one is really suggesting that the physical type of an individual or a group may in some way signify a special criminal propensity. In another form this relationship was discussed by Lombroso (13) in a manner which has had considerable historical significance. Lombroso, as is well known, suggested that there were certain physical signs, the so-called "stigmata of degeneration," by which the true criminal could be recognized—large projecting ears, a receding forehead, asymmetrical bodily proportions, and others. The signs of criminality were not directly racial, but Lombroso drew such frequent analogies between these and the characteristics used in racial classification as to suggest that indirectly at least race might be concerned. The prognathism, for example, which he found in 45.7 per cent of the criminals studied, is a Negroid trait, as are the woolly hair, thick lips and flattened nose, which are also of frequent occurrence; oblique eyelids and a scanty beard, which are Mongoloid traits, are also mentioned. The objection most frequently raised against this theory is that Lombroso paid too exclusive attention to the criminal population, and not enough to non-criminal groups of the same social and economic level, which might also have their share of the stigmata. Subsequent studies, of which that by Goring (7) is an outstanding example, have failed to confirm his findings, and the theory is now discredited in the minds of most scientists. There is one exception, however, in the person of Hooton,[1] who has recently revived the theory and adduced fresh evidence in its support. His data are not yet available, and so cannot at this point be properly evaluated. They seem, however, to show only slight and inconsistent differences between criminal and non-criminal populations.

BIBLIOGRAPHY

1. Aschaffenburg, G. *Crime and Its Repression*. Boston, 1913. (Trans.)
2. Baur, E., Fischer, E., and Lenz, F. *Human Heredity*. New York, 1931. (Trans.)
3. Burt, C. *The Young Delinquent*. London, 1925.
4. Giardini, G. I. "A Report on the Italian Convict," in *A Psychological and Educational Survey of 1916 Prisoners in the Western Penitentiary of Pennsylvania,* by W. J. Root, Jr., 1933.
5. Gillin, J. L. *Criminology and Penology*. New York, 1926.
6. Glueck, B. "A Study of 608 Admissions to Sing Sing Prison." *Mental Hygiene,* 2:1918, pp. 85-151.

[1] Preliminary Remarks on the Anthropology of the American Criminal. Radio Talk, April 22, 1932.

7. Goring, C. *The English Convict*. London, 1913.
8. Hankins, F. H. *The Racial Basis of Civilization: A Critique of the Nordic Doctrine*. New York, 1926.
9. Hartshorne, H., and May, M. A. *Studies in Deceit*. New York, 1928.
10. Laughlin, H. H. *Analysis of America's Melting Pot*. Hearings before the Committee on Immigration and Naturalization, House of Representatives, 67th Congress, 3rd session, Nov., 1922, serial 7-C, p. 790.
11. Lenroot, K. F. *Juvenile Delinquency*. Mimeographed Report, Children's Bureau, U. S. Department of Labor, Washington, 1929.
12. Levy, J. "Conflict of Cultures and Children's Maladjustment." *Mental Hygiene,* 17:1933, pp. 41-50.
13. Lombroso, C. *L'Uomo delinquente*. Turin, 1897. (5th Ed.)
14. Lombroso, C. *Crime, Its Causes and Remedies*. Boston, 1911. (Trans.)
15a. Maller, J. B. "Vital Indices and Their Relation to Psychological and Social Factors." *Human Biol.,* 5:1933, pp. 94-121.
15b. Maller, J. B. "The Trend of Juvenile Delinquency in New York City." *J. Juv. Res.,* 17:1933, pp. 10-18.
16. McDougall, W. *Is America Safe for Democracy?* New York, 1921.
17. Morrison, W. D. *Crime and Its Causes*. London, 1891.
18. Shaw, C. R., *et al. Delinquency Areas*. Chicago, 1929.
19. Shaw, C. R., and McKay, H. D. "Social Factors in Juvenile Delinquency." *Report on the Causes of Crime,* No. 13, Vol. II, p. 276. Washington, 1931.
20. Stofflet, E. H. "A Study of National and Cultural Differences in Criminal Tendency." *Arch. Psych.,* No. 185, 1935.
21. Sutherland, E. H. *Principles of Criminology*. Philadelphia, 1934.
22. U. S. Immigration Commission. *Immigration and Crime*. Washington, 1911.
23. Wickersham, G. W., *et al. National Commission on Law Observance and Law Enforcement*. Report No. 10, Washington, 1933.
24. Woofter, T. J., Jr. "The Status of Racial and Ethnic Groups," in *Recent Social Trends*, New York, 1933. Vol. I, Chap. 11, pp. 553-601.

Chapter XIII

MENTAL ABNORMALITIES

COMPLICATING FACTORS

THE scientific study of racial psychiatry has barely made a beginning. Although the question of the relation between race and mental disturbance is an interesting one, not only in itself, but in the light that it may throw on normal psychological differences, the available material is exceedingly difficult to interpret. For the most part, we are again dependent upon incomplete statistics, and as in the case of crime, there are many possible variables and many unpredictable ways in which they may enter.

Many of the complications are similar to those discussed in the preceding chapter. There is again the question of sampling in the case of foreign-born groups, the age distribution, relative concentration in urban and in rural districts, and social and economic status. Age distribution is even more important here than in the case of crime, as mental diseases are closely related to age. Table 36, from Winston (26), shows clearly how the incidence increases with advancing age:

TABLE 36: AGE INCIDENCE OF MENTAL DISEASE (WINSTON)

Age Group	Rate per 100,000 Population in 1922
Under 15 years	1.4
15–19	32.3
30–35	104.8
65–70	145.4

The median age of the general population in America in 1920 was 25.2 years, and the median age of first admissions

to psychiatric institutions in 1922 was 40 years. As the foreign-born are on the average older than the native-born, the
figures will have to be corrected for age in each case.

The foreign-born are proportionately much more numer-
ous in the large cities, where psychotic disturbances also are
more frequent. White (24) writes: "Density of population
and insanity go hand in hand. Mental disease is a disorder of
man as a social animal." The Federal Census in 1920 (7)
showed almost twice as many first admissions for urban
as for rural districts, the rate per 100,000 in the case of dementia precox being 15.1 and 8.0, respectively. It should be
kept in mind that these figures may also be affected by hospital facilities.

The importance of social and economic factors has been
demonstrated in the case of the Negro by Frazier (9) and
Bond (4), who find a close relation between occupational
status and the amount of family disorganization and psychological maladaptation. Smith (23) points out in a similar
connection that poor home conditions and lack of training
in the early years account for a large proportion of the delinquency and emotional instability found in many Negro
communities. That economic factors, directly or indirectly,
may influence the amount of abnormality very considerably
is suggested also by Frankwood Williams' (25) analysis of
the present situation in Russia (see Chapter XVI).

Another important complication in all of these statistics
is the degree and manner of hospitalization. There may be
marked differences in the willingness of a group to allow any
of its members to be committed to institutions; this may be
affected by economic as well as cultural factors, the wealthier
families having the means to care for the patient in their
own homes or in private institutions. In the case of the
Negro the figures may be disturbed by the inadequate hos-

pital facilities in the southern states; the Interracial Committee of Montclair, New Jersey (11), found that although the Negro constitutes about one-tenth of the population of the United States, he has available only about one-thirtieth of the hospital space. The figures for Negro psychoses derived from institutional records will therefore be incomplete. On the other hand, if the comparison is made in one of the northern states, care must be taken to give proper weight to the fact that the Negro tends to concentrate in the urban centers. It is obvious that a great many factors will have to be carefully controlled before racial comparisons of the total amount of mental disturbance have any meaning.

Insanity Among National Groups

Granting these difficulties, it may still be of interest to note the comparative figures for total insanity reported by Laughlin (13) in 1922. The figures in the following table are in terms of the ratio of insanity to the proportion which each group constitutes of the total population of the United States. A figure of 100 means that that group has exactly its proportionate share of insanity.

It need hardly be pointed out that the low rate of the Negro and the high rate of the total foreign-born may be explained by the factors indicated above. The other differences cannot always be so easily understood, and may well depend upon factors of selection or sampling with which we are not familiar, as well as upon the effect of the age distribution.

Although it has frequently been suggested that Jews have more than their share of psychotic disturbance, the available figures offer no support to this notion. Brill and Karpas (5) analyzed the admissions to the Manhattan State Hospital from 1908 to 1912, and found that the Jewish patients constituted .0009 of the total Jewish population of New York

TABLE 37: INCIDENCE OF INSANITY AMONG IMMIGRANT GROUPS (LAUGHLIN)

Group	Per Cent of the Quota Fulfilled
Japan	42
American Negro	57
Switzerland	69
Native White, both parents native	73
China	78
All native-born	83
Rumania	100
Native White, one parent native	104
Native White, both parents foreign	108
Canada	124
All Asia	130
Austria-Hungary	134
Mexico	137
Great Britain	156
Italy	157
France	158
All Balkans	162
Netherlands	171
Greece	172
Germany	174
West Indies	180
Portugal	181
Southeastern Europe	188
All foreign-born	192
Scandinavia	193
Northwest Europe	198
Turkey	200
Russia, Finland, Poland	265
Bulgaria	300
Ireland	305
Serbia	400

State, and the non-Jews, .0013 of the total non-Jewish population. Goldberg (10) made a similar analysis of the admission rate to the psychopathic wards of Kings County Hospital and Bellevue Hospital; in 1917 the Jews were 25.8 per cent of the population of New York City, but they were only 16.5 per cent of the psychopathic cases in these hospitals in 1918, and 14.5 per cent in 1919. In the entire state of New York in 1917, the Jews constituted 16.0 per cent of the population, and only 11.6 per cent of the total first admissions to the psychiatric wards of all state hospitals. Malzberg (14) also calculated that in New York City the Jewish first-admission rate was only 50-55 per cent of that among non-Jews. It is of course important to bear in mind that these figures may be influenced by social and economic status, and by the attitude of Jews toward hospitalization. It is also important to know what proportion of them attend private institutions. This does not imply any criticism of the figures above, but these possible sources of error need to be controlled.

More interesting than the total amount of mental disturbance within any one group is the relative frequency of occurrence of the individual psychoses. It has been suggested by Kretschmer (12), Pearce Bailey (1), Baur, Fischer and Lenz (2), and others that there is a close relation between the normal psychology of a group and the psychoses from which it suffers. If a group is habitually introvert, withdrawn from the world, "schizothyme," it should tend to show a rather large proportion of the introvert psychoses, particularly schizophrenia, or dementia precox. If it is normally extrovert, "cyclothyme," it should have more than its share of manic-depressive insanity. We noted in an earlier chapter (Chapter III) that Kretschmer has suggested a relation between the leptosome constitution and the Nordic and Mediterranean races, and that as a consequence these are more likely to be schizothyme and to show schizophrenia; the Alpines are pyknic, cyclothyme, and presumably more liable to manic-depressive insanity. The difference in the incidence of these diseases in northern and southern Germany is cited by Kretschmer as evidence in favor of this relationship.

Qualitative comparisons between hospital records in different countries, or even between different parts of the same country, suffer from the relative lack of objectivity in psychiatric diagnosis. The various psychotic conditions are not always so clearly separated from one another as to permit of a diagnosis upon which all psychiatrists would agree. The methods used in two different institutions may be sufficiently unlike to make a direct comparison of the figures impossible. May (15), for example, writes as follows: "The statement is, I think, also warranted that there is a considerable difference of opinion as to the classification of the different forms of manic-depressive insanity and that diagnostic procedure is far from being standardized. Many of these discrepancies are doubtless due to the difficulties in differentiating between certain cases of manic-depressive psychoses and dementia precox. . . . It must be admitted, moreover, that our fundamental conceptions of these two great groups do not permit of a hard and fast line of demarcation between them in all cases" (p. 426).

For this reason it is obviously not permissible to compare directly the figures reported by institutions in the various European countries in order to reach a conclusion as to national or racial differences. The comparison of these groups in the United States, on the other hand, suffers from our lack of knowledge of the selective conditions operative in migration. They are, however, the most satisfactory figures we have for these purposes, and it is interesting to analyze them for the light they throw on Kretschmer's theory.

The following figures are taken from the U. S. Federal Census of 1922 (8), but they have been arranged in the table in order to show possible racial differences. The terms Nordic, Alpine and Mediterranean at the head of each section have been placed there for convenience in comparison, but they are of course not strictly applicable. It is clear from the discussion in Chapter II that no European nation belongs entirely in one racial category.

The first table is for dementia precox, first admissions, per 100,000 population of the same nativity in the United States in 1922. The figures are taken from Pollock (19).

TABLE 38: INCIDENCE OF DEMENTIA PRECOX AMONG IMMIGRANT GROUPS
(U. S. CENSUS)

Nordic Groups	Number	Alpine Groups	Number	Mediterranean Groups	Number
England	13.4	Germany	14.6	Portugal	14.8
Scotland	14.3	France	19.7	Italy	24.6
Belgium	14.7	Jugoslavia	20.5	Ireland	31.9
Netherlands	15.4	Czechoslovakia	21.9	Spain	48.7
Denmark	16.7	Roumania	27.2	Greece	57.9
Norway	20.9	Switzerland	28.1		
Sweden	29.4	Hungary	28.8		
Finland	57.4	Russia	33.9		
		Poland	35.2		
		Lithuania	40.0		
		Austria	59.6		
Average	22.8		29.9		35.6

It needs very little observation of these data to show that Kretschmer's theory is not substantiated. There is almost the same range and the same variability in all three groups. There appears to be rather more dementia precox among the Alpine groups than among the Nordic, although Kretschmer's characterization would suggest the opposite result. Unfortunately, the individual patients were not diagnosed for either their constitutional or their racial habitus, and this comparison rests entirely on the racial composition of the groups in Europe. As far as they go, however, these figures argue definitely against any relationship of the kind Kretschmer suggested between race and psychosis. It may be noted incidentally that the only "Nordic" group with a really high incidence of dementia precox is the Finns, whose racial history is very complicated, and who probably have far less Nordic blood than the other groups listed; while the Austrians, who show the highest rate of all, come from one of the most purely "Alpine" countries of Europe. (It should be noted, however, that the Austrian group contains a substantial number of Jews.)

It may be added that these figures lend just as little support to the theory of McDougall (16), who regarded the Nordics as predominantly introvert, and the Mediterraneans as extrovert. The figures for schizophrenia among the Mediterranean groups are, as a matter of fact, higher than those for the Nordics.

An analysis of the statistics for manic-depressive first admissions yields a similar result. The following table is based upon first admissions per 100,000 population of the same nativity in the New York State hospitals between 1918 and 1922. They are taken from the New York State census of 1922, and arranged according to racial groups as in the table above. The same cautions in interpretation should be exercised. The figures are from Pollock (19a).

TABLE 39: MANIC-DEPRESSIVE INSANITY AMONG IMMIGRANT GROUPS
(NEW YORK STATE CENSUS)

Nordic Groups	Number	Alpine Groups	Number	Mediterranean Groups	Number
England	11.2	Poland	9.5	Italy	16.5
Scotland	11.2	Germany	10.0	Greece	19.9
Sweden	17.0	Czechoslovakia	13.1	Ireland	16.7
Denmark	18.3	France	13.1	Spain	20.7
Norway	21.0	Roumania	15.0		
Finland	25.6	Hungary	15.6		
		Russia	16.8		
		Switzerland	18.6		
		Austria	28.7		
Average	17.4		15.6		18.4

It is clear that there are no significant differences among the three racial groups.

With reference to the Negro, the results appear to be somewhat conflicting. The Federal and State Censuses for 1922 and 1924 (8) give the following distribution of Negro and White dementia precox first admissions per 100,000 of the same color in those two years. See Pollock (19).

TABLE 40: DEMENTIA PRECOX AMONG NEGROES AND WHITES (U. S. AND STATE CENSUS)

	Year	Negro	White
United States	1922	12.5	15.0
New York	1924	48.6	16.9
Illinois	1924	57.1	15.6

Pollock (19) believes the Negroes to be more susceptible to this disease, and regards the state figures as more typical than those for the country as a whole. It has been pointed out by Rosenthal (20), however, that these figures are affected by so many adventitious factors as to make this interpretation doubtful. In these two states there is a marked concentration of Negroes in the large cities which would raise their rate disproportionately. In the case of manic-depressive insanity, the New York State Census for 1918-22 (17) also gives a high figure for the Negro; even after the figures have been standardized for age and environment, they are still 15.48 for Negroes and 7.37 for native Whites per 100,000 of the respective races. It may be added that if the Negro is markedly extrovert, as is popularly believed, he should show a relatively greater amount of manic-depressive insanity. In New York State, however, his excess over the White figures is much more marked in the case of dementia precox, and this theory also will have to be abandoned.

One other group may be mentioned in this connection. Shaw (21) made a study of 100 hospital cases and 50 private cases among the Parsees of India. He found among the former, 52 cases of dementia precox to 17 of manic-depressive insanity, a proportion not much higher than that found in many White communities. Among the private cases, however, there were 24 of dementia precox to 3 of manic-depression. There is a suggestion here of a tendency for an apparently introvert people to develop more than the usual proportion of introvert psychoses; but the number of cases is small, and the demonstration is by no means to be regarded as conclusive.

Certain other qualitative differences between groups of various national origins in America emerge somewhat more clearly from the data. The figures used in the following discussion are from the United States Army draft statistics, which cite the percentage of draft rejections in each nativity group due to various mental abnormalities. These figures may be seen in detail in the article by Pearce Bailey (1) and will not be reproduced at this point. They show, for example, that whereas the general United States average for alcoholic psychoses is 3.0 per cent of all psychoses, the figure for the foreign-born Irish is 18.0 per cent; at the other extreme, the foreign-born Italians show 0.2 per cent, Negroes, 0.3 per cent, and Hebrews, 0.5 per cent. These differences are so large as certainly to be significant, although they do not by themselves prove the presence of a racial factor. It is interesting to note that the native-born Irish show a drop to 9.4 per cent, suggesting that here too, as in the case of crime, there may be a tendency to take over the psychotic "mores" of the native American. The Scandinavian figures for the same psychosis change from 6.6 to 2.8 per cent in one generation, and the Italian figures move in the opposite direction, rising from 0.2 to 1.2 per cent. These changes are suggestive, but care must be taken not to regard this theory as proved. There are notable exceptions, as, for example, in the change of the Italian figure for drug addiction, which increases from 2.6 per cent for the foreign-born to 19.1 per cent for the native-born, the American average being only 3.0 per cent. In all of these comparisons, however, it is important to keep in mind the possible effect of a different age distribution in the foreign- and native-born groups.

Among other qualitative differences it may be noted that Jews show the highest rate for psychoneuroses, 25.2 per cent, as compared with an American average of 17.0 per cent. The American Indians, the Mexicans and the Negroes show the highest rate for mental deficiency, and the foreign-born German and Irish the highest rates for the psychoses. The other differences are for the most part negligible.

There is little more at present to be said about qualitative psychiatric differences. The attempts made by O'Malley (18) and Bevis (3) to give a psychiatric characterization of the Negro are absolutely without foundation. The statements by O'Malley, for example, that freedom from slavery has only resulted in releasing all the Negro's "animal appetites," or that "all Negroes have a fear of darkness," or that involutional melancholia and depression are rare because of the Negro's lack of a "moral standard" hardly give the impression of an objective scientific attitude. The same may be said for the statement of Evarts (6), that outcrops of phylogenetic elements in the insane are much more common in the Negro, because "the colored race is so much nearer its stage of barbarism." These value-judgments offer no satisfactory basis for the development of a racial psychiatry.

Conclusion

The safest conclusion in this field is perhaps the one expressed by Sitsen (22), who states that, as his experience with the problem increases, his doubts as to the presence of a racial factor in psychiatry increase correspondingly.

BIBLIOGRAPHY

1. Bailey, P. "A Contribution to the Mental Pathology of Races in the United States." *Mental Hygiene,* 6:1922, pp. 370-391.
2. Baur, E., Fischer, E., and Lenz, F. *Human Heredity.* New York, 1931. (Trans.)
3. Bevis, W. M. "Psychological Traits of the Southern Negro, with Observations as to Some of His Psychoses." *Amer. J. Psychiatry,* 1:1921, pp. 69-78.
4. Bond, H. "Insanity Among Negroes." *Opportunity,* 10:1932, pp. 304-308, 324.
5. Brill, A. A., and Karpas, M. J. "Insanity Among Jews." *J. Nerv. and Mental Dis.,* 41:1914, p. 512.
6. Evarts, A. B. "The Ontogenetic *vs.* the Phylogenetic Elements in the Psychoses of the Colored Race." *Psychoanal. Rev.,* 3:1916, pp. 272-287.
7. Federal Census, 1920.
8. Federal and State Census, 1922-1924.
9. Frazier, E. F. "Psychological Factors in Negro Health." *Social Forces,* 3:1925, pp. 488-490.
10a. Goldberg, J. A. "Incidence of Insanity Among Jews." *Ment. Hygiene,* 6:1922, pp. 598-602.
10b. Goldberg, J. A., and Malzberg, B. "Mental Disease Among Jews." *Psychiatric Quarterly,* 2:1928, pp. 194-213.
11. Interracial Committee of Montclair, N. J. *J. Nat. Med. Assn.,* 23:1931, pp. 97-109.
12. Kretschmer, E. *The Psychology of Men of Genius.* New York, 1931. (Trans.)
13. Laughlin, H. H. *An Analysis of America's Melting Pot.* Commission of Immigration and Naturalization, Nov. 21, 1922. Washington.
14. Malzberg, B. "Prevalence of Mental Disease Among Jews." *Ment. Hygiene,* 14:1930, pp. 926-947.
15. May, J. V. *Mental Diseases.* Boston, 1922.
16. McDougall, W. *Is America Safe for Democracy?* New York, 1921.
17. New York State Census, 1918-1922.

18. O'Malley, M. "Psychoses in the Colored Race." *Amer. J. Insanity,* 71:1914, pp. 309-337.

19. Pollock, H. M. "Frequency of Dementia Precox in Relation to Sex, Age, Environment, Nativity and Race." *Mental Hygiene,* 10:1926, pp. 596-611.

19a. Pollock, H. M. "Prevalence of Manic-depressive Psychosis in Relation to Sex, Age, Environment, Nativity and Race." *Res. Pub. Assn. for Res. in Nerv. and Mental Dis.,* 11:1931, Ch. XXX.

20. Rosenthal, S. P. "Racial Differences in the Incidence of Mental Disease." *J. Negro Educ.,* Yearbook III:1934.

21. Shaw, W. S. J. "The Heredity of Dementia Precox." *Brit. Med. J.,* 2:1928, pp. 566-568.

22. Sitsen, A. E. "Ueber den Einfluss der Rasse in der Pathologie." *Virchow's Arch. f. path. Anat.,* 245:1923, pp. 281-294.

23. Smith, A. P. "Mental Hygiene and the American Negro." *J. Nat. Med. Assn.,* 23:1931, pp. 1-10.

24. White, W. A. "Social Significance of Mental Disease." *Arch. Neur. and Psychiatry,* 22:1929, pp. 873-900.

25. Williams, F. *Russia, Youth and the Present-Day World.* New York, 1934.

26. Winston, E. "Essential Techniques in the Analysis of the Relationship of Mental Disease with Age." *Mental Hygiene,* 15:1931, pp. 761-765.

PART III

THE CULTURAL APPROACH

Chapter XIV

THE "FUNDAMENTAL DRIVES"

THE IMPORTANCE OF CULTURE

THE search for an objective basis for a racial psychology has so far been unsuccessful. We have examined the available material in a number of different fields and assembled by a number of different methods, and we have failed to find any certain evidence of psychological differences among races. The problem must not, however, be left at this point. Groups do differ; the behavior of a Chinese certainly differs markedly from that of a Hottentot. If race—that is to say, physical type—is not responsible, the explanation must be sought elsewhere.

In the following chapters the attempt will be made to show something of the variability in behavior which may result from *cultural* rather than racial differences. The term culture has been defined in a great many ways; in its popular and literary connotation, for example, it suggests a form of behavior showing a high degree of cultivation or refinement. As it is here used, it is entirely free from any value-judgment, and applies to that whole "way of life" which is determined by the social environment. To paraphrase Tylor (58, p. 1), it includes all the capabilities and habits acquired by an individual man as a member of a particular society. In that sense we may as correctly speak of the culture of a simple Eskimo as of the culture of the most highly educated European; in that sense also universities and night-clubs are equally aspects of American culture.

There is clearly an intimate relation between psychology,

the science of the activities of the individual, and ethnology, the science of culture. One ethnologist (Radin, 46) has recently written that in his opinion the core of all investigations of culture is the attempt to arrive at a "satisfactory knowledge of what constitutes human nature" (p. 267). This is also the most important concern of the psychologist, and the pertinent data need to be collected both in the psychological laboratory and by ethnological field studies. For the most part, psychologists have not made sufficient use of ethnological material. Kantor (26) has written that "psychologists are oblivious of the fact that much of the data they require in order to clarify their problems the anthropologist is able to furnish" (p. 267).

There are two distinct, though related, ways in which the study of culture may be of real value to the psychologist. In the first place, when the psychologist speaks of "human nature," he usually fails to realize that what he knows is merely the nature of those human beings in his own culture or civilization. The books on "general psychology" in present use should more accurately add the subtitle "western Europe and America," since their generalizations have rarely been checked in other parts of the world. Even when the problem is recognized, little is done about it. Thorndike (57) concludes in his discussion of man's native tendencies: "The original nature of man is roughly what is common to all men *minus* all adaptations to tools, houses, clothes, furniture, words, beliefs, religions, laws, science, the arts. . . . From human nature as we find it, take away, first, all that is in the European but not in the Chinaman, all that is in the Fiji Islander but not in the Esquimaux, all that is local and temporary" (p. 198). Yet it is not unfair to say that the rest of Thorndike's book, like all other psychologies, is written as if the Chinese and the Fiji Islanders had never existed.

In the second place, however, the psychologist can learn from the study of culture something of the ways in which peoples differ, as well as the ways in which they are alike. Instead of "taking away" all that is in the Fiji Islander but not in the Eskimo, it may be precisely that which is in the one and not in the other that may be of special interest. There is no sharp line between these two approaches, but there is a difference in emphasis; and it is with the variations, rather than the uniformities in human behavior, that we are now concerned.

In this chapter we shall consider those activities which were called "instinctive" by the older psychologists, and which have more recently been discussed under the name of "fundamental drives," "dependable motives," and similar descriptive phrases. They presumably make up the core of human nature, and give the dynamic basis to behavior. Mc-Dougall (37), Thorndike (57), and others have given long lists of these activities which they regard as innate in the individual, and not dependent for their existence upon experience or upon the social environment. Other psychologists, like Watson (61), Kuo (27), and Bernard (3), have questioned their existence in this innate form. This is not the occasion for taking sides in this controversy. The probability seems to be that many of these activities do have an innate basis; but, as we shall see, they vary tremendously according to the cultural setting in which they develop.

THE MATERNAL DRIVE

One of the most important of these drives is the so-called maternal instinct, which is presumably responsible for the care and protection which a mother manifests toward her offspring. The strength or weakness of this drive may obviously have a vital effect on the life of a community.

The relation of parent to child differs greatly from one society to another. Rivers (50), for example, noted that in Murray Island in the Torres Straits it was very difficult to obtain genealogies from the natives because of the great prevalence of adoption. It is a common practice to adopt the child of another, sometimes even before the child is born, and it is customary in these cases to keep the child ignorant of his real parents. Even after reaching adult life, the child will give the name of his adopted father. Of the Andaman Islanders, Man (36) reports that it is of rare occurrence to find any child above the age of six or seven residing with its own parents, "because it is considered a compliment and also a mark of friendship for a married man, after paying a visit, to ask his hosts to allow him to adopt one of their children" (p. 125). The foster parents treat their adopted children with exactly the same kindness and consideration as their own. On the Banks Island the child belonged to the man who made the necessary payment to the midwife; on the Island of Merlav, the man who first planted the leaf of the cycas tree in front of the house in which the child was born was regarded as the father. (Rivers, 50.)

These last examples come from Melanesia, and it might seem as if Melanesians in general possess a very strong, racially determined love of children, independent of the sense of consanguinity. Adoption is by no means restricted to that particular group. It is found in North America and South Africa as well, although not to the same degree. On the other hand, even in Melanesia it is by no means universal. Malinowski (35) reports that it is rare among the Trobrianders, and Fortune (12) says the same of the Islanders of Dobu. When adoption does occur among the

Dobuans, it is never felt to be as binding as blood kinship, and a foster parent will refer publicly and freely to an adopted child as a "bastard" or an "orphan." (Fortune, 12, p. 17.)

It is also of interest to note that in ancient China (see Granet, 17) the concept of maternity was radically distinct from every tie of blood. Family life was based upon the principle that there can be only one wife, and therefore only one mother. In consequence, all the children of the secondary wives were regarded as the sons of the principal wife, and to her alone they paid the respect due a mother; she received the title of mother, while the blood mothers were "aunts" to all the children alike. In order for a woman to have a son, therefore, it was not necessary to bring a child into the world; it was enough to be the first wife, and for the second wife to have a son. If, for one reason or another, the principal wife was repudiated, all the children called her successor "mother."

The treatment of children as reflected in the attitude toward corporal punishment also differs greatly. In England until about one hundred years ago (Lowie, 33) the rod was widely used as an essential part of the child's education, and even today parents are generally regarded as having the right to punish their children in moderation when they seem to deserve it. There are some societies, however, which regard any form of corporal punishment as definitely inhuman. Le Jeune wrote of the American Indians that "all the savage tribes of these parts . . . cannot chastise a child or bear to see one chastised. What trouble this will cause us in carrying out our intention of instructing their young!" (See Briffault, 8, v. 1., p. 131.) The Eskimo do not consider that White people deserve to have children since they are so heartless as to strike them; and in a New Guinea village the natives

almost killed a White trader for beating his own child.
(Lowie, 33.)

These examples do not necessarily mean that among primitive peoples the parental attitude is more highly developed
than in our society. There are other instances which appear
to indicate just the opposite. Many peoples, for example,
were in the habit of selling their children. The Botocudo in
South America often were willing to sell their children to
the Brazilians; in the Upper Congo children were surren-
dered in payment of a debt; among the Aztecs they were
sold as slaves. Infanticide was also widespread. Among the
Kuni in South Africa, it is said that there is not a woman
who has not killed one or more children; this is the custom
of their ancestors. (Miller, 41.) In Australia the women often
plead that they cannot suckle and care for two children
together. One woman is reported to have said, "Oh, too
much young fellow Jimmy; no good two fellow picka-
ninny," as explanation for calmly killing her second child
by knocking his head against a tree. Haddon (19) reports
that in the Torres Straits Islands, after a certain number of
children had been born, all the succeeding ones were destroyed lest the food supply become insufficient. If the children were all of one sex some were destroyed from shame,
since it was considered proper to have an equal number of
boys and girls. In one of the Solomon Islands it is reported
that the Coast people kill their own children and purchase
young adults from the Bush people of the interior to save
themselves the trouble of rearing the young. Infanticide may
be directed against either sex. In British New Guinea girls
were preserved to be sold in marriage; in Tahiti they were
killed because they were of no use in fishing or war. (Sumner and Keller, 56.)

Unfortunately, it is not always possible to discover the

attitudes of the parents in these cases, and it may be that they are not always so indifferent to the loss of their children as these examples would suggest. At any rate it is clear that parental behavior is shaped by the particular forces— economic, social, traditional—operative in any community. Within our society one psychologist (Leta S. Hollingworth, 23) has discussed some of the social devices which impel women to bear and rear children. There are the forces of public opinion and the approval of leaders of the state like Mussolini and others; the law against the dissemination of birth control data; the law that sterility in the wife may be a cause for divorce; the drastic laws against infanticide and abortion; the religious forces tending to idealize motherhood; the dangers of "only children," and so on. In other societies the motives may differ. In Dahomey in West Africa (Miller, 41) the child is a practical asset; a son helps to fish or hunt, and a daughter is sold to a suitor for considerable material return. Every head of a family desires sons so that they may in time build their huts near his and add to his influence and importance. It is also for economic reasons that the Ugogo husband in East Africa claims all the offspring of his wife even when he is not the father. A woman in the Marshall Islands said, "Only wait until next spring, then I shall come with another child. Children are good, because my eldest is already earning money and brings it to me every month. As soon as all the children are grown, then I will become a rich woman." (Miller, 41, p. 63.) The Bakongo desire sons to bury them properly, and daughters to cry for them. "They prefer daughters to sons, for there is not only the portion of their marriage money, but they cry longer and better than boys and men." (Weeks, see Miller, 41, p. 64.)

There undoubtedly is in addition some biological basis

for maternal behavior. Among animals, for example, it has been shown (Giard, 14) that the reactions of the mother take place in response to gross physical stimuli. Suckling is sought by the female as a relief for uncomfortable pressure in the mammary glands, and maternal care ceases when the glands are depleted. Warden and his associates (60) have shown the great strength of the maternal drive in the white rat during the first few days after the birth of the offspring, and its gradual weakening and disappearance as the physiological state returns to normal. Rabaud (45) showed that the interest of female mice in the young of the species does not make its appearance until the end of gestation, and that it disappears entirely about six weeks after the birth. Even adoption among animals may similarly be explained as due to the unrelieved pressure of the mammary glands of a mother robbed of her young. (Geddes and Thomson, 13.) In addition there appear to be changes in metabolism and in the endocrine balance of the organism which may also play a part in the pattern of maternal behavior.

In the human mother it is probable that similar mechanisms are normally operative. Over and above these purely physiological conditions, however, there exist the strong cultural forces which shape the behavior into socially prescribed forms. There is no reason to believe that the mammary glands, for example, function differently in Tahiti and Australia; yet in one society there may be a great deal of adoption, and in the other, infanticide. The best indication that there is no physiological basis for this difference is the fact that in certain parts of Melanesia adoption and infanticide co-exist. It must be cultural, not physiological, factors that are responsible for group differences in maternal behavior.

Aggressiveness

There is the same variability in aggressive behavior. Cases are reported, for example, of peoples who engaged in combat for no apparent reason. In Korea it was customary every spring for the men and boys to go to the open places where stones were plenty, form sides and have regular pitched battles in which many were killed or wounded. (Saunderson, 52.) An Iroquois chief is reported to have asked a neighboring ruler to allow their young men to have a little war in order to keep in practice.

At the other extreme, Hobhouse and his associates (22) report at least ten cases of primitive tribes to whom war appeared to be unknown. Waitz (59) says that the people of the Lower Carolinas in the South Seas live at peace, and that in the islands of the Tokilan and Ellice groups there are no weapons except those that have been washed ashore, and these are stored in the temples. In Borneo the Kubu groups are not known to fight (Hose and McDougall, 24). The Bantus in one region of southwest Africa do not like to fight; and the tribes leave between them, wherever possible, wide uninhabited stretches. (Sumner and Keller, 56.) The Eskimo of Baffinland knew no warfare and could not be made to understand the meaning of battles. (Reclus, 49.) Nansen (42) quotes an interesting letter written by an Eskimo who evidently cannot understand how it is that men are hunting one another like seals and stealing from people they have never seen or known. He apostrophizes his own country: "How well it is that you are covered with ice and snow! How well it is that, if in your rocks there is gold and silver, for which the Christians are so greedy, it is covered with so much snow that they cannot get at it. Your unfruitfulness makes us happy and saves us from molestation." He expresses his surprise that Europeans did not learn better manners among the Eskimo, and proposes to send medicine men as missionaries to teach them the advantages of peace (p. 180).

Even where wars occur they vary greatly in ferocity and destructiveness. In a large number of cases the casualties were insignificant. A fight between two groups of Australians usually ended when one warrior had been killed; sometimes even a slight wound was enough to settle the issue. Among most primitive peoples a loss of five men would be regarded as a serious disaster. "A savage would stand aghast before the wholesale slaughter of civilized warfare, and beside some of its methods, his own are those of a gentleman." (Sumner and Keller, 56, v. 1., p. 370.)

Occasionally a people may *become* warlike as conditions change. Grinnell (18) believes that the Cheyenne probably did not fight very much before the White man came. The only incentive for fighting was the desire for revenge, and this was comparatively unimportant. The introduction of the horse furnished a new and strong motive for war because now something could be gained by it, and taking horses from the enemy became a regular profession. Many brave and successful warriors specialized in capturing horses, and their interest in war developed as a consequence.

This suggests that aggressiveness, as a trait of a particular society, may be determined by a number of secondary causes. Material interest probably plays the most important part. On Chatham Island there were not many fights except over the possession of the flesh of whales and other sea animals. (Weiss, 62.) The Hottentots fought only when their neighbors tried to take their property from them. (Sumner and Keller, 56.) In parts of South Africa wars were over the possession of cattle, and several tribes refused to keep livestock so as not to tempt their enemies. (Livingstone, 30.) Woman has often been the cause of war. Hobhouse (22) points out that in forty or more peoples marriage by capture is a full reality, and the possession of women is the direct object of a war or raid. Hagen (20) says of the Papuan region which he studied that war plays no great rôle, but that feuds occasionally arise over the possession of women. On the other hand, it is said of the Latoukas of Abyssinia (Baker, 1) that the capture of their women hardly disturbs them, but that they will risk their lives to save their animals!

Religious causes play an important part. It is a widespread belief that the eating of certain parts of a dead man transmits his virtues to the conqueror, and among the Yoruba hearts are sold in order to produce courage. In parts of Melanesia the hunting of heads was prevalent in order to acquire special power, or "mana." The Aztecs of Mexico carried on a continual warfare with the Tlaxcalans for the sole purpose of obtaining human sacrifices to renew the strength of their gods. (Payne, 44.)

One of the most important of all causes was the desire for glory. "Primitive man is not a miser nor a sage nor a beast of prey but, in Tarde's happy phrase, a peacock" (Lowie, 31, p. 357). The Cheyenne were taught from their earliest days to long for the approbation of their elders, and this was most readily earned by success in war. The applause of the public was the highest reward they knew. Among the Plains Indians in general the quest for military renown was hypertrophied. Each tribe had special rules for "counting coup," or showing evidence of great bravery. In most cases killing an enemy was relatively unimportant, and his scalp was merely a trophy to dance over. A really brave act was to touch or strike a living, unhurt man, and leave him alive. The bravest act of all was to go into war armed only with a "coup" stick. A man's standing in the community was proportional to his war record, and at tribal gatherings he would recite the list of his exploits and receive the honors which were due him. War was a game that had to be played according to definite rules, not an indiscriminate attempt to overcome the enemy at all costs. Its goal was glory, and victory or spoils were of secondary importance.

Racial differences cannot possibly be the explanation of these wide variations in aggressive behavior. Physical anthropologists regard as the same "race" the Eskimo who did not understand the meaning of war, and the Plains Indians who made war the center of their entire social organization. There are both peaceful and warlike groups among the Africans. Some Papuan tribes live at peace, others seem to revel in taking life. The amount of aggressive behavior is determined by the whole set of life conditions, and by the interplay of the forces of tradition and practical necessity. Physical type or race is apparently irrelevant.

Quarrels between individuals may also be settled in a host of ways. Culture may make the same form of behavior natural in one society and unthinkable in another. Livingstone (30) says that during his whole period of residence in the Bechuana country he never saw unarmed men strike each other. Their disputes are carried on with volubility, but never involve physical combat. When the Mrus of India have a difference of opinion, they do not fight, but call in an exorcist who finds out from the spirits how the matter should be decided. (Lewin, 29.) The Indians of Santa Marta in Colombia are peaceable, and carry no arms. When there is a grievance between two of them they go to a rock or large tree, each one carrying a stick, and "they strike ardently at the tree or rock, uttering a multitude of insulting words until one cracks or breaks his stick. To this one is accredited the victory, his enemy recognizing him as the braver; and, embracing, they return to their homes, renewing friendship and drinking." (Father de la Rosa; see Sumner and Keller, 56, Vol. IV, p. 129.) Among the Crow Indians personal brawls were looked upon with contempt, and a man would not "readily imperil his social position and invite the public derision of his joking-relatives by engaging in fisticuffs with a fellow-tribesman." (Lowie, 31, p. 398.)

When a dispute happens to arise among the Eskimo, they will frequently arrange to have a public duel or contest of a special kind. The contestants appear before the little village community and sing satirical and abusive songs about each other, each one doing his best to humble and ridicule his enemy in the eyes of the judges. The victory goes to the one who sings the more effective song. Occasionally it may be necessary for the contest to be renewed a number of times before the matter is settled, and in the intervening periods the two "enemies" are on perfectly friendly terms. (Reclus, 49.)

Among the Indians of British Columbia (northwest coast) there is still another interesting way of settling a dispute. They have an institution known as the "potlatch," in which the purpose appears to be to give away or destroy as large an amount of property as possible. In a quarrel, one man may give a potlatch to show that he is really superior, and his opponent will be regarded as the loser until he can restore his prestige by giving a greater potlatch himself. A Kwakiutl chieftain once said: "The white man fights with his hands, but we fight with property." (Boas, 6, p. 571.) This fighting with property may take place informally, as well as in the regular potlatch, as is described in the story told of the Tlingit of Alaska. "Two women were quarreling. In a rage one of them said to the other, 'I'll shut you up.' At that she rushed into her house, came out with both hands full of silver money, and scattered it to the crowd that was watching the proceedings. This did shut the mouth of her opponent as she could not do likewise." (Jones, 25, p. 95.) When natives quarrel it is a common thing for one to tell the other to shut up, unless he has something to destroy in order to get even.

Conflict may be inevitable, but culture determines its mode of expression. Whether an individual fights with satire or with property or with his fists will be decided by the traditions and customs of his group. A form of behavior which makes him a hero in one society will bring him ridicule in another. There will still be differences between individuals, but the broad lines of behavior will be determined by the group. The "hot-headed" Sicilian and the "phlegmatic" Englishman are in all probability cultural products.

ACQUISITIVENESS

Acquisitive behavior, regarded as instinctive by Mc-Dougall (37), has recently been subjected to very careful scrutiny by Beaglehole (2). He points out that the reaction to property is so tied up with a host of other cultural factors that it may take very different form in different societies. There are many peoples who practice a complete or partial communism, with almost complete disregard of any form of individual ownership. There are groups (for example, in Melanesia, see Rivers, 51) in which those objects which are made by the united efforts of a community are held in common, while those manufactured by an individual may be his private property. This rule is not universal. For example, in Baffinland, the hunter distributes among all the inhabitants the flesh of the seal he has caught himself. Similarly the Chukchi and the Koryak in Siberia share their spoils with the whole community. The same comparative disregard for personal property is shown by the Eskimo of Bering Straits, who do not hold a man to account if he fails to return what he has borrowed; they believe that if a man is in a position to lend something, he should wait until the borrower is ready to return it. (See Lowie, 31.)

Private property in food is unthinkable to many primitive peoples. Sumner writes of the Yakuts that they would not believe the ethnologist who told them that in his country there were rich and populous cities in which people sometimes died of starvation. They asked why anyone should die when he could go to eat with his neighbors (54). On the other hand, the Trobriand Islanders in Melanesia obtain social prestige through the individual ownership of food, which is stored and displayed. (Malinowski, 35.) It is a great insult there to say of someone that he is a "man with no food."

Among the British Columbia Indians private ownership of property constituted the very core of their society. Prestige went, however, not with the possession, but with the distribution of property. In order to obtain social status, property had to be destroyed or given away, and meanness or stinginess in the "potlatch" was regarded as a vice. Property had meaning only as an instrument for obtaining prestige. (Boas, 6.)

Indifference to private property is not invariably a trait of primitive peoples. There is probably no part of the world in which the principle of individual ownership was carried further than in the relatively simple society of the Torres Straits Islands. There every rock and water hole had its owner, the only piece of common land being the village street. (Lowie, 31.) The Australians also see an intimate relation between a man and what he possesses. Property is so charged with the owner's personality that when changing camp a native will leave valuable utensils lying about the ground and be absolutely sure of finding them when he returns. (Beaglehole, 2.)

There are peoples who care little about private ownership of material things, but who are very strict about the rights over incorporeal property. The Andaman Islanders regard songs as belonging exclusively to the man who has composed them, and a song that has once been received with applause will not again be sung except by the composer. The Koryak have private property in magical formulæ and incantations; the Torres Straits Islanders, in local legends; the Kai, in poetic compositions; and the Nootka Indians, in rituals, dances and carvings. (Lowie, 31.)

From his study of property in Melanesia, Rivers (51) concludes that "an instinct of acquisition in the interest of the individual can be so greatly modified in response to gregarious needs that it practically disappears or only appears under special circumstances" (p. 272). One may even question whether there is such an instinct to acquire, and Beaglehole (2) believes that his analysis shows the answer to be in the negative. With reference to cultural forces, he writes: "Human nature moulds its individualism into conformity with social ways of acting, its sentiments of ownership to group patterns of behavior" (p. 237).

Sex Behavior

Variations in sex behavior have been described in such detail by Hobhouse (22), Westermarck (63), Crawley (10), and others, that only brief mention is required at this point. These writers agree that in all communities the relationship between the sexes is subject to a very large number of restrictions and regulations, and that complete promiscuity has nowhere been reported. The rules often differ from ours, but on the whole they are followed with approximately the same strictness. We have no right to regard their rules as immoral, since the concept of right and wrong is entirely a function of the folkways of the group. Lowie (31) writes that his informant twitted him with the fact that while White men censured the Indians' immorality, a brother would not hesitate to speak freely with his sister, which no decent Crow would do.

The form of marriage prevalent in a community may bring about interesting differences in the psychological re-actions of the persons concerned. In our own society, which has idealized romantic love, a girl would be horrified at the thought of being bought and paid for by her suitor. Where marriage by purchase is the custom, a girl is proud of the price she brings. The Kaffir despises a wife taken for "love," that is, without payment. A Yakut girl would not consent to go to a husband until he had paid the bride-price. (Beaglehole, 2.) Occasionally a husband may complain of his bargain. Haddon (19) tells the amusing story of a Torres Straits Islander who told him his wife had cost a camphor wood chest with seven bolts of calico, one dozen shirts, one dozen singlets, one dozen trousers, one dozen handkerchiefs, two dozen tomahawks, one dozen hooks, two fish-lines, one long fish spear, one pound of tobacco, two pearl shells—and added sorrowfully, "By golly, he too dear!" (p. 231).

Jealousy in our sense of the word may frequently be lack-ing. The case has already been mentioned of the African tribe in which the husband recognizes his wife's children as his own, even when he knows that he is not their father. The habit of wife-lending as part of the entertainment of a guest, which has been reported for a great many peoples (the Eskimo are perhaps the best-known example), shows that marriage does not always imply exclusive possession. Spencer and Gillen (53) report that wife-lending is habitual among the Australian Arunta, and that jealousy is rare. One of the most striking examples of complete lack of the type of jealousy common in our society is seen in the case of the Kirgiz or the South African woman, who may actually ask her husband to get a second wife to share with her the work in the fields and in the house. (Lowie, 31.) Among the Hindus it is not unusual for a childless husband to compel his wife to bear him a child by another man. (Hobhouse, 22.) "Men who have no marital property in women, but sow their seed in the soil of others, benefit the owner of the woman" (Manu, ix, 51). Certain West African tribes, instead of prizing chastity in their brides, do not consider a girl fit for marriage until she has successfully borne a child. (Mead, 39.)

The extent of homosexuality in a community is dependent partly, if not entirely, on cultural attitudes. Among many North American Indian tribes this form of "abnormality" was quite frequent, the Berdache, or transformed shaman, having special power and influence. (Goldenweiser, 16.) Among the Chukchi in northeast Siberia this form of transformation occurred frequently. Shamans of this type seem to have been at first normal people who, after being inspired by the spirits, later changed their sex, and even on occasion entered into a homosexual marriage. They are known as "soft men," but they are among the most powerful members of the community. More rarely, a woman has shown a similar change. (Bogoras, 7.) It is clear that this social acceptance is at least partly responsible for the prevalence of these transformations.

SELF-PRESERVATION

Even the attitude toward life and death may be markedly influenced by culture. McDougall (38) has explained the tendency to suicide as a racial (Nordic) characteristic, but variations in this respect cannot be so simply explained, as Hankins (21) has adequately shown. There are Nordic peoples whose suicide rates are as low as those of any other racial group. On the other hand, the Japanese have institutionalized suicide to a greater degree than any other people (see Brinkley, 9, and Nitobe, 43), making it an important part of preserving "face," so that it is the only conceivable response to certain situations. The neighboring Chinese, of the same race, have not developed this custom to nearly the same extent, and commit suicide much less frequently. There appear to be fashions in suicide as in every other form of behavior. A recent study by Dublin and Bunzel (11) finds suicide exceedingly rare among the American Negroes. Before this is explained as an extrovert racial trait, it should be noted also that African Negroes have been known to commit suicide because of something which we should certainly regard as comparatively trivial—the death of a cow. (Lowie, 33.) Livingstone (30) says of the natives of Angola that if a woman who has had no children is taunted because of her barrenness, it is not uncommon for her to rush away and commit suicide. (See Miller, 41.) Among the Dobuan Islanders in Melanesia suicide or the threat of suicide is used to settle almost any domestic difficulty. (Fortune, 12.)

CONCLUSION

So it is with all the fundamental drives. Culture can produce and maintain profound differences even in those reactions which psychologists have usually regarded as basic to all behavior. To describe a race or a people as innately aggressive or peaceable, sedentary or nomadic, promiscuous or puritanical, overlooks the fact that culture may be entirely responsible. It is culture which can make the same form of behavior taboo in one society and apparently indispensable in another.

BIBLIOGRAPHY

1. Baker, S. W. *The Nile Tributaries of Abyssinia, and the Sword Hunters of the Hamran Arabs.* London, 1866.
2. Beaglehole, E. *Property: A Study in Social Psychology.* London, 1931.
3. Bernard, L. L. *Instinct: A Study in Social Psychology.* New York, 1924.
4. Boas, F. *Handbook of American Indian Languages.* Washington, 1911-1922. (3 vols.)
5. Boas, F. *The Mind of Primitive Man; A Course of Lectures Delivered Before the Lowell Institute, Boston, Mass., and the National University of Mexico, 1910-11.* New York, 1911.
6. Boas, F. *Contributions to the Ethnology of the Kwakiutl.* New York, 1925.
7. Bogoras, V. "The Chukchee," in *Publications of the Jessup-North Pacific Expedition,* Vol. VII. New York, 1904-09.
8. Briffault, R. L. *The Mothers; the Matriarchal Theory of Social Origins.* New York, 1927. (3 vols.)
9. Brinkley, F. *A History of the Japanese People from the Earliest Times to the End of the Meiji Era.* New York, 1915.
10. Crawley, E. *The Mystic Rose, a Study of Primitive Marriage.* London, 1902.
11. Dublin, L. I., and Bunzel, B. *To Be or Not to Be; a Study of Suicide.* New York, 1933.
12. Fortune, R. *Sorcerers of Dobu; the Social Anthropology of the Dobu Islanders of the Western Pacific.* London, 1932.
13. Geddes, P., and Thomson, J. A. *Evolution.* London, 1912.
14. Giard, A. "Les Origines de l'Amour maternel," in *Œuvres diverses,* Vol. I. Paris, 1911.
15. Goldenweiser, A. A. *History, Psychology and Culture.* New York, 1933.

16. Goldenweiser, A. A. *Early Civilization; an Introduction to Anthropology.* New York, 1922.

17. Granet, M. *Chinese Civilization.* New York, 1930. (Trans.)

18. Grinnell, G. B. *The Cheyenne Indians, Their History and Ways of Life.* New Haven, 1923.

19. Haddon, A. C. *Report of the Cambridge Anthropological Expedition to Torres Straits.* Vol. V, 1904.

20. Hagen, B. *Unter den Papua's.* Wiesbaden, 1899.

21. Hankins, F. H. *The Racial Basis of Civilization.* New York, 1926.

22. Hobhouse, L. T. *Morals in Evolution; a Study in Comparative Ethics.* London, 1906.

23. Hollingworth, L. S. "Social Devices for Impelling Women to Bear and Rear Children." *Amer. J. Sociol.,* 22:1916, pp. 19-29.

24. Hose, C., and McDougall, W. *The Pagan Tribes of Borneo.* London, 1912.

25. Jones, L. F. *A Study of the Thlingets of Alaska.* New York, 1914.

26. Kantor, J. R. "Anthropology, Race, Psychology and Culture." *Amer. Anthrop.,* 27:1925, pp. 267-283.

27. Kuo, Z. Y. "Giving Up Instincts in Psychology." *J. Phil., Psych. and Sci. Methods,* 18:1921, pp. 645-664.

28. LeJeune, Father C. *Jesuit Relations and Allied Documents.* Paris, 1897-99. (Trans.)

29. Lewin, T. H. *Wild Races of Southeastern India.* London, 1870.

30. Livingstone, D. *Missionary Travels and Researches in South Africa.* London, 1858. (2 vols.)

31. Lowie, R. H. *Primitive Society.* New York, 1920.

32. Lowie, R. H. *Primitive Religion.* New York, 1924.

33. Lowie, R. H. *Are We Civilized? Human Culture in Perspective.* New York, 1929.

34. Malinowski, B. *Sex and Repression in Savage Society.* London, 1927.

35. Malinowski, B. *Argonauts of the Western Pacific.* London, 1922.

36. Man, E. H. "On the Aboriginal Inhabitants of the Andaman Islands." J. Royal Anthrop. Inst., 12:1882.

37. McDougall, W. *Introduction to Social Psychology.* Boston, 1920.

38. McDougall, W. *Is America Safe for Democracy?* New York. 1921.

39. Mead, M. "Jealousy: Primitive and Civilized," in *Woman's Coming of Age.* New York, 1931.

40. Mead, M. *Sex and Temperament in Three Primitive Societies.* New York, 1935.

41. Miller, N. *The Child in Primitive Society.* New York, 1928.

42. Nansen, F. *Eskimo Life.* London, 1893. (Trans.)

43. Nitobe, I. *Bushido: The Soul of Japan.* New York, 1905.

44. Payne, E. J. *History of the New World Called America.* Oxford, 1892-1899. (2 vols.)

45. Rabaud, E. "L'Instinct Maternel chez les Mammifères." *Bulletin de la Soc. Zoölogique,* 46, Paris, 1921.

46. Radin, P. *The Method and Theory of Ethnology.* New York, 1933.

47. Radin, P. *Primitive Man as Philosopher.* New York, 1927.

48. Radin, P. *Crashing Thunder; the Autobiography of an American Indian.* New York, 1926.

49. Reclus, E. *Primitive Folk.* New York, 1891.

50. Rivers, W. H. R. *Report of the Cambridge Anthropological Expedition to Torres Straits.* Vol. V, 1904.

51. Rivers, W. H. R. "The Instinct of Acquisition," in *Instinct and the Unconscious.* Cambridge, 1920.

52. Saunderson, H. S. "Notes on Corea and Its People." *J. Royal Anthrop. Inst.,* 24:1894.

53. Spencer, Sir B., and Gillen, F. J. *The Native Tribes of Central Australia.* London, 1899.

54. Sumner, W. G., and Sieroshevski, M. "The Yakuts." *J. Roy. Anthrop. Inst.,* 31:1901, pp. 65-110.

55. Sumner, W. G. *Folkways.* Boston, 1907.

56. Sumner, W. G., and Keller, A. G. *The Science of Society.* New Haven, 1927. (4 vols.)

57. Thorndike, E. L. *Educational Psychology.* New York, 1903. (3 vols.)

58. Tylor, Sir E. B. *Primitive Culture.* London, 1871. (2 vols.)

59. Waitz, T., and Gerland, G. K. C. *Anthropologie der Naturvölker.* Leipzig, 1859-1872. (6 vols.)

60. Warden, C. J., et al. *Animal Motivation; Experimental Studies on the Albino Rat.* New York, 1931.

61. Watson, J. B. *Psychology from the Standpoint of a Behaviorist.* Philadelphia, 1919.
62. Weiss, B. *Mehr als fünfzig Jahre auf Chatham Island.* Berlin, 1901.
63. Westermarck, E. *The History of Human Marriage.* London, 1921. (3 vols.)

Chapter XV

EMOTIONAL EXPRESSION

The Causes of the Emotions

The first and most obvious way in which culture may affect the emotions is by determining what situations will give rise to them. Depending upon its cultural context, the same external occurrence may arouse diametrically opposite responses in two different societies. The birth of twins is hailed with rejoicing by the Bakuba and is regarded as a calamity by the East African Jagga. (Lowie, 13.) Being an orphan may arouse contempt among the Dobuans, and only sympathy among ourselves.

The emotion of shame, which McDougall (17) and others have attempted to explain on a sexual basis, may be aroused by a large variety of different situations. Briffault (4) has collected a number of interesting examples. There are many peoples who go about absolutely naked, or who wear clothing which does not cover those parts of the body which we consider it "modest" to conceal. The Fuegians wear a kind of cloak on their backs, with the front part of the body entirely exposed. There are groups of Australians among whom the sole article of clothing is a nose-ring. The story is told of a girl who was finally induced to sell hers to a White visitor, but she was obviously "ashamed" to be without one and ran immediately into her hut to get another. There are peoples who refuse to be seen eating; some Polynesians regularly turn their backs upon one another, or eat only in privacy. The cause of shame is determined entirely by custom, and the feeling appears to develop almost entirely as the result of being "out of fashion." Porteus (21) tells the illuminating story of a group of Australian natives who were sitting together quite naked, but who scurried to put on their clothes as soon as a White man approached. Clothes were for the protection of the White man's modesty, not their own. It was merely one of the White man's rules.

Death is among us perhaps the most sorrowful of all occasions, but it may be accepted with rejoicing by groups as different from each other as the northern Siberians and the Fiji Islanders. It is reported that on one occasion a young Fiji Islander invited a White man to attend his mother's funeral, which was about to take place. The invitation was accepted, and the procession started for the burying ground. No corpse was to be seen, however; and when the stranger inquired about it, the young Fijian pointed out his mother who was walking along with them, as lively as anyone in the procession. The relatives and friends took an affectionate farewell and buried her alive. (Hunt; see Lubbock, 14.) This custom rests upon the belief that an individual spends eternity in the next world in possession of the bodily powers with which he leaves this one. It is an advantage, therefore, to die in the prime of life, and the greatest service a son can render his parents is to kill them before they are weakened by old age.

There is the same variability in the causes of all the emotions. Fear, for example, may be aroused by ghosts or by death or by menstruation; ridicule may be a man's punishment for being a coward in battle or for speaking to his mother-in-law.

Amount of Expression

Culture may also determine the amount of emotional expression permitted. The Plains Indian and the Englishman are known for their reserve, the Sicilian for his lack of it. These habits can be taught if the training begins sufficiently early in life. The English schoolboy may start out by being expressive, but it is not long before he learns that the tradition of his group demands self-control. If the Plains Indian cries the first time he is hurt, the disapproval of his older comrades will cause him to bear his pain silently on the next occasion. "Imperturbability, in all situations, is one of the most striking and general traits of the Indian character. To still his muscles, to resist the expression of all emotion, seems to be the point of attainment. . . . Neither fear nor joy are permitted to break this trained equanimity." (Schoolcraft, see Lubbock, 14a, 520.)

There is no indication that this form of behavior is racially determined. Not all American Indians react in the same way. There is no stoical tradition, for example, among the Pueblos of the Southwest, or among many of the Mexican tribes; the Huichol in Mexico are lively and vociferous, differing greatly from the usual American Indian stereotype. They are described as "a gay and sociable group, emotional, laughing easily and often, quickly aroused to anger and as quickly appeased." (Klineberg, 12, p. 447.) Another indication that "imperturbability" is not an Indian racial characteristic is found in the fact that even among the Plains Indians there are occasions in which the culture not only permits, but actually demands, an emotional outburst. The death of a near relative, for example, resulted in an abandonment to grief in marked contrast to the traditional stoicism and reserve which is expected at other times.

The Negro, at least in America, is usually regarded as highly emotional and expressive, with relatively little control over his feelings and their manifestations. Of the Kipsigis, in Kenya (Central Africa) it is, however, reported that noise, excitement, anger, or any display of feeling are "the attributes of children left behind at initiation or rebirth." (Orchardson, 19, p. 471.) They say: "Be silent till your anger has abated," and they act so. "It is extraordinary how this calm behavior irritates some Europeans."

These examples show that two groups belonging to the same race may differ greatly in the amount of emotional expression which is habitual. The contrast between the proverbial reserve of the Englishman and the exuberance of the Anglo-Saxon American of the Middle West is another illustration of a difference which can be due only to culture.

MEANS OF EXPRESSION

The problem of variations in the nature of emotional expression was raised by Darwin (8), who sent out a questionnaire to missionaries and other travelers who had the opportunity of making observations among different peoples. "It seemed to me highly important to ascertain whether the same expressions and gestures prevail . . . with all the races of mankind. . . . Whenever the same movements of the features or body express the same emotions in several distinct races of man, we may infer with much probability, that such expressions are true ones,—that is, are innate or instinctive. Conventional expressions or gestures, acquired by the individual during life, would probably have differed in the different races, in the same manner as do their languages" (p. 15).

The intimate connection between emotional expression and language was also recognized by Tylor (23), who pointed out that a frown or a smile does not necessarily imply the presence of the corresponding emotions, but may be voluntarily assumed in order to simulate these emotions, or merely to convey the thought of them to others. "Physical expression by feature . . . thus serves as an important adjunct to spoken language" (p. 165). More recently, Dumas (9) has stressed the fact that most expressions, whatever their origin, have become language, and are constantly used in social life to express emotions which we feel only slightly or not at all. There is ample evidence in ethnological literature that emotional expression varies in the same manner, though perhaps not to the same degree, as language, and that it is also to some extent a conventionalized form of communication.

The shake of the head from side to side as a sign of negation is explained by Darwin (8) as an extension from the child's earliest refusal of food. When the child has had enough, it moves its head to one side; when food is again offered, it moves its head to the other. This is the child's first "no." Darwin himself pointed out, however, that this lateral shake is by no means universally equivalent to a negation. The Abyssinians say "no" by jerking the head to the right shoulder, and "yes," by throwing the head back and raising the eyebrows. The Dyaks of Borneo raise their eyebrows to mean "yes," and contract them slightly to mean "no." The Maori say "yes" by raising the head and chin; the Sicilians say "no" in exactly the same manner.

Assent and dissent as expressed in the inflections of the voice appear to show similar variability. Porteus (21) asked his interpreter one night to request a group of Australian natives to do a special dance for him. The man broadcast his question to the encampment. "From near and far, east, west, north and south of us, came a volley of replies, apparently in terms of the most vehement refusal. . . . I felt that this language needed no interpretation, and our spirits fell accordingly. Albert (the interpreter), however, merely inclined his ear to each direction in turn, and then when the clamor suddenly ceased turned to us and to our surprise remarked: 'Them feller say makem cobba-cobba all right' " (p. 58). The Kaingang of Brazil make use of what sounds to us like a whining or complaining sound to indicate a long-continued action, without any of the emotional significance which a similar sound has in our society. (Dr. Jules Henry, personal communication.)

Tears may have a very special function in some societies, and it is a mistake to assume that they always imply grief or pain. Among the Maori of New Zealand it was not etiquette to make any demonstration at the departure of a friend; tears were reserved for his return. When a group of visitors arrived, there was a mournful weeping and wailing which might continue for hours. "The copious shedding of tears at such a function is marvelous." (Best, 2, Vol. I, p. 377.) Brown (5) says the same of the Andaman Islanders. When two friends or relatives meet after a separation, they greet each other by sitting down, one on the lap of the other, with their arms around each other's necks, weeping and wailing for two or three minutes. Among both groups there are a number of other situations in which weeping is customary. For example, when two hostile local groups make peace, a day is fixed for a special ceremony during which both parties shed floods of tears. Brown points out that in these instances weeping is not simply the spontaneous expression of feeling, but a rite, the proper performance of which is demanded by custom. Some of the occasions are sorrowful, others happy. In certain circumstances men and women are required to weep, and if they neglected to do so, it would be an offense condemned by all right-thinking persons in the community.

This is an interesting example of the way in which culture may develop control over reactions usually regarded as involuntary. In our own society it is relatively rare for an individual to have the power of producing tears at will; among the Maori and the Andamanese, this power seems to be general. In all cases, as Brown points out, it is real weeping; a man wails or howls, the tears streaming down his face. "On one occasion I asked the natives to show how it was done and two or three of them sat down and were immediately weeping real tears at my request" (p. 117). Maning (15), who observed a peace-making ceremony among the Maori, writes: "How they manage to do it is more than I can tell to this day, except that I suppose you may train a man to do anything" (p. 62).

Even when tears are used on sorrowful occasions there may still be a high degree of conventionalization and artificiality. Mauss (16) points out that Australians cry for the dead only at certain definite hours, and that only certain relatives are required to cry. In many cases these are not the closest relatives, in our sense. There is often also a conventional number of tears and cries to which they must give expression. Sincerity is not excluded, but it is by no means essential. Granet (10) has shown how there developed in ancient China a true "language of sorrow," a detailed orderly symbolism with established rules. A person is forbidden to have a grief which cannot be expressed in this definite symbolism. He must use the words which everyone else uses, and only those gestures and lamentations which are prescribed and regulated. The amount of food to be eaten, the clothes, the conversation—all are exactly determined. A nobleman speaks less during his period of mourning than does a commoner; silence in the latter would mean that he was presuming beyond his class. "The gestures of grief . . . constitute a technique and a symbolism; they form a practical language which has its requirements of order, correctness, clarity, its grammar, syntax and philosophy" (p. 96).

Laughter has probably much the same function in all societies, although relatively little is known in detail of the conditions which arouse humor. There is undoubtedly a great deal of amusement among primitive peoples, as among ourselves, at the sight of the discomfiture of others, or when things happen in a strange or unusual fashion. (Klineberg, 12.) In the American Southwest, particularly among the Zuñi, there are clowns who take part in the dances and amuse the people by obscene or satirical or childish pranks. (Bunzel, 6.) They disregard all rules and arouse much laughter by their mimicry and burlesque. (Parsons, 20.) This laughter is undoubtedly much like our own. It has been suggested that certain peoples—the Japanese, for example— really have a different sense of humor, but this has not as yet been adequately studied. It is said that the Japanese will keep an absolutely straight face under conditions which would convulse Europeans, but this is more likely a matter of self-control than a lack of humor. The Chinese, too, will usually not show any amusement at the mistakes made by foreigners in their presence, but as soon as they are alone they will enjoy the joke to the full.

It is quite possible, however, that a smile or a laugh may have a different meaning for groups other than our own. Lafcadio Hearn (11) has remarked that the Japanese smile is not necessarily a spontaneous expression of amusement, but a law of etiquette, elaborated and cultivated from early times. It is a silent language, often seemingly inexplicable to Europeans, and it may arouse violent anger in them as a consequence. The Japanese child is taught to smile as a social duty, just as he is taught to bow or prostrate himself; he must always show an appearance of happiness to avoid inflicting his sorrow upon his friends. The story is told of a woman servant who smilingly asked her mistress if she might go to her husband's funeral. Later she returned with his ashes in a vase and said, actually laughing, "Here is my husband." Her White mistress regarded her as a cynical creature; Hearn suggests that this may have been pure heroism.

Just as foreigners object to the Japanese smile as being insincere, so the Japanese are surprised at the irritated faces of foreigners which reflect too closely what they feel. This is only one instance of a misunderstanding between groups who have learned a different "language" of emotional expression.

Kissing appears to us a natural expression of affection. Steele wrote: " 'Tis certain nature was its author, and it began with the first courtship." (See Lubbock, 14a, p. 563.) It is unknown, however, in many groups, and shows different forms in others—the rubbing of noses among the Maori and the Eskimo, the face rubbing of the Australians, and the nose-to-cheek caress of the Chinese and other Mongolian peoples. It may obviously be a mistake, therefore, to conclude with Monteiro (18) that affection is lacking when it is not expressed in the way to which we are accustomed. He writes: "In all the long years I have been in Africa I have never seen a Negro manifest tenderness to a Negress. I have never seen a Negro put his arm around a woman's waist, or give or receive any caress whatever that could indicate the slightest loving regard or affection on either side." (v. 1, p. 243.)

We find it natural to stand up in the presence of a superior; the Fijians and Tongans sit down under similar circumstances. The inhabitants of the Friendly Islands would take their clothes off as a sign of respect. (Lubbock, 14a.) Among the Maori it was a sign of friendship and often of protection to double the forefinger of the right hand and place the projecting second joint to the tip of the nose. (Best, 2.) The Todas raise the open right hand to the face, resting the thumb on the bridge of the nose. To them it means respect; but almost exactly the same sign is used in our society to signify something quite different. Darwin (8) writes that "spitting seems an almost universal sign of contempt or disgust" (p. 260); it represents originally the rejection of anything offensive from the mouth. The Jaggas of East Africa, however, regard it as a kind of blessing in critical situations, and a medicine man will spit four times on a patient or a new-born baby. (Lowie, 13.)

There is no doubt that emotional expression, apparently so natural and so direct, is to a large extent a learned reaction—a bodily language which must be known if it is to be understood. Under the controlling influence of tradition and training, it may vary so greatly in nature and in amount as to make the overt behavior of two different groups mutually unintelligible. It is not going too far to say that it is in part responsible for the misunderstanding between groups of differing culture.

CONCLUSION

Culture appears therefore to determine the situations that will arouse an emotional response, as well as the extent to which the response is overtly expressed, and the particular forms which the expression may take. It may make death an occasion of sorrow in one society, and in another a matter of rejoicing. It may demand of a people (like the Sioux) the violent demonstration of grief and the suppression of any sign of physical suffering. It may attach a muscular or a glandular response to any one of a number of situations so that a form of behavior becomes "second nature" in one society and unthinkable in another. It may make one people "emotional" and another "phlegmatic," altogether apart from their biological constitution. This does not mean that there are no innate factors in emotional expression. Young children in all societies probably laugh and cry under much the same conditions. As they grow older, however, they learn to "speak" the particular language of emotional expression that has been institutionalized by their group.

It is probable that the very emotions felt by one people may not occur in that same form elsewhere. When a Kwakiutl child dies, the father's emotional experience is a peculiar combination of grief and shame—grief at the loss of his child, and shame because he has been "insulted" by the universe, and because his prestige and security have been threatened. (See Boas, 3; Benedict, 1.) It may be that the Kwakiutl father never feels grief without its accompaniment or overtone of shame, and that as a consequence his felt emotion really differs markedly from what ours would be under similar circumstances. On the physiological side, all we really know is that in emotional excitement the organism is prepared for some activity which will meet the existing emergency. (Cannon, 7.) This function of the emotions is probably universal; the nature of the overt activity, however, as of the subjective experience which accompanies it, varies greatly from one culture to another.

BIBLIOGRAPHY

1. Benedict, R. F. *Patterns of Culture*. New York, 1934.
2. Best, E. *The Maori*. Wellington, N. Z., 1924. (2 vols.)
3. Boas, F. *Contributions to the Ethnology of the Kwakiutl*. New York, 1925.
4. Briffault, R. *The Mothers; the Matriarchal Theory of Social Origins*. New York, 1927. (3 vols.)
5. Brown, A. R. *The Andaman Islanders, a Study in Social Anthropology*. Cambridge, 1922.

6. Bunzel, R. L. "Introduction to Zuñi Ceremonialism." *47th Annual Report,* Bur. Amer. Ethnol., 1932.

7. Cannon, W. B. *Bodily Changes in Pain, Hunger, Fear and Rage.* New York, 1916.

8. Darwin, C. *The Expression of the Emotions in Man and Animals.* New York, 1873.

9. Dumas, G. *Traité de Psychologie.* Paris, 1923-1924. (2 vols.)

10. Granet, M. "Le Langage de la Douleur d'après le Rituel funéraire de la Chine classique." *J. de Psych.,* 19:1922, pp. 97-118.

11. Hearn, Lafcadio. "The Japanese Smile," in *Glimpses of Unfamiliar Japan.* New York, 1894. (2 vols.)

12. Klineberg, O. "Notes on the Huichol." *Amer. Anthrop.,* new ser., 36:1934, pp. 446-460.

13. Lowie, R. H. *Are We Civilized? Human Culture in Perspective.* New York, 1929.

14a. Lubbock, J. (Lord Avebury). *Prehistoric Times.* New York, 1872.

14b. Lubbock, J. (Lord Avebury). *The Origin of Civilization and the Primitive Condition of Man.* London, 1870.

15. Maning, Judge F. E. *Old New Zealand.* London, 1876.

16. Mauss, M. "L'expression obligatoire des sentiments." *J. de Psych.,* 18:1921, pp. 425-434.

17. McDougall, W. *An Introduction to Social Psychology.* London, 1908.

18. Monteiro, J. J. *Angola and the River Congo.* London, 1875. (2 vols.)

19. Orchardson, I. Q. "Some Traits of the Kipsigis in Relation to Their Contact with Europeans." *Africa,* 4:1931, pp. 466-474.

20. Parsons, E. C. "Notes on Zuñi." *Memoirs, Amer. Anthrop. Assn.,* 4:1917, Pt. II.

21. Porteus, S. D. *The Psychology of a Primitive People; a Study of the Australian Aborigine.* New York, 1931.

22. Tylor, Sir E. B. *Anthropology: An Introduction to the Study of Man and Civilization.* London, 1888.

23. Tylor, Sir E. B. *Primitive Culture.* London, 1871. (2 vols.)

Chapter XVI

THE ABNORMAL

THE SIGNIFICANCE OF THE ABNORMAL

ETHNOLOGISTS have recently made it clear that even the line between the normal and the abnormal may be culturally determined. Sapir (14) writes that cultural anthropology is sceptical of the validity of the concept of normal behavior. The external form of normal adjustment is very elastic, and needs to be redefined for every culture in turn. Benedict (2) has also pointed out that many types of personality which seem to us to be clearly abnormal have been accepted by different civilizations as the very foundations of their institutional life. "Normality, in short, within a very wide range, is culturally defined. It is primarily a term for the socially elaborated segment of human behavior in any culture, and abnormality, a term for the segment that that particular civilization does not use" (p. 73).

It has previously been suggested (Chapter XIII) that although racial factors probably play no very important part in the incidence of various types of abnormality, there are important differences in behavior, abnormal as well as normal, that need to be explained. The ethnological material to which we now turn shows that this explanation may be found in the effect of culture, which not only determines what forms of behavior shall be considered normal, but even introduces certain "fashions" in abnormality.

VARIETIES OF "NORMAL" BEHAVIOR

There are undoubtedly important differences between individuals in every culture, as a result either of constitutional factors, or of early experiences and conditioning. These differences may mean that any particular individual might be a deviant in one community and a perfectly normal or even a superior person in another. For example, a man who is definitely homosexual is condemned in our own society, but he might have an honorable career as a shaman or a religious leader in Siberia or among some North American Indians. Whether the personality traits of any individual fit into the forms demanded by his community may be largely a matter of accident, but it is an accident which will determine his status. There, is, therefore, no abnormality as such; there is simply deviation from the accepted pattern, whatever that may be.

In the case of most people, however, normality is no accident. As Benedict (2) puts it, the vast majority of the individuals in any group are shaped to the fashion of their particular culture. They can be molded in any direction. They can be made to act in the fashion which the culture institutionalizes, even when that is one which we in our society regard as abnormal.

There is, for example, the disease known to psychiatrists as paranoia. It is characterized by the presence of a delusional system which completely fills the mind of the patient. In typical cases there is a combination of delusions of grandeur, delusions of persecution, and delusions of reference. (This last describes the patient's belief that everything happening in his environment has some direct reference to himself.)

The American Indians of British Columbia (the so-called Northwest Coast) illustrate, according to Benedict, a definite paranoid form of behavior. In their speeches at the potlatches (see Chapter XIV) the chiefs frequently refer to themselves in grandiose terms which in our society would not be found outside the institutions for the insane. A few extracts follow (see Benedict, 2):

I am the great chief who vanquishes
I am the great chief who vanquishes
I sneer at the chiefs below the true, real chief.
I am the great chief who makes people ashamed.

Our chief brings shame to the faces
Our chief brings jealousy to the faces
Our chief makes people cover their faces by what he is continually
    doing in this world, from the beginning to the end of the year.
I am the only great tree, I the chief.
I am the only great tree, I the chief.

"Delusions of reference" are closely associated with this megalomania. All of existence is seen in terms of insult. Not only derogatory acts performed by a neighbor or an enemy, but all untoward events, like a cut when one's axe slips, or a ducking when one's canoe overturns, are insults (Benedict, 2). When some such thing happened, the only proper course was to give a potlatch and distribute property enough to wipe out the stain. If the misfortune were more serious, someone might have to be killed in order that the "insult" might be avenged. This is the accepted mode of behavior; the one who follows it "acts nobly because he has not been downed. He has thrust back in return" (p. 71). If someone were to behave in the same manner in our society, he would certainly be committed to an institution.

There are many other similar examples. Among the Dobuan Islanders (see Fortune, 9) fear and suspicion are the dominant attitudes, and each man suspects every other to an extent unknown in any other society; no one will touch the food belonging to anyone else for fear that it has been magically poisoned. Among most Polynesian tribes taboos are so extensive and serious that there is a host of things which a native is afraid to touch, in much the same manner though to a greater degree than an hysteric patient with the neurosis known as "défense de toucher." Epileptoid trance phenomena and homosexual behavior, both abnormal in our society, may help to confer power and prestige on religious leaders in many primitive communities.

The psychoanalyst, Franz Alexander (1), makes a similar point with reference to Buddhistic training in India. The complete withdrawal of interest from the external world which is the goal of Buddhistic self-absorption is in his opinion very similar to an artificial schizophrenia. There is a deliberate cultivation of a form of behavior which in our society is characteristic of what is perhaps the most severe kind of functional mental disorder. It may require years of careful training to reach a state which we would regard as the greatest of all misfortunes. Those who are successful may be able to perform certain physiological miracles which are typical of the catatonic; the body may be held in a stereotyped position for hours or days, and Alexander says that there may be a suspension of metabolism which will permit burial alive for a considerable period. (Note: The phenomena as they are usually described are so difficult to explain on the basis of our present knowledge of physiology, that we must be cautious before we accept these statements as they stand. It seems probable, however, that Alexander's analysis is essentially accurate.) In the case of both the Hindu mystic and the catatonic, there is a complete withdrawal from reality, a complete absorption in the self. In the latter it represents a disease; in the former, an enviable accomplishment.

These examples do not necessarily signify that there is no constitutional basis for abnormality. They do show, however, as in this last case, that the same constitution may be a misfit in one society and an ideal in another. The schoolboy who spends all his time daydreaming is a problem child in America; if he is a Hindu he may be regarded as a potential religious leader. There are undoubtedly certain individuals who would not fit into any culture; but it is probable that most cases of abnormality are relative to the environment in which they happen to occur.

Extent of Abnormality

Similarly, even the extent of abnormality in any community may depend at least in part upon the demands which it makes on its members. Frankwood Williams (16) believes that the sweeping effort now being made in Russia to relieve "anxiety pressures," those things causing anxiety, has meant a parole for hundreds of thousands of potential neurotics and psychotics. The reduction in economic responsibility and competition has been the most important single factor, though other influences, particularly the freeing of parents and children from too great an emotional attachment to the home, have also contributed. Williams says that although it is too early for accurate figures, the incidence of nervous and mental diseases in Russia appears to be falling, and there seems to be a similar decline in prostitution and divorce and other symptoms of maladjustment. Even when peasants come to the cities in large numbers they show no special behavior problems; they "won't even go crazy when they should!" (p. 139). One Russian psychiatrist told Williams that he had searched in vain for three months in all Moscow to find a new case of depressed manic-depressive insanity to show his students. "In Russia mental hygiene is inherent in the social organization, in America such mental hygiene as we have is injected into the individual and the social body by a group of professional experts" (p. 149).

Williams believes that the comparison is all in favor of the Russians.

·As he says, however, accurate statistics are not available, and a final judgment on the incidence of abnormality in Russia must be postponed. There is an interesting possibility that it is not so much the amount as the character of abnormality which has been affected. There is reason to believe that while the important psychoses, like manic-depressive insanity and schizophrenia, may not occur so frequently, there is a considerable increase in the number of fatigue and exhaustion neuroses. The culture may make life easier in one direction and increase the strain in another. In any case, the nature and extent of the abnormality cannot be understood except in the light of cultural factors.

In this same connection it has been pointed out by Harry Stack Sullivan (personal communication) that there is an acute curable form of schizophrenia which in his experience frequently develops in an individual who rushes into a romantic marriage that soon turns out to be unsatisfactory. He suggests that in communities in which marriages are arranged by the parents (as in China) and in which romantic attachments are relatively rare, that particular form of disturbance might not occur.

Malinowski (12) compares the incidence of abnormality in two neighboring Melanesian Islands and comes to the conclusion that the difference can be explained by the different attitudes of the two groups. The Amphlett Islanders have a very strict sexual morality; they regard pre-nuptial intercourse with disapproval and have no institutions to support sexual license. The Trobrianders, on the other hand, look with kindly indulgence on the sexual experimentation of children, and allow the young men to visit the girls under conditions of almost complete freedom. It is probably no accident, says Malinowski, that among the Trobrianders there appears to be no hysteria or neurasthenia, and that during his long visit among these people he observed no cases of nervous tics or of obsessive behavior. The Amphlett Islanders, however, were a community of neurasthenics. It should be added that these two groups are similar in race and in language, and that their cultural differences refer almost exclusively to their attitude toward sexual morality.

"FASHIONS" IN ABNORMALITY

There are interesting qualitative differences in the psychoses shown by different groups, and highly complex disturbances in behavior which appear to be characteristic of certain societies and not of others. In some cases these can be shown to be influenced very directly by the culture of the group. Cooper (7), for example, has described what he calls the "wihtigo psychosis," which appears among the northern Cree Indians in the vicinity of James Bay. The wihtigo in Cree mythology is a supernatural being who is much feared because of his cannibalistic tendencies. Occasionally, particularly in times of famine, a man may have the delusion that he has been transformed into a wihtigo and may develop a craving for human flesh; he either goes through the motions of eating it or actually does so. This type of psychosis is clearly a cultural phenomenon, and could not appear in that form among any other people.

Other "fashions" in abnormality are not quite so easy to explain. One of the most interesting is the so-called "Arctic hysteria," of which an excellent account has been given by Bogoras (5) and which has been critically summarized by Čzaplička (8). It is found chiefly among northern Siberians, and its most important feature is the tendency of the sufferer to repeat the words and actions of those in his immediate vicinity. There is a high degree of suggestibility, almost hypnotic in intensity, although the subject is perfectly wide awake in the process. If the victim sees someone throw an object away, or even pretend to throw it away, he himself will repeat the action with whatever he happens to have in his hand. He will imitate as if by compulsion indecent gestures made by another, and will often repeat every word that is addressed to him. There is even one account of a whole regiment of Siberian natives repeating the orders of a Russian officer, who was not aware of the existence of this malady and whose anger was not appeased when even his reprimands were shouted back at him.

The cause of this affliction is obscure. Novakovsky (13) suggests that it is the reflection of the Siberian environment. The long winter with its cold and darkness and extreme quiet; the sudden change of season; the short summer period necessitating strenuous and anxious labor to provide enough food for the winter season—all these conditions create an "environment which is responsible for a highly disorganized nervous system" (p. 127), of which Arctic hysteria is one manifestation. People from other parts of Siberia or from Russia become subject to this same hysterical condition when they migrate to these regions. Huntington (10) accepts this explanation and finds in it a welcome support of his views regarding the importance of environment. Unfortunately for the theory, however, there is a very similar disease found in equatorial regions, particularly in the Malay peninsula, where the climate and the geographical environment differ as much from the Arctic as it is possible to imagine. It is known as "lattah" and also is characterized by great imitativeness of much the same variety. Clifford (6) believes that it is present to some extent at least in every adult Malay. It should be added that this imitative mania can hardly be explained as a racial characteristic, since the Malays and the northern Siberians are not identical in physical type. It is true that they are both Mongoloid; but the rest of that widely scattered race appears to be free from this disorder, and its sporadic occurrence in these two distinct areas precludes a racial explanation.

Arctic hysteria is therefore not necessarily Arctic, nor does it seem to be a true hysteria. One of the typical characteristics of hysteria is that the patient almost invariably retains enough control over his actions to avoid hurting himself. A man with hysterical epilepsy, for example, differs from a true epileptic in that his fits rarely do him any real harm. This is not true of the imitative mania found in the Arctic. If the sufferer sees someone else apparently jump into the water, he will jump in himself even at the risk of his life, and he will often sustain serious injury. The true nature of the disease is still not clearly understood.

In the case of lattah, Van Loon (15) notes that 85 per cent of the Malay women suffering from it in East India had lived most of their life as servants in European or in the wealthier Chinese or Malay households. They had learned to obey automatically, without question, and without any initiative of their own. The disease in their case may thus be simply an extension and an exaggeration of an habitual mode of behavior.

Van Loon also discusses the well-known condition of "amok," which occurs with special frequency among the Malays. It is characterized by a sudden attack of mad rage in which the man who "runs amok" blindly attacks everyone he meets, often injuring or killing a great many before he can be stopped. Kraepelin (11) regarded amok as an epileptic dream state; but Van Loon states that the majority of cases are not caused by epilepsy, and that the epileptics whom he observed in the Dutch East Indies did not run amok. In amok the cause is not temper or rage as in epilepsy, but an agony of fear, the patient in his hallucination imagining himself to be attacked by a tiger, a snake or a human enemy. It frequently occurs in many infectious conditions, but the exact cause of these particular symptoms is still obscure.

These few instances of local psychoses suggest an interesting and fruitful field of investigation. There are undoubtedly others which have not as yet been adequately described, the careful study of which would undoubtedly throw light on the intricate relation between culture and abnormality. There is room here for important work by the ethnologically trained psychiatrist whose mind is open to the possible effects of culture, as well as to the manifestations of mental disturbance in our own society.

Conclusion

The writer is not suggesting that the concept of abnormality has an exclusively cultural significance. It may be argued, for example, that the analogy between paranoia in our society and the behavior of the Northwest Coast chieftain is at best a superficial one. The external manifestation may be similar, but the paranoiac is characterized by a fundamental lack of orientation which gives him a totally different personality constellation. There is likewise a very real difference between the Hindu mystic who has achieved a *voluntary* control over the posture of his body, and the catatonic who remains rigid in response to some inner uncontrollable need. The Hindu is an integrated, the catatonic a disintegrated personality.

Granting all this, it is still important to note that in the overt behavior at least there is a close similarity between what is normal in one society and abnormal in another. Perhaps the clearest case is that of homosexuality, where the abnormality consists entirely of a certain form of behavior, so that the resemblance between the Siberian shaman and the pervert in our society may hardly be dismissed as superficial. It is true that in some cases the shaman may be feared and disliked, but he is accepted as an important person in the community. (See Čzaplička, 8.) His position is an enviable one, and it is more than probable that many people who would otherwise show no such tendency are encouraged to do so by the prestige and power which will result.

Racial factors can play no part in determining what is normal or abnormal in the life of a community. The megalomanic tendencies of the Northwest Coast and the homosexuality of the Plains Indians are equally foreign to the behavior of the Pueblos. (For further discussion of the differences between Indian groups, see Chapter XVIII.) As we have seen, race cannot be responsible for the incidence of abnormality, for Malinowski (12) has shown that two neighboring Melanesian peoples may differ greatly in this respect, and Williams (16) has indicated that the same people (the Russians) may show a marked decrease in mental disturbance when anxiety pressures have been relieved. Finally, race cannot account for the occurrence of what we have called "fashions" in abnormality. The wihtigo psychosis of the Cree is not found in other American Indian communities. The imitative mania known as Arctic hysteria has a distribution which does not correspond with that of any particular type. These various group differences may be accounted for only by the molding influence of culture.

BIBLIOGRAPHY

1. Alexander, F. "Buddhistic Training as an Artificial Catatonia." *Psychoanal. Rev.,* 18:1931, pp. 129-145.
2. Benedict, R. F. "Anthropology and the Abnormal." *J. Genet. Psych.,* 10:1934, pp. 59-82.
3. Benedict, R. F. "The Vision in Plains Culture." *Amer. Anthrop.,* 24:1922, pp. 1-23.
4. Benedict, R. F. *Patterns of Culture.* New York, 1934.
5. Bogoras, V. "The Chukchee," from *Publications of the Jessup North Pacific Expedition,* Vol. VII. New York, 1904-1909.
6. Clifford, H. *Studies in Brown Humanity.* London, 1898.
7. Cooper, J. "Mental Disease Situations in Certain Cultures: A New Field for Research." *J. Abn. and Soc. Psych.,* 29:1934, pp. 10-18.
8. Čzaplička, M. A. *Aboriginal Siberia.* Oxford, 1914.
9. Fortune, R. *Sorcerers of Dobu: The Social Anthropology of the Dobu Islanders of the Western Pacific.* London, 1932.
10. Huntington, E. *The Character of Races.* New York, 1924.
11. Kraepelin, E. "Vergleichende Psychiatrie." *Zentralbl. f. Nervenheilk. u. Psychiatrie,* 27:1904, p. 433.
12. Malinowski, B. *Sex and Repression in Savage Society.* London, 1927.
13. Novakovsky, S. "Arctic or Siberian Hysteria as a Reflex of Geographic Environment." *Ecology,* Vol. 5, April, 1924.
14. Sapir, E. "Cultural Anthropology and Psychiatry." *J. Abn. & Soc. Psych.,* 27:1932, pp. 229-242.
15. Van Loon, F. H. G. "Amok and Lattah." *J. Abn. & Soc. Psych.,* 21:1927, pp. 434-444.
16. Williams, F. *Russia, Youth and the Present-Day World.* New York, 1934.

Chapter XVII

CHILDHOOD AND ADOLESCENCE

THE IMPORTANCE OF CHILD STUDY

THE study of children in different communities has a special significance for the problems of race and culture. When adults only are compared, it is not always possible to tell to what extent the differences between them are due to innate and to acquired factors respectively. When the comparison is made between children, the differences may be seen in the process of formation, and something may therefore be learned about the educational forces which are operative. This genetic approach is of value in almost every problem which we have so far considered. In the case of emotional expression, for example, it is important to know when the observed differences between various peoples develop; if they are racial in character there should be some evidence of their presence at a very early age; if cultural, they should be negligible at first and become progressively greater. When, in addition, something can be found in the environment or in the culture to explain the differences, the case in favor of their acquired character becomes all the stronger.

This may be illustrated by an interesting observation regarding sex differences made by Margaret Mead (6) in her study of the children on the island of Manus in New Guinea. These children do not play with dolls. On one occasion Miss Mead brought to them some little wooden statues from a neighboring tribe, and it was the boys, not the girls, who treated them as dolls and crooned lullabies to them. This hardly argues that sex differences in Manus are fundamentally opposed to those in other peoples; and if we free ourselves from the old notion that little girls play with dolls as a sort of biological prophecy of later motherhood, it is not very difficult to understand. As Miss Mead points out, the pattern in Manus is for the men to play with the children, while the women are busy with their regular duties. The division of labor is such that the women are continuously occupied throughout the day, while the men have a great deal of leisure time between their activities of hunting and fishing. The father attends to the child and plays with it, and the Manus boy in Miss Mead's experiment is merely imitating the behavior of his father in what we might regard as a *cultural* "prophecy of later fatherhood." This fits in with the theory of Groos (3), who considers play as a preliminary experimentation in forms of behavior that are important in adult life, except that we regard the determining factors as cultural and not biological. For our purposes the essential thing is that a sex difference which in one society might be regarded as innately determined, is completely reversed when a culture imposes other patterns of behavior.

This point is carried further in Miss Mead's latest book (7), in which the relation between sex and temperament is studied in three primitive societies. Among the Arapesh, both men and women are trained to be co-operative, unaggressive, responsive to the needs and demands of others. In marked contrast, both men and women among the Mundugumor are ruthless, aggressive, "positively sexed individuals." In the third tribe, the Tchambuli, there is "a genuine reversal of the sex-attitudes of our own culture, with the woman the dominant, impersonal, managing partner, the man the less responsible and the emotionally dependent person" (p. 279). It is concluded that "the personalities of the two sexes are socially produced" (p. 310).

In the present chapter we are concerned primarily with two problems in child psychology. The first is the question of child thinking, and the way in which it may vary under the influence of cultural factors; the second is the problem of adolescence. In both of these the work of Margaret Mead (5, 6, 7) has been of great importance.

THE THINKING OF THE CHILD

In a significant series of studies the Swiss psychologist Piaget (9, 10) has described the formation of concepts in the mind of the child, and has skillfully analyzed the relation of the child to the world in which he lives. At first, says Piaget, the child does not distinguish the psychical from the physical world, and regards as living and conscious a large number of objects which are for us inanimate. This phenomenon he calls "animism," defined as "the tendency among children to consider things as living and conscious" (p. 380). There are four successive stages; in the first everything that is in any way active is conscious, even though stationary; in the second, consciousness is attributed only to things that can move—the sun and a bicycle are conscious, a table and a stone are not; in the third stage, things that move of their own accord, like the sun and the wind, are conscious, whereas objects that receive motion from outside, like a bicycle, are not; in the fourth and final stage, consciousness is restricted to the animal world. The same stages are described in the case of attributing "life" to objects. Children may vary in the age at which these stages appear, but they are apparently all animistic for some time at least. Piaget suggests that animism is an essential aspect of the child's thinking.

There is of course the alternative possibility that the child thinks animistically as a result of the training and education he receives in one particular society. It is not difficult to find a number of factors which tend in that direction. When Tommy hurts himself against a chair, he is usually comforted when his mother scolds the chair for being so naughty. He is told stories of the wind and the sun competing with each other in order to make a man remove his coat, or of magic tables which "set themselves," or of a door which opens in response to the right command. The language which he learns speaks of the "sun rising," the "wind moaning in the forest"; it speaks of a ship as "she"; and in its poetry it asks, "What are the wild waves saying?" In other languages like French and German where masculine and feminine gender are ascribed to inanimate objects, there would be an even greater encouragement of this tendency. The question then arises as to whether the child would still think animistically if his early training and his language were free of all these influences.

Margaret Mead (6, 8) is of the opinion that personalizing the universe is not inherent in child thinking, but is a tendency bequeathed to him by his society. She found animism foreign to the mentality of the children she studied in the village of Peri, of the Manus tribe in the Admiralty Islands. She writes: "I found no evidence of a child's attributing chance events, such as the drifting away of a canoe, the loss of an object, an unexplained noise, a sudden gust of wind . . . to supernatural causes" (8, p. 173). When she attempted to blame the canoe for drifting away, she would receive an answer like, "No, it wasn't fastened," or "Popoli is stupid; he didn't fasten it right." When a child made a bad drawing, Miss Mead attempted to blame the pencil, but the child would answer in surprise, "I made it badly," or "I drew it like that." She obtained from the children over thirty thousand drawings, and not once in the entire set did she find a natural phenomenon personified or an inanimate object treated as if it were alive. All her attempts to discover signs of animistic thinking among these children were unsuccessful.

In explanation she points out that the Manus child is forced at a very early age to make a correct physical adjustment to his environment. If he hurts himself the fault is not that of the object, but his own; instead of being petted and comforted, he is scolded for his clumsiness. If he hurts himself a second time, he hopes that no one has seen him, instead of crying for help. One result of this is that he quickly achieves a self-reliance and a physical proficiency far in advance of children of the same age in our society. "He grows up to be an adult wholly admirable from a physical standpoint, skilled, alert, fearless, resourceful in the face of emergency, reliable under strain" (6, p. 47).

The language also is free from personalizing tendencies. It is a simple language without figures of speech, sex gender or rich imagery. It makes no distinction between "he," "she" or "it," and therefore in her opinion gives no suggestion of life to inanimate objects. (On this point, however, Miss Mead's analysis is not convincing, since a language of this kind might render even more probable the confusion between the physical and the mental which Piaget regards as the basis of the child's animism.)

Manus adults are animistic, although in a slightly different sense. Their world is peopled by spirits whose activities explain sickness and death and all other kinds of misfortune. The children apparently are little affected by this traditional point of view. Even when the adults describe the spirits or devils to them, the children pay little attention. They "reject the supernatural in favor of the natural" (6, p. 108). Piaget, however, seems to be of the opinion that the animism of children is far removed from the religious attitude which Tylor (11) discussed under the same name, and which consists of peopling the world with spirits. Tylor's animism is presumably due to the idea of a soul or spirit, which results from a person's experiences with death and dreams. It is an attempt to explain and understand the difference between the animate and the inanimate. The child's animism, on the other hand, is due precisely to a confusion between these two. When, usually between the ages of eight and ten, he becomes conscious of the difference, he ceases to think animistically. Miss Mead's point, therefore, that Manus children are not animistic because the adults in the community do not share with them their traditional material, would seem to be due to the identification of these two quite different forms of animism. Even if the children did people their world with spirits, they might still not personalize inanimate objects. It may be, however, that the two forms of animism are not so distinct as Piaget suggests.

In any case, our present concern is not with the details of Miss Mead's interpretation, but with her demonstration of the fact that the thinking of Manus children is not identical with that of children in Geneva or in New York. Even in the case of something apparently as fundamental as a thought process, culture and education may be seen creating marked divergences between different groups.

ADOLESCENCE

In our society a number of psychologists have testified to the difficulties of adjustment attendant upon the period of adolescence. G. Stanley Hall (4), in his monumental treatment of this subject, spoke of adolescence as a period of storm and stress and likened its manifestations to the symptoms of hysteria and other forms of mental disturbance.

It is supposedly a time of turmoil when the individual tries to escape from tradition and family influence, or experiences a disturbing religious conversion, or discovers that he is a misfit in society. Other psychologists have regarded this picture as somewhat exaggerated, but they agree that this period is a difficult one, and that profound alterations in the personality are of frequent occurrence.

Here, too, groups differ. Margaret Mead (5), who has studied Samoan society from this point of view, writes that there the adolescent girl differs from the non-adolescent only in the fact of bodily changes; there is no conflict, no revolt, no mental disturbance or neurosis; only an easy transition to a new status. There are several reasons for this, as Miss Mead points out. The problem of sex, which in one form or another creates difficulties for almost every adolescent in our society, is practically non-existent. Samoan society permits pre-marital intimacies, and shortly after puberty almost every young boy and girl enters into a series of "affairs." These can hardly be called "love affairs," because love in the romantic sense in which we know it rarely enters; but they are for that reason no less able to satisfy an urge which in our society is probably the most important single source of torment and disturbance.

In addition, the transition to adult life in Samoa, as among almost all of the so-called primitive peoples, is made much easier for the adolescent because he is not faced with the same problem of finding a way of adjustment to his new status. The choice of a vocation and a career, of a religion and a moral code, of friends—all constitute issues in a world where the process of becoming an adult is so difficult precisely because it is so imperfectly defined. The adolescent is uncertain of his status. He is trying to be a man among people who still regard him as a child, and who will not treat him with the seriousness to which he thinks he is entitled. Conflict, though not inevitable, occurs easily under such conditions, especially because of the lack of uniformity which makes it possible for some adolescents to have more freedom and greater independence than others. Adult status in our group cannot be achieved without a struggle.

In the case of the "primitive" adolescent the problem is simpler. There is still room for individuality, but on the whole there are few choices for him to make. Revolt of any kind is so rare as to present no difficulty. There are not many religions to choose from, only the one which is accepted by all. There is often only one way of earning a living, and usually a fixed time for marrying and building his own house. His attitude toward his parents, his place in society, his status as an individual, the amount of freedom which he may enjoy, are all determined for him.

This does not mean that the more primitive peoples pay no attention to the fact of adolescence. There are some who do not, but they are in the minority. In most cases there is definite recognition of the fact that the youth is becoming an adult, preparing to act as a full-fledged member of the group, and no longer to be treated as a child and a dependent. With this recognition there are many ceremonial observances varying from tribe to tribe. (See Van Waters, 13, 14.) In Australia the boy must undergo severe physical ordeals; in British Columbia both boys and girls perform certain rites to train them for their future occupations; among the Plains Indians the boy used to seek a vision experience and torture himself in order to win prowess in war. Other groups make their young men and women act in a play or allegory in which they die and are born again. Still others make them change their place of dwelling, or permit them new types of decoration, or keep them in seclusion for a time, or give them tests of skill and endurance, or instruct them in the manners and customs of their people. In general, therefore, coming-of-age is regarded as having real importance, although interestingly enough the ceremonies occur at different ages in different groups, depending more on the social significance of the rite than on the sudden occurrence of a biological change. (See Benedict, 1.) In any case it rarely brings with it much conflict or disturbance. The change in status is an important one for the individual, but it is determined in almost every detail by the unchallenged conventions of the group and offers no special psychological problem. It seems reasonable to conclude, therefore, that when problems do arise, as among our own adolescents, they are created by culture rather than by biology.

Conclusion

The material briefly summarized in this chapter raises the important question of the extent to which the typical psychological development of the child is a function of his social environment. Piaget's suggestion of an early animistic period in the child's thinking may not hold, as Margaret Mead suggests, in a community in which the language and the parental admonitions are not so rich in animistic allusions. It would be interesting to make parallel observations in several primitive communities of other stages through which the child is said to pass. One such study might be made of Piaget's distinction between an earlier "egocentric" or a later "socialized" speech, the former being quite independent of the responses of the other children present, whereas the latter represents a true exchange of ideas. Furfey's (2) concept of Developmental Age, which is presumably a measure of emotional maturity, would certainly not be equally applicable to all groups. There are very probably differences in the developmental curve, depending on the demands placed upon the child by his society.

This is particularly true in the case of adolescence, the psychological significance of which does not depend mainly upon a physiological change, but rather upon a culturally defined form of behavior. Adolescent conflict is a phenomenon of our society, not of human nature. Even in this case, it is important to note that the conflict does not usually occur at the time of physiological puberty, but some time later, when the real transition to adult life takes place, and when the worries attendant upon social and economic relationships begin to appear. Not only the nature of the problems of adolescence, but even their very existence as well as the time of their occurrence, will differ according to cultural influences.

BIBLIOGRAPHY

1. Benedict, R. F. *Patterns of Culture*. New York, 1934.
2. Furfey, P. H. *The Growing Boy*. New York, 1930.
3. Groos, K. *The Play of Man*. New York, 1901. (Trans.)
4. Hall, G. S. *Adolescence*. New York, 1905. (2 vols.)
5. Mead, M. *Coming of Age in Samoa*. New York, 1928.
6. Mead, M. *Growing Up in New Guinea*. New York, 1930.
7. Mead, M. *Sex and Temperament in Three Primitive Societies*. New York, 1935.
8. Mead, M. "An Investigation of the Thought of Primitive Children with Special Reference to Animism." *J. Roy. Anthrop. Inst.*, 62:1932, pp. 173-190.
9. Piaget, J. *The Child's Conception of the World*. New York, 1929. (Trans.)
10. Piaget, J. "Children's Philosophies," in Murchison, *A Handbook of Child Psychology*. Worcester, Mass., 1931.
11. Tylor, Sir E. B. *Primitive Culture*. London, 1871.
12. Van Waters, M. *The Adolescent Girl Among Primitive Peoples*. Worcester, Mass., 1914.
13. Van Waters, M. "Adolescence," in *Encycl. of the Soc. Sci.*, Vol. I, pp. 455-459. New York, 1930.

Chapter XVIII

PERSONALITY

The Individual and Society

THE problem of the relation between culture and personality
is implicit in a great deal of the material which has been
presented. If we think of personality as the integration of all
behavior patterns of the individual, it is clear that it has already been discussed in part under several headings. The
strength of the fundamental drives, the emotional attitudes,
the ideas as to what constitutes normality, the presence or
absence of conflict, all make their contribution to the nature
of the individual. It may be questioned whether we have
any right to speak of personality apart from these and similar aspects.

There have, however, been several interesting attempts to
look at the relation between personality and culture in a
different way. Some of these have found their inspiration
in the point of view of psychoanalysis, and have approached
the problems of personality in a primitive culture by the application of Freudian mechanisms. Others have been impressed by the manner in which total cultures are integrated,
and have tried to understand the complete pattern of behavior by seeing it as a functioning dynamic whole. These
approaches have opened up new and significant problems,
and point the way to further important work in this field.

The "Œdipus Complex"

In the Freudian approach to personality, the Œdipus complex occupies perhaps the central position. It receives its

name from the tragic story of Œdipus who, having grown up far from his native Thebes, returned to kill unknowingly his father Laius and marry his mother Jocasta; when they discovered what they had done, Jocasta killed herself and Œdipus put out his eyes. We are still moved by this tragedy, says Freud, because there is in every one of us, though in varying degrees of attenuation, the desire to kill the father and possess completely the love of the mother. This is apparently a fundamental and universal "complex" which undergoes more or less successful repression, the degree of this repression being of great importance in the development of the personality. (For the place of the complex in the whole Freudian scheme, see Freud, 8.)

The Œdipus complex has been used as a principle of explanation not only in the case of normal and abnormal individual personality, but also in the interpretation of social and ethnological phenomena. There have been a number of essays in this latter field, of which Reik's psychoanalytic studies of ritual (23), Roheim's analysis of Australian Totemism (24), and the interpretation of myths by Otto Rank (22) and Karl Abraham (1) may be mentioned as representative. Freud himself has written in *Totem and Taboo* (9) what has been called an "ethnological psychoanalysis," which is an attempt to explain incest taboos and other totemistic proscriptions on a psychoanalytic basis. The assumption is here made that society once consisted of a primal horde, in which a violent and jealous father kept all the females for himself, and drove away the growing sons. "One day the expelled brothers joined forces, slew and ate the father, and thus put an end to the father horde" (p. 235). Then the suppressed tender impulses toward the father asserted themselves in the form of remorse; and the sons tried to undo their deed by declaring that the killing of the father substitute, the totem, was not allowed, and they renounced the fruits of their victory by denying themselves the liberated women. This is the origin of the incest prohibition, according to Freud, as well as of the taboo against killing or eating the totem animal. (For a critical discussion of this theory see Goldenweiser, 11, and Kroeber, 19.) Roheim (25) is of the opinion that with *Totem and Taboo* a new science has appeared. "We sometimes call it psychoanalytical anthropology, but we all believe it will be the only anthropology of the future" (p. 6).

This historical reconstruction of Freud's has been challenged by the anthropologists, and there is no doubt that from the scientific point of view the evidence which Freud adduces is very meager. However, the application of the Œdipus complex to the understanding of certain mechanisms of human behavior has been made with much greater success, and though we may question its universality there appears to be no doubt about its importance. Here as elsewhere the problem arises as to whether the complex is to be regarded as an inevitable component of human nature, or as an effect of the particular family system under which we live. In the latter event, we should expect the complex to take a different form in those cultures which have institutionalized a different set of family relationships.

Malinowski (20) has shown how the "nuclear complex" (an alternative name for the Œdipus complex) may be affected by a matrilineal society like that of the Trobriand Islanders. Whereas among us the father represents authority, among the Trobrianders he has no rights or prerogatives, and his relation to his children is purely social. It is his duty to "receive them in his arms" (p. 10). He assists in looking after them and tending to their needs, and is regarded by them as an affectionate friend. The authority over them is centered in the mother's brother. It is he who is held up as an ideal to be followed. He introduces into the life of the boy social ambition, glory, pride in lineage, and the promise of future wealth. He must be obeyed unquestioningly.

The relation to the mother also shows certain differences. In our society weaning is usually very sudden and painful for the child; it is a real trauma. From that time on the child is separated more and more from the mother, and there is a gap in his life that is not easily filled. In New Guinea weaning takes place much later, at a time when the child neither wants nor needs the breast, and gives it up voluntarily. There is no sudden wrench and no trauma, and presumably no unfulfilled longing for the mother.

Childish sex curiosity is taken for granted and not looked upon as reprehensible in any way. The children are left to themselves, and there is a great deal of sex experimentation even before puberty. There is, however, one important taboo. Brothers and sisters are separated from an early age and are never together socially on a free footing. Above all, there must not be the slightest suspicion of an interest of one in the love affairs of the other. At puberty the taboo is particularly strict, and there are special houses inhabited by groups of adolescent boys and girls separately. The sister is therefore a mysterious being, near but never intimate. She is the only spot in the sexual horizon that is permanently hidden. She is forbidden, "indecent." This taboo causes the thought of the sister to be constantly present and constantly repressed.

Malinowski suggests that these differences in the relationships within the family give to the nuclear complex a very special form. "In the Œdipus complex there is the repressed desire to kill the father and marry the mother, while in the matrilineal society of the Trobriands the wish is to marry the sister and kill the maternal uncle" (p. 81). The evidence is not entirely convincing; but it is interesting to note that when the natives were asked whether they ever dreamed of incest with their sisters, they became very much disturbed and refused to discuss the matter, whereas the thought of incest with the mother was apparently ridiculed and dismissed without any show of emotion.

The mythological material is significant from this same point of view. In one heroic legend Tudava, the hero of many tales, revenges himself upon his maternal uncle for having abandoned Tudava's mother when she was too ill to flee with him from the ogre who was laying waste the country. Another story tells how love magic originated when a sister and brother became infatuated with each other and died in each other's arms; "through their linked bodies grew the sweet-smelling plant which is the most powerful of love magics" (p. 128).

This interesting attempt by Malinowski to derive the nature of the nuclear complex from the family organization has been challenged by a number of psychoanalysts, particularly Ernest Jones (14). He believes that the important problem is to understand why the Trobrianders should have this system of mother-kinship and should trace their descent through the mother rather than through the father. One possible explanation is ignorance as to the part which the father plays in procreation, and Malinowski had indeed noted that the Trobrianders seemed to lack knowledge on this point. Jones cannot believe that they are really ignorant; he suggests that the observation of the behavior of animals could hardly fail to enlighten them. (This is not entirely convincing, however, since also among animals the birth of the young occurs so long after the performance of the sexual act.) In Jones' opinion, the Œdipus complex is fundamental, and the hatred against the father results in a repudiation of the father's part in procreation. Mother-right and the apparent ignorance of paternity are due to the same motive—to soften and deflect the hatred against the father. Many neurotics also refuse to admit to themselves the part which is played by the father in procreation, and in religion the frequently recurring theme of the virgin mother may be similarly explained. The maternal uncle is chosen as a sort of scapegoat. "The matrilineal system with its avunculate complex arose . . . as a mode of defense against the primordial Œdipus tendencies." The complex is the cause, and the whole sociological structure is the effect.

Any attempt to decide between the alternatives presented by Jones and Malinowski would necessarily lead to a critical discussion of the whole structure of psychoanalysis, and this is obviously impossible here. Malinowski's position seems to the writer to be rather more convincing. In any case it constitutes a significant effort to understand the relations among individuals in a family on the basis of the specific influences at work in one particular culture. Since in our society personality development is regarded by the Freudians as largely the result of the earliest experiences of the child in the home, the relations with the parents determining most of its ideals and social attitudes, it is obvious that Malinowski has raised an issue of the greatest importance.

Psychoanalytic Personality Types

Largely as a result of the ethnological field work of Geza Roheim (25), considerable interest has been aroused in the possibility of understanding the personality of primitive peoples in terms of psychoanalytic mechanisms. Karl Abraham (2), for example, developed the notion of the "oral character," which Roheim applies to the understanding of the characteristics of the natives of central Australia. The theory on which this application rests is that the very early experiences of the child, and particularly those associated with feeding, may be of the greatest importance in determining the adult character.

According to Abraham, if in the suckling stage the pleasure derived is marked and undisturbed, the individual's whole attitude toward life is apt to be an optimistic one. His dominant feeling is one of expectation that some kind person (a mother representative) will care for him, and that the mother's breast will flow for him eternally. He will tend to be generous and care-free; an "oral optimist." Failure to achieve gratification in the suckling period may result in a later asking or demanding social attitude, a tendency to cling to others, a dislike of being alone, and a marked impatience and apprehensiveness. This is the "oral pessimist." (For convenient description and criticism, see Healy, Bronner and Bowers [12], pp. 310 ff.)

The Central Australian, according to Roheim, is predominantly an oral optimist. His mother is invariably good and kind, generous with her breast to all children. The child is never weaned until he weans himself. The people grow up generous, friendly, happy. The type that has lost faith in the world because of the trauma of weaning (the oral pessimist) does not exist among them. There are no eternal grumblers, no persons who are continually being slighted or offended. They are all on the best possible terms with one another and with the world.

Freud (7) and Jones (15) have both discussed what they call the "anal character." The child in whom anal erotism is strong derives great pleasure from the various activities associated with the excretory processes, and feels intensely the strong taboos imposed by his environment upon all direct modes of expression of these interests. As a result of symbolization and sublimation, several personality traits may later develop which express the same tendencies in an indirect fashion. Freud believes that there are three cardinal anal characteristics—(1) orderliness (bodily cleanliness, reliability, conscientiousness, pedantry), (2) parsimony or avarice, (3) obstinacy or defiance.

The Central Australians are perfectly natural about all their excremental functions. There are no taboos or restrictions of any kind associated with them. Consequently, says Roheim, the anal character does not occur among them. They have no care for the morrow, and time means nothing to them. Instead of being stingy, they share everything with their fellows.

This approach has interesting possibilities which it is hoped will be developed by further research. It would be a particularly good check upon the psychoanalytic theories of character formation to try them out upon a large number of primitive societies. There are many of these among whom feeding and excretion arouse attitudes different from those reported for the Australian Arunta, and it would be worth while noting with considerable care their relation to personality formation. It is obvious, however, that the description of the character of a primitive people is a very subjective matter, and the method is difficult to apply without being affected by one's own bias. Even if there were complete agreement about the Arunta, one would still have to retain a certain scepticism until the relationship had been verified in several other communities. This does not mean that Roheim's interpretation is incorrect, but merely that all subjective generalizations are necessarily open to question. There is, however, enough plausibility in his analysis to warrant the further application of a similar technique.

CULTURE PATTERNS AND THE INDIVIDUAL

In an earlier paragraph personality was tentatively defined as "the integration of the behavior patterns of the individual." No two individuals, with the possible exception of identical twins, are ever entirely alike in these behavior patterns, but the similarities which do exist have led to several attempts to divide individuals into types. Perhaps the best known of these is Jung's (16) division into extroverts, whose interest and energy is directed outward, usually upon the external world, and introverts, whose interest is directed primarily upon themselves. There are many other type classifications; William James (13) speaks of the tender-minded and the tough-minded; Nietzsche (21), of the Apollonian and Dionysian; Spranger (27) has six types, the economic, the æsthetic, the theoretic, the religious, the social and the political; Kretschmer (18) speaks of schizothyme and cyclothyme. Still others might be cited, but these have attracted the most attention.

It is possible that cultures, too, may be classified in a somewhat similar fashion. If we take Jung's types as a starting point, there will probably be almost complete agreement in the description of the culture of the United States of today as predominantly extrovert. There might not be the same unanimity in the choice of a typically introvert culture, but it is more than likely that India, with its emphasis upon subjective religious experience and withdrawal from the world, would generally be regarded as falling in that category. This may not be the best classification to use in the case of cultures, but it at least indicates one possible approach. As far as the individual is concerned, it seems reasonable to believe that his introversion may be determined at least in part by the prevailing patterns of his culture.

There is no doubt that cultures, like individuals, are totalities. They, too, constitute an integration which is more than the sum of its parts, and which cannot be understood if attention is focused on the parts alone. In the social sciences the concept of integration was stressed by Dilthey (5), but its rôle in the understanding of culture was given more definite recognition by Oswald Spengler (26) in his *Decline of the West*. Spengler draws an interesting contrast between the Apollonian world-view which is characteristic of the classical period, and the more modern Faustian attitude. For the Apollonian, the soul is a cosmos ordered into a group of excellent parts. Life is under the shadow of threatening catastrophe from outside, and there is no place for individual will or conflict. For the Faustian, on the other hand, the soul is a force endlessly combating obstacles and striving for the infinite; life is an inner development and conflict is its essence. All aspects of culture—painting, music, mathematics, architecture—express these two opposed philosophies.

A significant attempt to understand cultures as integrations has recently been made by Ruth Benedict (3). She rightly points out that Spengler's characterizations are not entirely applicable to the complex and heterogeneous civilizations which he sought to describe. She believes that the integrated character of societies may better be studied where there are not so many cross currents and divergencies of behavior, and she turns her own attention to the simpler, more "primitive" cultures.

Her starting point is Nietzsche's discussion in his studies of Greek tragedy of two opposed ways of arriving at the values of existence. The Dionysian pursues these values through the "annihilation of the ordinary bounds and limits of existence" (3, p. 78). He seeks to escape from the boundaries set by his senses and to break through to another order of experience. He presses to achieve excess and values the illuminations of frenzy. The Apollonian distrusts all of this. His law is *measure*, and he keeps to the middle of the road. He does not meddle with disruptive psychological states. Even in the exaltation of the dance, he "remains what he is, and retains his civic name" (3, p. 79).

In Benedict's opinion this typology appears to be particularly applicable, though not in every Nietzschean detail, to the cultures of the North American Indians. She believes that on the whole the American Indians were Dionysian. They valued violent experiences and had a highly developed individualism. They obtained their supernatural power in a dream or vision which was sought at times (as on the western plains) with hideous tortures. Drugs and alcohol were used freely; intoxication meant exaltation, and was a synonym of religion. Life was filled with intense and disturbing experiences.

On the other hand, the Pueblo Indians of Arizona and New Mexico are distinctly Apollonian. The Zuñi, for example, are described (following Dr. Bunzel, 4) as a ceremonious people valuing sobriety and inoffensiveness. Their religious life is formal and established, consisting of the performance of neatly dovetailed ceremonies which occupy a great deal of their time and attention. Their prayers are formulæ, the effectiveness of which comes from their faithful rendition. Instead of being an intense outpouring of the human heart they are always mild and ceremonious, asking for orderly life, pleasant days and shelter from violence.

Among the Pueblos, visual or auditory hallucinations are to be avoided. Individuals do go out at night to listen for a voice, but merely as a mechanical taking of omens rather than a search for a particular experience. Fasting is merely a requirement for ceremonial cleanliness and is not connected with any sort of exaltation. Drugs are used very rarely, and alcohol constitutes no problem among them as it does on almost all other Indian reservations. There is no torture; the boys are lashed in the initiation ceremonies, but not severely enough to draw blood. The dancing shows none of the frenzy found elsewhere. It is merely an effort to influence nature by a monotonous reiteration of prescribed movements. Even the well-known Hopi Snake Dance is not a Dionysian courting of a dangerous or repulsive experience, but a sober and formal ceremonial.

There is almost no individualism among the Zuñi, and personal authority is perhaps the trait most vigorously discouraged. The ideal man is a person of affability and dignity, who has never tried to lead and who has never called forth comment from his neighbors. Even in contests of skill, like foot races, if a man wins habitually he is debarred from running. A good man is one about whom one never hears anything. Even when he has office thrust upon him, he must avoid the appearance of leadership. There are no shamans conspicuous for peculiarity or instability of personality, only priests who are depositories of ritual and administrators of cult activities. Death is faced realistically, as a bereavement, but the mourning is nothing like that of the Plains Indians, among whom it was a Dionysian indulgence in uninhibited grief. The Pueblos have made a "civilization whose forms are dictated by the typical choices of the Apollonian, all of whose delight is in formality and whose way of life is the way of measure and of sobriety." (Benedict, 3, p. 129.)

Other cultures may similarly be described in terms of their total pattern or integration. We have already seen that for the Northwest Coast Indian, life was mainly a pursuit of megalomanic drives, and everything was seen and interpreted from the standpoint of the prestige of the individual.

Among the Dobuan Islanders the dominant traits (according to Dr. Fortune, 6) are fear and suspicion, and every person lives in continual dread of the black magic of his associates. It need hardly be pointed out that in these as in all other cultures there is still room for individual differences, but in most cases and for most characteristics the individual is definitely the product of his culture. The accident of being born in Dobu results in one type of personality; and in Zuñi, another. Here again it may be noted that race plays no important part in these differences in cultural integrations. American Indians furnish the best examples of Apollonian culture at one extreme, and Dionysian at another. The Trobriand Islanders (see Malinowski, 20) and the Orakaiva (see Williams, 28) are both Melanesian communities, neighbors of the Dobuans and of exactly the same physical type, but they are both happy care-free peoples without any of the paranoid reactions which are characteristic of Dobu. It is reported that the Trobrianders are exceedingly uncomfortable when in the presence of the Dobuans, and are always anxious to return to their own community. The difference in the behavior pattern is marked, and it has nothing to do with race.

The attempt to describe the total pattern of culture as Dr. Benedict has done, and to note its effect upon the individual, is undoubtedly of very real importance in this whole field. The great difficulty is that the method of approach is one of interpretation, and that it is questionable whether different observers would describe the integration of a culture in the same terms. An ethnologist among the Plains Indians might conceivably be so impressed by their sobriety and unemotionality in the ordinary affairs of life, that he would hesitate to describe them as fundamentally Dionysian. It is difficult in any general characterization of this kind to do justice to the complexities and cross currents which exist even in one of the "simpler" cultures. Quite possibly exceptions will be overlooked because of the interest of the ethnologist in the general pattern. It may be that in time a method will be devised sufficiently objective to eliminate differences of opinion and to give greater reliability to this significant development of a cultural typology. There can be no doubt as to the importance of integration in the intelligent analysis of a culture.

Bibliography

1. Abraham, K. "Dreams and Myths." *Nerv. and Ment. Dis. Mono.*, Ser. 15, 1913. (Trans.)
2. Abraham, K. *Selected Papers of Karl Abraham, M.D.* London, 1927. Chaps. 23 and 24, pp. 370-406.
3. Benedict, R. F. *Patterns of Culture.* New York, 1934.
4a. Bunzel, R. L. "Zuñi Texts." *Publications of the Amer. Ethnol. Soc.*, 15:1933.
4b. Bunzel, R. L. "Introduction to Zuñi Ceremonialism." *Forty-seventh Annual Report of the Bureau of Amer. Ethnol.*, Washington, 1932, pp. 467-544.
5. Dilthey, W. *Gesammelte Schriften,* Vols. II and VIII. Leipzig, 1914-1934. (9 vols.)
6. Fortune, R. *Sorcerers of Dobu; the Social Anthropology of the Dobu Islanders of the Western Pacific.* London, 1932.
7. Freud, S. "Character and Anal Erotism," in *Collected Papers,* Vol. II, Chap. 4, pp. 45-50. London, 1924.
8. Freud, S. *A General Introduction to Psychoanalysis.* New York, 1920. (Trans.)
9. Freud, S. *Totem and Taboo.* London, 1919. (Trans.)
10. Freud, S. *New Introductory Lectures on Psychoanalysis.* New York, 1933. (Trans.)
11. Goldenweiser, A. A. *Early Civilization; an Introduction to Anthropology.* New York, 1922.
12. Healy, W., Bronner, A. F., and Bowers, A. M. *The Structure and Meaning of Psychoanalysis as Related to Personality and Behavior.* New York, 1930.

13. James, W. *Pragmatism; a New Name for Some Old Ways of Thinking.* London, 1911.
14. Jones, E. "Mother-right and the Sexual Ignorance of Savages." *Int. J. Psychoanal.,* 6 Pt. II:1925, pp. 109-130.
15. Jones, E. "Anal-Erotic Character Traits." *J. Abn. Psych.,* 13:1919, pp. 261-284.
16. Jung, C. G. *Psychological Types.* New York, 1926. (Trans.)
17. Jung, C. G. *The Psychology of the Unconscious.* New York, 1916. (Trans.)
18. Kretschmer, E. *Physique and Character.* New York, 1925. (Trans.)
19. Kroeber, A. L. "Totem and Taboo: An Ethnological Psychoanalysis." *Amer. Anthrop.,* 22:1920, pp. 48-55.
20. Malinowski, B. *Sex and Repression in Savage Society.* London, 1927.
21. Nietzsche, F. *The Birth of Tragedy.* New York, 1924. (Trans.)
22. Rank, O. "The Myth of the Birth of the Hero." *Nerv. and Ment. Dis. Mono.,* ser. no. 18:1914.
23. Reik, T. *Ritual: Psycho-analytic Studies.* New York, 1931. (Trans.)
24. Roheim, G. *Australian Totemism.* London, 1925.
25. Roheim, G. "Psychoanalysis of Primitive Cultural Types." *Internatl. J. Psychoanal.,* 13: 1932, pp. 2-224.
26. Spengler, O. *The Decline of the West.* London, 1926-1928. (Trans.)
27. Spranger, E. *Types of Men.* Halle, 1928. (Trans.)
28. Williams, F. E. *Orokaiva Society.* London, 1930.

Chapter XIX

PRIMITIVE MENTALITY

INTRODUCTION

THE material presented in these last few chapters has dealt largely with the behavior of the "simpler" or "primitive" peoples. There are of course striking differences between this behavior and our own in many cases, and it is important to decide whether these may be explained by certain special qualities of the primitive mind. Primitive mentality has been frequently described, but in a variety of ways, and it may be of interest to review critically some of the more important theories.

Historically this problem has been complicated by moral and social issues. The well-known descriptions of the primitive by Rousseau (18) and Hobbes (8), for example, had their principal motivation in a specific theory of society. Hobbes was interested in showing how political institutions arose out of enlightened self-interest, which transformed the "nasty, brutish and short" life of the savage into the more ordered, regulated existence of civilized man. Rousseau, and to a lesser extent also Voltaire, were more concerned with the evils of their own society, which they contrasted with the peaceful, idyllic life of the "noble savage." None of these writers had any direct experience with primitive peoples, and the published material gave little support to their extreme views. In any case, they were probably not concerned with the objective accuracy of the pictures they drew.

In more recent times theories of primitive mentality have usually been affected by the doctrine of evolution. Herbert

Spencer's (19) application of a biological point of view to sociology had suggested that evolution might be used in the explanation of psychological phenomena. It led directly to the notion that the mind of civilized man is a relatively recent product, and that it had been preceded by a more primitive type of mentality. Spencer himself attempted no clear-cut distinction between primitive and civilized mentality. He implied that the mentality is fundamentally identical, the differences depending rather on the amount of knowledge possessed by one community or another. "The laws of thought are everywhere the same; given the data as known to him, primitive man's inference is a reasonable inference." (Spencer [19], p. 100.)

Other writers have spoken with greater assurance of the qualities which they regard as characteristic of the mind of the primitive.

Lévy-Bruhl

One of the most widely known of these theories is that developed by the French sociologist and philosopher, Lévy-Bruhl, who has written a series of volumes (12, 13, 14) that have aroused considerable interest. He starts from Durkheim's (6) notion of "collective representations," ideas which depend for their existence on the group, rather than on any individuals within the group. Among primitive peoples these representations are emotional, not logical. They are also mystical, in that they imply belief in forces and influences which, though imperceptible to the senses, are nevertheless regarded as real. They show a belief in a mystical causality in which anything can be the cause of any effect; so the natives of New Guinea thought that a picture of Queen Victoria could do them harm, and that drawing shadow pictures on their walls increased the food supply. This mystical causality results in a belief in omens and other forms of magic, all of which we know to have no meaning.

Primitive mentality shows also a characteristic that Lévy-Bruhl calls the "law of participation." This makes it possible to believe that phenomena can be both themselves and other than themselves at the same time, and is another way of saying that natives are indifferent to the "law of contradiction." The Bororo of Brazil (von den Steinen, 20), for example, think of themselves both as men and as red parakeets, and the Huichol Indians of Mexico (Lumholtz, 16) regard the deer and the peyote as identical. The same mechanism is shown in the phenomena of sympathetic magic; the native burns an image of his enemy thinking to do him harm, although in reality the enemy may be far away. He is "there" and "not there" at the same time.

Lévy-Bruhl describes this process as "pre-logical" and as qualitatively different from the thinking of civilized man. "The difference between the mystic and pre-logical mind of the primitive and the white man's way of thinking is so far-reaching that any abrupt transition from the one to the other is inconceivable" (12, p. 409). For that reason it is almost impossible for a civilized man really to understand the mental world of the primitive. "Confronted by the collective representations in which it expresses itself, the pre-connections which link them together, the institutions they objectify, our conceptual and logical thought moves with difficulty, as in the presence of some mental entity which is foreign and even hostile to it" (12, p. 445). As a result, our explanation of what we see the natives doing will be the wrong one nine times out of ten. The world in which primitive mentality operates only partially coincides with our own.

When no logical thought is required, says Lévy-Bruhl,

primitive mentality functions successfully. The tracking feats of the Australian, the perfect reproductions of long and complicated rituals by American Indians, indicate, for example, that their memory is often extraordinary. When thinking is needed, however, there is no objectivity, but rather a belief in occult powers and mystic influences which have little to do with the actual world.

Lévy-Bruhl has been criticized (see, for instance, Goldenweiser, 7) principally on the ground that the mechanisms which he regards as primitive are still to a considerable extent operative in our own society. Any one of our widespread superstitions shows the type of thinking in which the "cause" has no visible connection with the "effect." The casting of horoscopes, the fear of unlucky numbers, the belief in the prophetic nature of dreams, the seven years' bad luck that follows the breaking of a mirror, the magical power of a rabbit's foot and a four-leaf clover, the knocking-on-wood to avert misfortune—these and a host of others are at least as mystical as anything found among primitive peoples. Even the "law of participation" is by no means absent among us. If one believes that God is everywhere and in everything, it must follow that a thing can be itself and God at the same time. Sympathetic magic, as exemplified by burning in effigy, is still occasionally found in our peasant communities.

What Lévy-Bruhl has done is to compare the most logical, most advanced type of thinking of our society with the magical and religious beliefs of primitive peoples. Logic is by no means universal in so-called civilized communities; it is more probably the exception than the rule. Nor is it correct to say that primitive man is invariably pre-logical or mystical. In the practical problems of his daily life he may show a high degree of caution and objectivity in reaching his conclusions. As Radin (17a) has shown (see below), he is even capable at times of a highly reflective and critical analysis which would do credit to anyone in our own society.

It may be added that Lévy-Bruhl's interpretations are unfortunately not always exact. A recent study of the Huichol, for example (11), has shown that they regard the deer and the peyote not as identical, but as having a common origin. Further, it is only to those who have eaten the drug that the field of peyote resembles a herd of grazing deer. In this instance, as in others, Lévy-Bruhl has had to rely on indirect testimony.

ENTWICKLUNGSPSYCHOLOGIE

The psychologist Werner (22) has written an *Entwicklungspsychologie*, an outline of psychology from the developmental point of view, in which a parallel is drawn between the thinking of the primitive, the child and the psychopathic. All three, for example, are characterized by an inability to differentiate between the real world and the world of imagination. The child wakes up after a dream, complaining that he has lost something. The Dayak of Borneo punishes his wife because in his dream she was unfaithful. The Cherokee dreams he was injured, and next day must be treated for his wound. So, too, the schizophrenic lives in an "autistically" created reality which has nothing to do with the world outside.

Abstract thinking is in Werner's opinion impossible to all three. The primitive, the child and the psychopathic all think concretely, in terms of perceived form. A native of New Mecklenburg refused to translate "the white man shot six bears today" because it had not happened. The child will interrupt a question that begins, "If your brother were . . . ," by saying, "But I have no brother." The Bra-

zilian natives ascribe the flat and split shell of a certain tortoise as due to a fall from heaven. "The Indian will not
explain this in terms of any general zoological or biological
causation, but will seek the explanation in a story which
tells how this happened" (p. 224).

Children and schizophrenics practice magic in a manner
quite analogous, says Werner, to that of primitive peoples.
A three-and-a-half-year-old girl put a stone on top of her
head in order not to grow. Many schizophrenics believe that
they can manipulate the invisible forces of the world by a
series of rites and ceremonies. A taboo may have the same
force for a neurotic as it has for a Polynesian. (See Chapter
XVI.)

Werner's entire theory is largely an argument from
analogy, and the resemblances which he notes do not always
survive closer examination. Those who have had any contact
with primitive peoples will certainly reject his identification;
the objective, sensible way in which practical problems are
often handled by the native is neither childlike nor psychopathic. There is perhaps only one important similarity
in the thinking of the primitive and of the child, namely,
that they both lack the scientific knowledge required for the
explanation of many phenomena. We cannot expect either
of them to speak in terms of "general zoological or biological causation" for the obvious reason that they know nothing
about it. There, however, the analogy ends. The child and
the psychotic would be equally at a loss when faced with
the difficult problems of adjustment solved daily by an
Eskimo or a Hottentot.

Werner argues that the inability to think abstractly is reflected in the absence of abstract terms in primitive languages. Boas (4) has shown, however, that this is not the
case, and that even when the term is missing, the abstract

idea may still be comprehended. Similarly, a Huichol informant gave the word for "my father" and for "your father," and said there was no word for "father," but he showed clearly that he understood what the investigator meant (11). Vendryès (21) notes that the modern Greek and Bulgarian languages have no infinitive, but no one would suggest that these people lack the faculty of conceiving a verbal action abstractly.

Werner's point that primitives fail to distinguish between a real and an imaginary world has been made in a different form by Jaensch (9) in connection with his theory of eidetic imagery. This is a particularly vivid form of imagery, approximating sense perception in clarity of detail; in our society it occurs with some frequency among children, but is relatively rare among adults. Jaensch notes the prevalence of visions and other imaginary experiences among primitive groups, and states that the eidetic disposition seems "on the average far more widely prevalent in primitive civilizations, even among adults, and that in particular a much closer relation between eidetic images and perceptions exists for them" (p. 22). This is presumably because like children they are at an earlier stage of development in which image and reality have not yet been clearly differentiated.

It is not difficult to demonstrate, however, that the vision experience is definitely under the influence of culture, and that not all primitive peoples are equally subject to it. Benedict (3) has shown, for example, how closely it is bound up with other aspects of the culture and to what extent it may be modified by the prevailing traditions of the group. Lowie (15a) points out that among the Crow Indians everyone strives for a vision; among certain tribes in California, it is principally the women who have visions; among some South American tribes and in Siberia this experience is restricted to a few special, highly suggestible individuals. Culture determines not only who shall have a vision, but also the form which it must take. The Crow, for example, always see something happen four times, four being their mystic number. The Ojibwa regularly have visions of cosmic exploration. The Huichol under the influence of the peyote always see their saints, brightly colored replicas of the pictures used in their religious ceremonies (11). It is also highly probable that many who report visions do so to avoid admitting failure, and that therefore the vision experience is not quite so prevalent among primitive peoples as is generally believed. (Radin, 17b.) It may be added that during the Middle Ages vision experiences were by no means rare among devout Christians in European countries; it is hardly necessary to assume that they were at a primitive stage of development.

The variations in the nature and prevalence of vision phenomena cannot be explained by the presence or absence of a simple eidetic disposition. As far as primitive peoples are concerned, it may be noted that a study of American Indian children by Klüver (personal communication) failed to reveal any special tendency toward this form of imagery.

THE COLLECTIVE UNCONSCIOUS

In recent psychiatric literature, particularly in that inspired by psychoanalytic teaching, considerable use has been made of the concept of a "collective unconscious." Just as the individual's unconscious is the repository of his forgotten experiences, so the collective or racial unconscious contains the early experiences of humanity. These latter reveal their presence within the individual through their representation in symbols, as well as in the bizarre beliefs and practices which characterize the neurotic. The unconscious of the individual contains therefore not only what he has once known and forgotten, but also considerable material of which he has never been conscious, and which constitutes a universal heritage.

It is Jung (10) who has placed the greatest emphasis on this concept of the collective unconscious. His follower, Aldrich (2), has described his theory by comparing human beings to buildings. The part that is above the ground may be likened to the "conscious"; the cellar below the ground is the "personal unconscious," partly accessible, partly hidden; there is a trapdoor in the cellar leading into a subterranean labyrinth which underlies all the houses—the "collective unconscious."

The primitive mind represents for Jung an infantile stage of development, corresponding to dream and fantasy rather than to directed thinking. Primitivity is in fact regarded as a racial childhood, and the mentality which characterizes it is said to be similar to that of children in our own society. Infantile thinking recapitulates that of our ancestors; it is merely a re-echo of the prehistoric and ancient. This fantastic type of mentality also occurs in modern adult man as soon as directed thinking ceases, as in fatigue or during sleep; while in psychotic disturbance there is a reversion to an earlier stage, a replacement of civilized behavior by an earlier mode of adaptation. Our minds bear the marks of the evolution through which we have passed. The child and the psychotic (as in Werner's scheme) have the mentality of the primitive.

Psychoanalysts have made use of the concept of the "collective unconscious" in an attempted explanation of the meaning of mythology. Just as dreams are the expression of unfulfilled wishes in the individual, so myths contain in disguised form the wishes of the childhood of the race. The myth is a "retained fragment from the infantile life of the infantile psyche of the race." (Abraham, 1, p. 72.) The race experiences in the myths "the fulfilling of its wishes" (p. 70). Thus the origin myths of various peoples who trace their descent from the gods are considered to be the projection of a grandiose complex of the group, just as a delusion of noble birth is part of the daydreams of many individuals.

Jung is not clear as to whether the "collective unconscious" is truly universal, or differs from one race to another. It is more probably the former, although Aldrich's (2) suggestion that it results from the experience of one generation after another argues for the possibility that the inheritance of two racial groups may differ. In any case, the whole concept may be dismissed as unproved. Until we know more about the manner in which experience may be inherited, and until we have more precise understanding of how a mystical "collective unconscious" may contain within itself symbols and archetypes, it hardly seems necessary to take this whole theory seriously.

Primitive Man as Philosopher

As has been suggested above, the theories of Lévy-Bruhl, Werner, Jung, and others, rest upon those accounts of primitive people which have shown them to be least rational in their thinking or their behavior, and comparisons have then often been made with the most logical and objective thinking of our own intellectuals. If the material is chosen differently, the contrast between primitive and civilized may not be nearly so significant. It has already been pointed out that many of our persistent superstitions are just as mystical and illogical as any of the beliefs reported by Lévy-Bruhl. On the other hand, Radin (17a) believes that there is the same distribution of temperament and ability among primitive peoples as among ourselves, and he has succeeded in assembling a large number of excellent examples of the activity of "primitive man as philosopher."

Many of these examples constitute a direct refutation of the descriptions of primitive mentality summarized in this chapter. Werner says, for example, that the natives do not generalize; and he cites the case of the Brazilian Indian who was willing to say, "I die," and "We die," but would not say, "All men must die." (Werner, 22, p. 224.) Radin, however, gives a Crow song which says specifically, "Sky and earth are everlasting, men must die" (p. 103). There is also a Masai proverb, "Everything has an end" (p. 157).

Many proverbs of these and other peoples show how closely their thinking approximates our own. The Masai say, "Don't make a cloth for carrying a child in before the child is born" (Don't count your chickens before they're hatched), and "The zebra cannot do away with his stripes" (The leopard cannot change his spots). The Samoans say, "The many are the chiefs" (God is on the side of the strongest battalions). The Maori say, "Deep throat, shallow muscle" (Empty barrows make the most noise).

Lévy-Bruhl speaks of mystic causation, in which there is no direct connection between cause and effect. There is ample evidence, however, that savages are not always ignorant of true causal relations. The Baganda say, "The stick which is at your friend's house will not drive away the leopard"; and "The god helps you when you put forth your running powers." The belief in dreams is also supposed to indicate mystical thinking, but a sceptical Amazulu admitted that "among black men the real meaning of dreams is not known. For some dreams have every appearance of reality, but they are not true." (Radin, 17a, p. 383.)

Many other examples might be cited of the complex speculations of primitive philosophers on such problems as the inevitability of death, the origin of the world, the character of God, and the moral nature of man. Radin concludes that "the thinkers among primitive peoples envisage life in philosophical terms" (p. 386), and regards the material here presented as indicating definitely that Lévy-Bruhl is wrong in his insistence on an intrinsic difference between the mentality of primitive man and our own.

THE MIND OF PRIMITIVE MAN

This appears to be the only reasonable conclusion. As Boas (4) pointed out long ago, judgments of the characteristics of natives are frequently determined by lack of understanding on the part of the investigator. If the savage fails to appear promptly when he has made an engagement with the White man, it is concluded that he is fickle and unreliable; it may be that he is just not interested. The only way to compare him with the White in this respect is "to compare their behavior in undertakings which are equally important to each" (p. 107). The native is described as lacking in sustained attention, and as wearying quickly of a conversation requiring thought or memory on his part. Boas suggests, however, that the questions put to the native by the traveler often seem to him very trivial and he "naturally soon tires of a conversation carried on in a foreign language, and one in which he finds nothing to interest him" (p. 111). It is the same with all the other so-called traits of primitive mentality.

It should also be noted in this connection that in the relatively recent history of our own culture there are many instances of a type of thinking which seems now to be as far removed from modern science as anything reported for primitive peoples. They were Europeans, after all, who believed that witches would not sink in water, and that men could wander through the world at night as werewolves; or who exercised all their wit and ingenuity in arguments about the number of angels who could dance on the point of a needle. This was not so many centuries ago; and as far as we can tell, there has been no biological change in our society to account for the apparent increase in logic and objectivity. Here, as elsewhere, if we widen our horizon to include more than our particular moment in history, the distinction between "primitive" and "civilized" becomes much less convincing. (See Lowie, 15b.) There is a further chastening thought in the example of the Eskimo who wished to send missionaries to teach the White men how foolish (they might almost have added "how primitive") it is to war with one another.

When the psychology of a Hottentot is described as unlike ours, the difference has nothing to do with any particular stage of development. Two so-called primitive peoples may in most respects resemble each other just as little as either one of them resembles us, and the German scholar may find it as difficult to understand an educated Chinese as a native Australian. The contrast is not between primitive and civilized, but between one culture and another, and on occasion even between different periods or centuries within the same culture.

Bibliography

1. Abraham, K. *Dreams and Myths, a Study in Race Psychology*. New York, 1913. (Trans.)
2. Aldrich, C. R. *The Primitive Mind and Modern Civilization*. New York, 1931.
3. Benedict, R. F. *Patterns of Culture*. New York, 1934.
4. Boas, F. *The Mind of Primitive Man*. New York, 1911.
5. Catlin, G. *Letters and Notes on the Manners, Customs and*

Condition of the North American Indians. New York, 1841. (3rd Ed., 2 vols.)

6. Durkheim, E. *The Elementary Forms of the Religious Life: A Study in Religious Sociology.* New York, 1915. (Trans.)

7. Goldenweiser, A. A. *Early Civilization; an Introduction to Anthropology.* New York, 1922.

8. Hobbes, T. *Leviathan; or the Matter, Form and Power of a Commonwealth.* London, 1887. (3rd. Ed.)

9. Jaensch, E. *Eidetic Imagery and Typological Methods of Investigation.* London, 1930. (Trans.)

10. Jung, C. G. *Psychology of the Unconscious.* New York, 1916. (Trans.)

11. Klineberg, O. "Notes on the Huichol." *Amer. Anthrop.,* new ser., 36:1934, pp. 446-460.

12. Lévy-Bruhl, L. *Primitive Mentality.* New York, 1923. (Trans.)

13. Lévy-Bruhl, L. *How Natives Think.* New York, 1925. (Trans.)

14. Lévy-Bruhl, L. *The Soul of the Primitive.* New York, 1928. (Trans.)

15a. Lowie, R. H. *Primitive Religion.* New York, 1924.

15b. Lowie, R. H. *Are We Civilized? Human Culture in Perspective.* New York, 1929.

16. Lumholtz, C. *Unknown Mexico.* New York, 1902. (2 vols.)

17a. Radin, P. *Primitive Man as Philosopher.* New York, 1927.

17b. Radin, P. *Crashing Thunder; the Autobiography of an American Indian.* New York, 1926.

18. Rousseau, J. J. *Du Contrat Social.* Amsterdam, 1762.

19. Spencer, H. *The Principles of Sociology.* London, 1896.

20. von den Steinen, K. *Unter den Naturvölkern Zentral-Braziliens.* Berlin, 1897. (2nd Ed.)

21. Vendryès, J. *Language, a Linguistic Introduction to History.* New York, 1925. (Trans.)

22. Werner, H. *Einführung in die Entwicklungspsychologie.* Leipzig, 1926.

Chapter XX

CONCLUSIONS AND IMPLICATIONS

RACE AND CULTURE

THE preceding discussion has shown that race cannot be regarded as the cause of a particular culture, or as the cause of culture in general. Ignoring the question of cultural values for the time being, we have seen that folkways may differ fundamentally in the case of peoples who are racially identical. Among the American Indians, for example, we find many extremes of behavior; the Plains Indians have been described as introvert, and the Eskimo as extrovert; the Pueblos are peaceful and the Apache very warlike; the Sioux are stoical and reserved, the Huichol lively and emotional. These are only a few of the cases that might be cited. The group differences are very important, but they seem to have no relation to race.

If in spite of this the attempt is made to evaluate the cultural contributions of the various races, there arises the apparently insoluble problem of finding an adequate criterion. Value-judgments are necessarily subjective, and there appears to be no way of making them scientifically acceptable. The Chinese invented gunpowder, but instead of using it as a weapon of war they amused themselves by making fireworks. The Westerners adopted it to make themselves masters of a large part of the world. If we use power as a criterion we shall regard the Westerners as superior; if our values are æsthetic rather than political, at least as good a case can be made for the Chinese.

There are simple peoples who have moral standards which

must be considered superior even by our own criteria; as we have seen, the Yakuts of Siberia could not understand how it is possible in our cities for some to be starving while others have more than enough to eat. The Yakuts have the custom of sharing their food with the hungry, and a Yakut moralist might make a good case for the inferiority of our civilization. The same may be said also of the Eskimo who offered to teach the White men how to live at peace with one another. We have the right to speak of our civilization as more complex, but we have no evidence of its general superiority.

Even on the basis of our own standards it is difficult to make a clear case for the superiority of any race over another. We happen now to be in a period of history in which a great deal of political power is in the hands of northwest Europeans. If we take a longer historical view, however, their superiority even in that respect may certainly be questioned. We have seen how Aristotle doubted the abilities of the northern barbarians; Julius Cæsar spoke of them just as contemptuously. The Chinese had a rich culture, with a highly developed art and philosophy, at a time when most White peoples had not made any of the contributions which are now regarded as proving their superiority. One of the earliest and most important of all civilizations, the Egyptian, from which the western world borrowed so profusely, was the creation of Mediterraneans with a strong Negroid intermixture. The Renaissance, in spite of Woltmann and Chamberlain, was certainly much more a Mediterranean than a Nordic product. We cannot judge the superiority of a race by its supremacy at any given moment, and we can say nothing about the hierarchy of races in the future.

It becomes especially difficult to assume an intimate relation between race and cultural contributions when we note the tremendous difference in level of complexity of groups belonging to the same race. The highly developed Chinese and the simple North Siberian are both Mongoloid; the Mayas and the Incas of Central and South America were of the same race as the simplest tribes of California. Race, therefore, cannot be responsible. It is not easy to say why these differences developed. The answer may be found in a host of contributing factors—the physical environment, the history, the economic life, contact with other peoples, the presence of outstanding individuals, the fortunes of war, etc. An analysis of these is outside the scope of the present volume.

In one sense, the end of this investigation finds us not much farther advanced than its beginning. The subjective judgments of race differences, reviewed in the introductory chapter, were dismissed as having little significance for a scientific, impartial study. The search for something more objective led through a considerable quantity of material, collected by all the methods at the disposal of both the natural and the social scientist, and presumably not too directly influenced by the personal whims and prejudices of the investigators. The findings, however, though rich and varied, are either inconsistent or inconclusive, and the general conclusion can be only that the case for psychological race differences has never been proved. This is perhaps a negative result, but it has certain very definite and positive implications.

RATIONALIZATIONS

When the Spanish writers justified the exploitation of the American Indians (see Chapter I) on the grounds that they were racially distinct from and inferior to the Whites, they set a fashion which was widely followed. In the history of the treatment of the American Negro, for example, the notion of a racial inferiority played an important part, though it is not difficult to see in it the consequence of an economic system based upon slavery, rather than an honest attempt to evaluate the abilities of a people. The arguments in common use were often based on concepts which are now outworn, like that which saw in the inferiority of the Negroes a punishment for the sin their ancestor Ham had committed against his father Noah. (Priest, 3.) With a change in habits, the Bible was no longer considered adequate evidence; but the shift to the language of a more modern scientific era added very little soundness or objectivity. (Johnson, 2.) The conclusion came first, and the "facts" were found to justify it.

The wholly artificial character of the argument is clearly illustrated in the attitude toward Negro skilled labor after Emancipation. During slavery, a large part of the skilled mechanical work in the South was in the hands of Negro slaves. There are accounts of bitter protests made by White artisans against the practice of turning over the bulk of this skilled work to Negroes. After Emancipation, however, the theory was advanced and accepted that Negroes were constitutionally incapable of filling the very positions they had held during slavery! (Weatherford and Johnson, 5.) It would be difficult to find a clearer case of belief motivated by self-interest. In this instance there are historical facts which show the belief to be false, but these are conveniently ignored or forgotten.

There are many other examples of this type of rationalization. Professor Strong (4) has shown how, in the case of the Japanese on the Pacific Coast, every significant fact about them was seized upon and twisted about until it made a suitable weapon for causing them injury. "Hence, if they asked less than the going wage, they were threatening the American standard of living; if they demanded better wages, they were avaricious; if they were successful in farming and saved enough to buy their own ranch, they were driving the whites out; if they were unsuccessful, they were 'wearing out the land' " (p. 125). This is the stuff out of which racial theories are made. Man is a rationalizing, not a rational, animal.

That being the case, there may not seem to be much hope of affecting behavior by an appeal to science and objectivity. The materials presented in this volume and the conclusions to which they lead have certain implications for the practical problems of human relations, but making these implications felt is quite a different matter. It may still be of interest, however, to analyze them a little further.

Some Practical Implications

The general conclusion of this book is that there is no scientific proof of racial differences in mentality. This does not necessarily mean that there are no such differences. It may be that at some future time, and with the aid of techniques as yet undiscovered, differences may be demonstrated. In the present stage of our knowledge, however, we have no right to assume that they exist.

There is no reason, therefore, to treat two people differently because they differ in their physical type. There is no justification for denying a Negro a job or an education because he is a Negro. No one has been able to demonstrate that ability is correlated with skin color or head shape or any of the anatomical characteristics used to classify races. A man must be judged as an individual, not as a member of a group whose limits are arbitrary and artificial. Our racial and national stereotypes—the "pictures in our minds" of the Oriental, the Italian, the Jew, the Mexican—will be wrong much more often than right; they are based on current opinions which have never been verified, and they cannot be trusted in the treatment of human beings.

There is no reason to make our immigration laws stricter for one people than for another. It has never been demonstrated that groups differ fundamentally in their ability to adapt themselves to a new culture, or to make a contribution to their new country. If their culture resembles ours more closely, the process of adaptation may not take quite so long, but the whole history of the United States has shown that these differences are negligible. There is nothing more illuminating in this connection than the report of a congressional committee in 1838, which charged that "the country is being flooded with the outcasts of the jails, almshouses, and slums of pauper-ridden Europe," that the newcomers were "the most idle and vicious classes, in personal appearance most offensive and loathsome," and that the prisons were filled with them. There were, however, the ancestors of the Irish and German and British Americans who are now (or were until recently) most concerned about the character of the new immigrants. (See Feldman, 1, pp. 134-136.) There is something to be said for the careful examination of each individual immigrant, but no valid reason for accepting or rejecting an applicant because of his national origin.

There is no reason to pass laws against miscegenation. The human race is one, biologically speaking. There are no subvarieties whose genes are mutually incompatible, or whose crossing will necessarily lead to degeneration. Race mixture is not in itself harmful if the parent stocks are healthy, and if the hybrids suffer no special social disabilities. Certain groups may prefer, for reasons of cultural or religious loyalty, not to intermarry with others, but that is a matter of sentiment and not of biology. If two individuals of different stock wish to marry, any objection by the state is an unwarranted interference in a matter which concerns them alone, and which in any case has not been shown to have any harmful consequences. Laws directed against mixture in order to maintain race purity have no meaning, since every large population in the world already contains within it a varied assortment of physical types.

There is no innate aversion of races to one another. The very fact that race mixture has taken place everywhere and at all times is the best possible indication that this is so. Racial antagonisms must be understood in their historical and social setting; they have no basis in biology. The assumption that they are the inevitable result of group differences merely serves to hide their true causes.

THE RACE PROBLEM

What these causes are is by no means easy to determine, and it would be presumptuous on the part of the writer to attempt to analyze them in a few closing sentences. There is an increasing tendency to see in the race problem merely one aspect of the class war, in which those who are in a position of privilege make of unimportant differences in skin color or religion or language a convenient excuse for their own continued domination. Those who look upon race relations from this point of view see little hope of any real improvement until the present competitive system has been replaced by a new social order. They point with conviction to Russia, where the economic change has been accompanied by a more sympathetic treatment of minorities, and where the class struggle and the race problem seem to have disappeared together.

On this point the writer must reserve judgment. It may be that the analysis in terms of economics is an oversimplification, and that racial antipathies have a life and momentum which are to some degree independent of the economic structure. It may be, on the other hand,˙ that these antipathies are entirely secondary, and that if nothing more were to be gained by them, they would disappear of themselves.

In any case, that is not really our problem. Most of us live in a competitive society. We have no means of knowing whether in the near or distant future this competition will be replaced by something radically different. We are dealing with race conflict under conditions of competition, and we cannot wait for this conflict to be removed by an upheaval in our whole social structure. Even under conditions of competition there is something that can be done. It is quite possible, for example, to concede the irrelevance of cephalic index and pigmentation and nasal width, while maintaining a firm faith in "rugged individualism."

If the material collected in this volume were accepted as demonstrating the absence of any valid proof of racial differences in intelligence or character, it might conceivably lead to a more favorable attitude toward groups usually regarded as inferior. In time there might even be a change in race relations. This seems to assume that people do reason, although a little earlier it was suggested that they usually rationalize. There is hope, however, even in rationalization. The very search for reasons, even if that search is secondary, makes it possible for opinions to change, if one by one the foundations on which they rest are shown to be illusory.

Once science has demonstrated that there is nothing in the brain or blood of other races which justifies our ill-treatment of them, it becomes important to see that this knowledge is disseminated. In this respect, the schools have a particularly important function to perform. If attitudes are to be changed in the face of the forces tending to perpetuate them, the only hope is to reach them early, and to give to children habits of favorable reactions to other races which will stay with them through life. These habits may possibly result, in part at least, from the knowledge that every single one of the arguments used in order to prove the inferiority of other races has amounted to nothing. In any case, the educational experiment seems to the writer to be worth trying.

BIBLIOGRAPHY

1. Feldman, H. *Racial Factors in American Industry*. New York, 1931.
2. Johnson, C. S., and Bond, H. M. "The Investigation of Racial Differences Prior to 1910." *J. of Negro Education,* Yearbook III, July, 1934.
3. Priest, Josiah. *Bible Defense of Slavery*. Glasgow, Ky., 1852.
4. Strong, E. K., Jr. *The Second-Generation Japanese Problem*. Stanford University, 1933.
5. Weatherford, W. D., and Johnson, C. S. *Race Relations: Adjustment of Whites and Negroes in the United States*. New York, 1934.

INDEX OF NAMES